THE EU & KALININGRAD

Kaliningrad and the Impact of EU Enlargement

foreword by
The Rt. Hon. Christopher Patten

edited by
James Baxendale
Stephen Dewar
and
David Gowan

FEDERAL TRUST
europe's eastern borders

This book is published by the Federal Trust, whose aim is to enlighten public debate on federal issues of national, continental and global government. It does this in the light of its statutes which state that it shall promote 'studies in the principles of international relations, international justice and supranational government.'

The Trust conducts enquiries, promotes seminars and conferences and publishes reports and teaching materials. The Federal Trust is the UK member of the Trans-European Policy Studies Association (TEPSA), a grouping of fifteen think-tanks from member states of the European Union.

Up-to-date information about the Federal Trust can be found on the internet at www.fedtrust.co.uk

© Federal Trust for Education and Research 2000

ISBN 0 901573 18 3

NOTE: The views expressed should not be taken as a statement of British Government policy.

The Federal Trust is a Registered Charity No. 272241

Dean Bradley House, 52 Horseferry Road,

London SW1P 2AF

Company Limited by Guarantee No.1269848

Marketing and Distribution by Kogan Page Ltd

Printed in the European Union

Contents

PROBLEMS AND THREATS: REAL OR IMAGINARY?

THE WAY FORWARD

APPENDICES

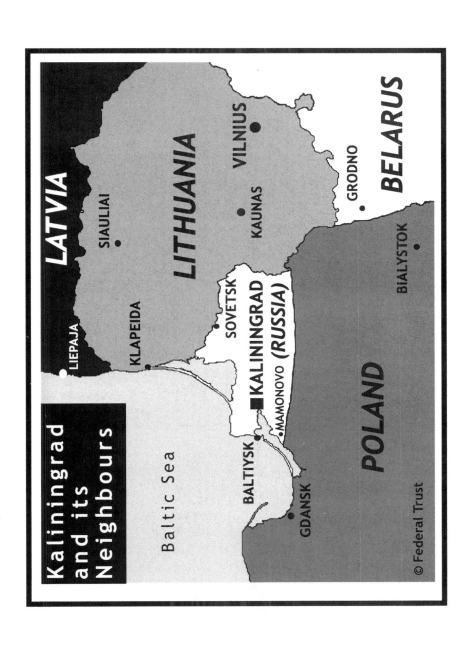

Kaliningrad and its Neighbours

Baltic Sea

LATVIA

LIEPAJA

SIAULIAI

KLAPEIDA

LITHUANIA

SOVETSK

KAUNAS

VILNIUS

KALININGRAD (RUSSIA)

MAMONOVO

BALTIYSK

GDANSK

POLAND

GRODNO

BELARUS

BIALYSTOK

© Federal Trust

Acknowledgements

This book is the result of a round table seminar jointly organised by TEPSA and the British Embassy, Brussels on *The Consequences of EU Enlargement for Kaliningrad.* This was held in Brussels on 29 March 2000.

The editors wish to extend their warmest thanks to Guy Vanhaeverbeke, former Secretary General of TEPSA and, in particular, to Margareta Theelen without whom this project would never have seen the light of day. Special thanks are also owed to Janet Gunn, the Head of Eastern Research Group at the Foreign and Commonwealth Office in London.

Foreword

The Rt. Hon. Christopher Patten
European Commissioner for External Relations

As the European Union expands its membership and as it seeks to develop closer relations with its neighbours, the situation of Kaliningrad merits particular attention. Its location is strategic but there are reasons for concern.

There is increasing risk of a development gap between Kaliningrad and its rapidly developing neighbours; the question of local cross-border movements; the growth of organised crime; the increasing regional integration with neighbouring countries as an engine of growth.

Kaliningrad is involved as part of the Russian Federation in the Partnership and Cooperation Agreement with the EU. Kaliningrad faces specific challenges and new opportunities as a result of the EU enlargement process. In this context, the 'Northern Dimension' initiative, which embraces at its core North West Russia and the neighbouring regions of an enlarged EU, is important, creating new avenues for cooperation at grass-roots levels between people, companies and local governments.

The expertise gathered during your Round Table is therefore timely and the views expressed at the Conference will make a valuable contribution to future EU-Russia discussions on Kaliningrad.

Introduction

James Baxendale
British Embassy, Brussels[1]
and **Stephen Dewar**
Independent economic consultant,
Moscow

When the three Baltic States of Estonia, Latvia and Lithuania regained their independence in 1991 and the Soviet Union was dissolved, a small part of Russia found itself physically cut off from the Russian mainland. This exclave is Kaliningrad.

Kaliningrad on the map

Kaliningrad is the most westerly of the 89 republics, territories and regions that constitute the Subjects of the Russian Federation. It is also, with a population of just under one million and an area of 15,200 square kilometres – about half the size of Belgium – one of the smallest. It is located on the shores of the Baltic Sea, with Poland to its south and Lithuania to its north and east. Beyond Lithuania lie Belarus and Latvia, so that Kaliningrad is a long way from the rest of Russia – almost 400 km from the nearest border.

Brief history[2]

Kaliningrad was forged out of the fortunes of war. The Potsdam Conference of 1945 accepted that what had previously been East Prussia should be split. Two-thirds of the territory was allocated to Poland and the northern third to Russia. The part of the German population that had not already fled in the final stages of the war was deported by Stalin, and the land was resettled by Soviet immigrants, predominantly Russians.

In 1946, the capital city – previously known as Königsberg – was renamed Kaliningrad, after Mikhail Kalinin, latterly President of the Presidium of the Supreme Soviet of the USSR. The region took the same name.

Outside military circles, little was heard about Kaliningrad once it became Soviet territory. It was the main base for the Soviet Baltic Fleet and an important military zone and, hence, a closed area – forbidden to foreigners and to non-resident Soviet citizens without permits. But the successive shocks of *perestroika* in the late 1980s and the collapse of the Soviet Union changed all that. In 1991, with the independence of the Baltic States, Kaliningrad became a Russian exclave. The dissolution of the Warsaw Pact and the repatriation of Russian troops from central and eastern Europe (CEE) also robbed the region of much of its former military significance.

These forces combined to lead to Kaliningrad opening up once more to the outside world. In January 1991 the first direct train service between Berlin and Kaliningrad since 1945 recommenced and foreigners returned – over 90,000 former East Prussians initially, though these numbers have subsequently declined enormously. Since then, Kaliningrad has taken on a new kind of identity – although in the early years, a somewhat confused one.

The 1990s

On the one hand, Kaliningrad continued in the early 1990s to have a strong, albeit reduced and changed, military significance. It remained the base of the - now Russian - Baltic Fleet; it was a staging post for Russian troops withdrawn from eastern Europe; and it continued to maintain a strong military presence of its own. All this caused worries in neighbouring states, notably Lithuania, as troop and munition movements between Kaliningrad and mainland Russia had to pass through her territory.

From the mid 1990s, however, the military issue declined in importance as the Baltic Fleet lost much of its strength in parallel with the general deterioration in the Russian armed forces and as a result of deliberate cuts. The transit troops went home peacefully - transit issues with Lithuania being resolved on a pragmatic basis - and the military population fell from an estimated 200,000 troops at its height to between 16,000 and 30,000 troops now.

On the other hand, Russia needed to find a way of ensuring the region's economic prosperity. While the rest of Russia was going through economic turmoil, Kaliningrad, as an exclave which had been part of the now defunct Soviet-era Baltic economic area, was threatened by its own specific restructuring and transition problems. To overcome these geographic and economic disadvantages, Kaliningrad was granted the status of a Free Economic Zone (FEZ), effectively able to import duty-free just about everything from raw materials to consumer goods. The idea was to use these incentives to attract investment, Russian and foreign, boost international trade and, thereby, turn the region into a 'Baltic Hong Kong' and gateway between Russia and the West.

But the hoped-for economic miracle failed to materialise. Despite the efforts of the Regional Administration, led by Yuri Matochkin, Governor from 1991 to 1996, to develop the region as an internationally open economy, numerous difficulties frustrated these aims. Not least of these was the ambivalent attitude to free market economic activity characteristic of Russia as a whole. On top of this, President Yeltsin cancelled the FEZ in 1995, only to restore most of these privileges in the form of a Special Economic Zone (SEZ) early the next year. Such uncertainties over the Federal Russian Government's commitment to the SEZ have remained, with periodic attempts made to curtail the privileges, if not eliminate the SEZ altogether. The International Monetary Fund (IMF) has also at times advocated the elimination of the SEZ. Such see-sawing from Moscow between support, indifference and opposition has not created investor confidence. Compared to the Baltic States and Poland, Kaliningrad attracted little in Foreign Direct Investment (FDI) in the 1990s.

Economy[3]

Resources

Kaliningrad has some natural resources, including modest oil reserves (on and off-shore, though only the former are currently exploited) which currently yield 650,000 tons a year. Salt, sand, clay, gravel, brown coal and peat are also found in reasonable quantities, but these are low value bulk commodities and do not represent either a present or future basis for an economic miracle.

Being part of the great central and east European plain, there is a large area of potentially arable land. However, a combination of environmental deterioration and the generally poor state of post-Soviet agriculture have led Kaliningrad to become a net food importer, rather than a successful producer.

The most important resource in Kaliningrad is amber. Over 90% of the world's known resources of prime amber are in Kaliningrad, mostly concentrated in a coastal area in the north-west of the region where it is mined in open-cast fashion. Unfortunately, contested privatisations in the aftermath of the dissolution of the Former Soviet Union (FSU), investment shortages, lack of profitability affecting the ex-state monopoly that held exclusive mining and processing rights, and large-scale smuggling, have combined to deprive the region of any significant economic benefit from exploiting this resource.

Manufacturing and industry

The bulk of Kaliningrad's manufacturing sector is based on traditional and, to a large extent, decaying industries. Paper and pulp, machine-building, ship-building and repair are major but declining employers. Fishing and fish processing remain very important sectors. Kaliningrad used to land over 10 % of the total fish catch brought into the FSU. There is also a modest electronics manufacturing sector derived from the important defence-related industry that thrived in previous times. Overall, however, all these traditional industries have been in structural decline since the advent of *perestroika* and there have been no major developments in new industries. A large number of small and medium-sized enterprises (SMEs) have sprung up over the last ten years or so, notably in furniture making, but the total numbers are low compared with the progress made in other transition economies in CEE countries, although somewhat higher than in Russia as a whole. There is a promising growth in the information technology area, which gives grounds for genuine optimism concerning the future for this sector, but it is still modest in size.

One of the most impressive areas has been the burgeoning growth of firms in the trading sector and this is reflected in the extremely high growth in turnover of international trade. However, while exports grew reasonably throughout the 1990s until the Russian financial and economic crisis of August 1998, imports have grown explosively, to such an extent that Kaliningrad now runs current account deficit approaching one billion dollars a year - a one thousand dollars per man, woman and child.

In short, Kaliningrad's economy is not that dissimilar to that of many other parts of Russia - with a continuing reliance on increasingly obsolete industries, a decaying infrastructure, impoverished agriculture, and a lack of development of new industries. But all these problems are greatly exacerbated by the additional costs and difficulties posed by its position as an exclave.

Why Kaliningrad matters: both exclave and enclave

Why then should Kaliningrad matter? Why should the European Union be concerned? Kaliningrad matters for two reasons. Though not dissimilar to many other regions of Russia, its situation is made more acute by its exclave status. It is physically cut off from those Russian regions with which it might otherwise conduct internal trade and it feels neglected by Russia. But, in addition, at some stage in the next few years when both Poland and Lithuania accede to the European Union

(EU), Kaliningrad will become, not just an exclave *outside* Russia, but also a Russian enclave geographically *within* the EU. Its problems will become the EU's problems while, conversely, how the EU acts will have a huge impact upon Kaliningrad. How Russia and Kaliningrad address the issues of, for example, transit, crime, environment and trade, will inevitably affect, and require the involvement of EU member states. Equally, how the EU deals with such matters as infrastructural development, Schengen and the Single Market in the newly acceded member states will have a profound effect on Kaliningrad and hence Russian interests. The one cannot afford to ignore the other.

What are the problems that will affect both Kaliningrad and the EU? The brief list that follows will, we hope, serve as illustrations – almost a snapshot – of some of the main issues that are discussed in more detail in the book.

Transportation links

EU enlargement around the Baltic Sea region will give a significant boost to both the development of, and demand for, increasingly modernised and integrated transport systems. An important element of this is the Trans European Networks (TEN) programme which involves the modernisation of major road and rail networks linking the Nordic countries, Russia, the Baltic States, Belarus and Ukraine with central, eastern and western Europe. The programme involves huge investment and procedural reforms. It seeks to increase average speeds, simplify and facilitate cross-border clearance procedures and improve the efficiency of services. Kaliningrad, however, is not getting the financial resources from Moscow to keep up with the developments in the neighbouring states. And since Poland and Lithuania have a common border, there is a strong possibility that Kaliningrad will simply be isolated from these important trade routes.

Kaliningrad is poorly serviced by air. The local airline, Kaliningrad Avia, has just 6 aeroplanes in service at present, compared with 12 less than five years ago, and there is only one direct international service linking Kaliningrad to foreign destinations.[4]

And although Kaliningrad Sea Port is the only year-round, ice-free Russian port on the Baltic Sea, it accounts for just 5% of the total cargo traffic through Baltic Sea ports in Russia and the Baltic States.[5]

Visas, borders and freedom of movement

In 1999 there were 8.6 million border crossings to or from Kaliningrad.[6] But once Poland and Lithuania accede to the EU, Kaliningrad residents will need visas to travel overland outside the oblast, for instance to visit friends and relatives in the rest of Russia. The reason is that both countries must adhere to the Schengen Agreement on accession. Schengen rules are designed to facilitate internal cross-border movements within the EU and to do so primarily through tightening the external borders.[7] Poland intends introducing a national visa regime for Russian citizens in 2001 and is already tightening entry controls. And although Lithuania presently has a reciprocal visa-free regime for Kaliningrad residents, it too will have to introduce a Schengen-compliant visa regime on accession to the EU. Once members of the EU, neither country will be able to negotiate special visa regimes for the residents of Kaliningrad.

Energy supplies

At present, Kaliningrad obtains its electricity from Russia via Lithuania. But as Lithuania moves towards EU accession, it will disconnect from the Russian electricity grid and link up with the Baltic Energy Grid, thereby placing Kaliningrad in a serious quandary. As a net importer of around 80 percent of its energy needs, Kaliningrad will either have to buy energy from foreign states in hard currency, or negotiate with Lithuania an expensive new transit link directly with the Russian grid 400 kilometres away.

The Regional Administration has a policy commitment to build a new gas-fired, combined heat and power station in the oblast, which would significantly reduce its dependence on imported electricity. However, this project will require an increased supply of natural gas and the construction of a second gas pipeline from the rest of Russia via Lithuania. This solution, though technically feasible, is costly, and there are no signs at present that the project will attract the necessary financial support.

Single Market standards

The EU requires that all accession countries adopt the Single Market regulations and standards as laid down in the *acquis communautaire*. Their adoption by Poland and Lithuania, and the other Baltic and CEE accession states, will have a significant impact on Kaliningrad, whose future economic prosperity is and will continue to be critically dependent on exports. In 1997, for instance, Poland and the Baltic States accounted for 36.2% of Kaliningrad's exports, whilst exports to Germany amounted to 24.2%.[8] Some of the more important manufactured exports from Kaliningrad – such as processed fish – may well be barred from the new EU markets unless they comply with the relevant standards. The costs to Kaliningrad's companies – a small region in economic decline – of acquiring the necessary information and adapting its technologies and processes accordingly could be high and thus could become an effective barrier against exports.

Crime, environmental pollution and AIDS

Kaliningrad's social and environmental problems unavoidably pose problems for its neighbours – and, therefore, for the enlarged EU. Kaliningrad has a reputation for high levels of crime, including organised crime. There is smuggling notably in amber, alcohol and cigarettes; drug trafficking; and a grey economy in second-hand and stolen cars. Environmental pollution is threatening: approximately 253 million cubic metres of human and industrial waste – two thirds of it untreated - is discharged into the Baltic Sea per annum.[9] And Kaliningrad is sadly now a major centre for HIV/AIDS. Official statistics indicate nearly 3,000 cases of AIDS, while experts estimate that it may be as much as 6-8 times higher.[10] Kaliningrad, on the basis of such statistics, has the highest level of infection of anywhere in Russia or, reportedly, the whole of Europe.

But if the will to act is there ...

This is just a snapshot of a few of the issues that are likely to have an impact upon Kaliningrad in the foreseeable future. Ideally, such a period of change and challenge in the region would provide the right opportunity and circumstances for Kaliningrad to begin the necessary task of economic and social restructuring. Unfortunately, at present, this does not appear to be the case. Many Russians are concerned that EU enlargement looks set to pose even greater difficulties, and hence hardship, for Kaliningrad.

Policy-makers in the EU, Russia and Kaliningrad need to confront these issues if they are to overcome any negative effects which the enlarged EU may have on Kaliningrad and to prevent any problems from spilling over into the region. At the same time, they need to consider what policies might enable Kaliningrad and Russia as a whole to benefit from the enlargement process.

The purpose of this book is to focus attention on these possible problems. It is a necessary starting point before taking any action. Failure to acknowledge that potential problems exist will only put off the 'evil day' when a reckoning may have to be made. There is time to address these problems – but only if the will to act is there.

With firm commitment on all sides, based on a shared understanding of the issues, Kaliningrad could well achieve the potential that President Putin spoke of at Helsinki in October 1999 - of being a 'pilot region' in EU-Russian relations. This will have lessons for both communities in how to develop prosperous and stable neighbourly relations.

---

[1] The following views are purely personal and do not in any way represent the official position of the British Government.

[2] A brief chronological listing of the more significant events in Königsberg/Kaliningrad's history is given in Appendix 1 at the end of the book.

[3] A brief statistical profile of Kaliningrad is contained in Appendix 2 at the end of the book.

[4] Provided by the Danish carrier, SAS, which operates 6 flights a week to Copenhagen.

[5] Tacis, *Kaliningrad Region : Proposed Strategic Development Framework* (December 1998).

[6] Kaliningrad Customs Agency figures. 51% of these crossings were made by non-Russians. Many are also the result of the so-called 'suitcase trade'.

[7] Although they will have to join Schengen immediately on accession, Poland and Lithuania will be subject to transitional arrangements until they are able to issue full Schengen visas.

[8] See Appendix 2.

[9] Tacis, *op cit*, note 4.

[10] Speech by Vygaudas Usackas to CBSS meeting, Kaliningrad, 17-18 February 1999.

Executive Summary

David Gowan
St Antony's College, Oxford

Kaliningrad is a challenging anomaly left by the collapse of the Soviet Union, an Oblast[1] of one million people ruled from Moscow but cut off from Russia proper and bordered by Poland and Lithuania. Despite its seemingly advantageous position on the Baltic, its considerable (but unfulfilled) agricultural and industrial potential and the world's largest deposits of amber, the region faces severe problems. These include pollution, economic isolation, growing levels of organised crime and drug-trafficking and one of the worst concentrations of HIV in Europe.

As the European Union enlarges to include Kaliningrad's neighbours, these difficulties are bound to impact on relations between Brussels and the Russian Government, which has proposed that Kaliningrad should be treated as a 'pilot region' for future co-operation. The issue was discussed during the summit meeting between President Vladimir Putin and EU leaders on 29 May 2000. The central, and so far unresolved, question is what sort of pilot relationship Moscow would be willing to countenance between the EU and this small region, which is destined to become an island (or exclave) within the EU. What are the implications for the EU's relations with Russia as a whole?

The Conference and the Book

This collection of papers, 'Kaliningrad and the Impact of EU Enlargement', is the product of a round table conference held in Brussels by the British Embassy to Belgium and the Trans European Policy Studies Association (TEPSA) on 29 March 2000.

The conference was chaired by René Nyberg, the Director for Eastern Affairs at the Foreign Ministry of Finland. The other participants included experts from Kaliningrad, Moscow and St Petersburg, Deputy Foreign Minister Vygaudas Usackas from Lithuania, representatives of the EU Commission, senior diplomats from Poland, Latvia, Denmark and Sweden and a range of specialists from universities, think tanks and research organisations.

The chapters in this book are grouped under five broad headings:

- Setting the scene: EU/Russia relations
- The Kaliningrad Oblast
- The Neighbours
- Problems and threats: real or imaginary?
- The Way Forward

The papers present a wide range of views from participants in the conference. There is general agreement that the EU needs to develop a coherent policy in respect of Kaliningrad, and that progress can be made only with the full support of the Federal Russian Government. However, some of the authors point out just how intractable some of the problems faced by Kaliningrad are. Igor Leshukov's paper is of particular value in that it sets Kaliningrad in the context of the wider relationship between Moscow and the regions.

On the options for future policy, there is a tension between those (notably Sylvia Gourova, Deputy Mayor of the City of

Kaliningrad, and Pertti Joenniemi) who argue for radical EU initiatives to offer preferential treatment to Kaliningrad, and others who argue that the issue has been over-dramatised and that the scope for EU involvement is limited. The papers by Vygaudas Usackas and Wojciech Zajaczkowski give insight into practical steps taken by Lithuania and Poland. The opening paper by René Nyberg and the paper by Dag Hartelius provide an insight into the likely future development of EU policy.

Key Issues

The issues discussed at the conference and in the contributions to this book arise directly or indirectly from Kaliningrad's geographical position. They include:

● <u>Isolation and dependence on transit through Lithuania for contact with the remainder of Russia</u>. This has major negative economic consequences for the viability of the port and for local industry. Despite brave attempts by some of Kaliningrad's apologists, there is no way in which it can be turned into a natural advantage.

The Federal Russian Government has tried to offset the Oblast's isolation by tax concessions, which constitute the main feature of the Special Economic Zone (SEZ). These are designed to encourage assembly of goods from imported components, and onward export of the finished product into 'mainland' Russia and abroad. They have so far worked moderately well in a handful of showcase investments (in the car and furniture industries), but the overall benefits of the SEZ have been limited and marginal. Although Kaliningrad's level of prosperity (reflected by net inward economic migration until 1998 or early 1999) is slightly above the average for Russia, overall levels of domestic and foreign investment are low and there has been little serious development of industry, agriculture or infrastructure – all of which are run down.

● <u>An extensive grey or black economy and a high level of organised crime (including drug trafficking) and corruption</u>. Smuggling is pervasive, and is largely based on the illegal import of cigarettes, cars and consumer goods. It also extends to trade in amber. Hitherto neither Moscow nor the local authorities have managed to reduce this illegal activity significantly.

● <u>Health problems</u>. These include HIV (in large part transmitted by used needles), multi-resistant tuberculosis and shortages of medical resources.

● <u>Severe and chronic environmental degradation</u>. Kaliningrad is one of the worst sources of pollution in the Baltic.

● <u>Political tensions</u>. There is considerable local opposition to the present Governor, and some apparent strains between Moscow and the Regional Administration. Much will depend on the outcome of the gubernatorial elections in November 2000.

● <u>The effects of Putin's policy towards the regions</u>. At a time when Putin is trying to strengthen the control of the centre over the regions, there must be considerable uncertainty over the extent to which he will be ready to permit autonomy and/or preferential arrangements in Kaliningrad. Russia participated in an EU conference on Kaliningrad held in Denmark in May under the auspices of the Northern Dimension[2] programme. However, it is still unclear how Putin and the Russian Federal Government will be prepared to implement the proposal (mentioned above) to treat Kaliningrad as a pilot region within the framework of EU-Russian co-operation.

● <u>The continuing, if latent, military significance of the Kaliningrad Oblast, which is home to the Headquarters of the Baltic Fleet</u>. If any future NATO enlargement were to include the Baltic States, the Oblast would once again be seen by many Russians as an embattled forward outpost.

The EU (through the Tacis programme) and individual countries have run technical assistance projects focused on water supply and waste, other environmental issues, transport, energy, health, social administration, business, education, agriculture, cross-border co-operation and good governance. The overall value of recent and current projects is estimated to be over 25 million euro. However, the effectiveness of these projects has, arguably, been very limited.

EU Enlargement

Lithuania and Poland are already uncomfortable about the knock-on effects for themselves of the problems experienced by Kaliningrad. The difficulties described above are likely to increase as the prosperity gap widens, and will be of direct concern to the EU after Polish and Lithuanian accession.

The Russian Government is anxious to stress that Kaliningrad should remain an integral part of the Russian Federation, but recognises the need for help, and also argues that the EU is under an obligation to find means of alleviating any additional problems caused to Kaliningrad by enlargement.

EU enlargement will bring with it one specific complication for residents of Kaliningrad travelling to mainland Russia. Lithuania's accession to the EU and adoption of the Schengen acquis will almost certainly necessitate the introduction of a visa regime in place of the existing arrangement under which residents of Kaliningrad can make short visits to (or transit journeys through) Lithuania without a visa[3]. Poland has already decided to introduce a visa regime in 2001 and is in the process of tightening its control over (and increasing the cost of) entry from Kaliningrad. However, both Lithuania and Poland accept the need to issue visas in a manner that will minimise the problems and expense for Kaliningrad residents.

More generally, Lithuania (which has significant economic links with Kaliningrad) has been keen to play a constructive role. In February 2000, the Lithuanian Deputy Foreign Minister

Vygaudas Usackas and the Russian Deputy Foreign Minister Ivan Ivanov signed a joint memorandum ('the Nida declaration') containing a list of projects for co-operation between Lithuania and Kaliningrad for possible inclusion in the Northern Dimension Action Plan. Although the issues (e.g. transport, energy, environmental protection and education) are at the uncontroversial end of the spectrum, they mark a significant departure in that they are the first example of practical joint action between an applicant country and the Russian Government over issues associated with EU enlargement.

Summary of papers

These and other issues are reflected and discussed in the papers that follow. In the remainder of this executive summary, I give a brief account of the line of argument and flavour of each of the contributions. The aim is to whet the reader's interest. Read as a whole, the collection of papers offer a lively debate about the problems faced by Kaliningrad and the ensuing policy issues both for Moscow and the EU.

Chapter 1 - René Nyberg: 'The Baltic as an Interface between the EU and Russia'

Rene Nyberg is a senior diplomat in the Finnish MFA. The paper draws attention to Russia's economic dependence on the EU. 60% of Russian GDP is generated by foreign trade. 40% of its foreign trade is with the EU, a figure that will rise to over 50% after the next phase of EU enlargement. It seems clear that Russia under President Putin has made a choice for co-operation with the EU and the West in general, and will not opt for isolationism or seek a non-existent 'Eurasian' option. However, Russia's relationship with the EU will be complicated by enlargement, the economic fault line between Russia and the EU and by friction with Latvia and Estonia.

For the first time, a genuine interest in the EU can be seen in Russia. But the Russian political elite is plagued by 'euro-ignorance' and an insufficient understanding of the process of integration. Events that have influenced Russia's perception of the EU include Finland's membership in 1995 (creating a common EU-Russia border), the prospect of Estonian membership, the introduction of the euro and the introduction of a European Security and Defence Policy (ESDP). Meanwhile, future commercial co-operation with European companies over development of gas deposits in the Barents Sea will underpin the EU-Russian economic relationship and give further meaning to Finland's successful initiative of 1997 to establish a 'Northern Dimension' policy for the EU.

Moscow has shown flexibility over Kaliningrad by proposing that it should be a 'pilot region' for EU-Russian co-operation. Lithuania has played an important role, and it is significant that Moscow has agreed to a joint Lithuanian-Russian proposal for projects for Kaliningrad in the context of the Northern Dimension.

Nevertheless, Kaliningrad remains the flash-point of the Baltic Sea region, and is simultaneously a microcosm of the problems of Russian society. The most difficult issue both for the EU and Russia will be arrangements for visas and transit through Lithuania for Kaliningrad residents travelling to and from Russia. A solution will have to be found that does not involve any derogation from the Schengen acquis. Finland will insist that all acceding countries sharing a common border with Russia adopt a border regime on a par with her own.

If Kaliningrad is the immediate test, St Petersburg is the key to a European future for Russia. It remains the largest metropolis in the Baltic Sea area, with the only major Russian port in the Baltic, a highly skilled labour force and significant scientific and cultural assets. It is Russia's gateway to an enlarging EU.

Chapter 2 - Yuri Borko: 'EU/Russian Co-operation: The Moscow Perspective'

Yuri Borko is one of the most prominent commentators in Russia on EU issues. His paper describes the architecture of the EU-Russia relationship. The Partnership and Co-operation Agreement, which came into effect on 1 December 1997, remains the main legal and organisational framework.

In June 1999, the European Council adopted a 'Common Strategy on Russia', and the Russian Government replied with a 'Medium Term Strategy for the Development of Relations between the Russian Federation and the EU (2000-2010)', which Putin presented (on behalf of Yeltsin) at the EU-Russia summit in October 1999.

The paper describes these documents, and examines the main elements of Moscow's approach to the EU. These include the political relationship, trade and investment, other forms of co-operation including infrastructure and technical assistance and the Russian approach to EU enlargement and cross-border co-operation.

The author quotes a public opinion survey to show that a policy of strategic partnership with the EU would receive widespread support from Russian society as a whole, not only among political and intellectual élites. Public opinion would support programmes with clear goals and tangible results, and - in this context - would welcome projects to help Kaliningrad.

The author nevertheless argues that developments could occur that would undermine EU-Russian relations. He mentions two possibilities: a drift towards a more authoritarian regime in Russia resulting in violation of human rights; or further eastwards enlargement of NATO.

Chapter 3 - Stephen Dewar: 'Kaliningrad: Key Economic Issues'

Stephen Dewar has a great deal of experience of technical assistance in Kaliningrad and in Russia more widely. He is a co-author of 'The Kaliningrad Puzzle'[4]. The following issues are discussed in the first part of his paper:

● How the trade patterns of Kaliningrad's neighbours have developed since 1993. <u>Poland's</u> main trade partner is the EU. Polish trade with Russia (including Kaliningrad) has remained low, but has not varied significantly. Her trade with the Baltic States is negligible. The <u>Baltic States</u> have increased their trade with the EU (especially with the Nordic countries), and their trade with Russia has fallen. None of these trends is of help to Kaliningrad. Trade is predominantly westwards from Poland and northwards from the Baltic States.

● Since 1993, the port of Kaliningrad has not handled more than 4-5% of the combined cargo passing through the Baltic ports in Russia and the Baltic States.

● Land transit traffic is limited. The development of Trans European Networks (TENs) is unlikely to lead to an improvement, as Kaliningrad will remain on spurs rather than on through routes. Lengthy customs and other border controls are in any case likely to remain a deterrent to through traffic.

● Kaliningrad is unlikely to become a transit mode for passenger air traffic or for air cargo. Further investment in the airport would not change this situation.

The paper analyses trade to and from Kaliningrad. Although Kaliningrad's international trade has grown since 1992, imports are almost three times the value of exports. Kaliningrad's main partners are Germany followed by Poland and Lithuania. There is a high level of volatility in reported trade, but this may reflect inadequacies in data collection and may also reflect the high volume of grey and black trade (which does not feature in the statistics).

The author discusses the breakdown of trade, including the predominance of cigarettes and other consumer goods in imports. He questions the usefulness of the Special Economic Zone (SEZ) as it currently operates. He concludes by suggesting some of the elements that would need to be addressed in any action plan.

Chapter 4 – Alexander Songal: 'Kaliningrad Oblast: Towards a European Dimension'

Alexander Songal was a senior member of the Oblast Administration under the previous Governor, Yuri Matochkin. The paper offers an insider's view of attempts during the past decade to identify and respond to the needs of the oblast. It describes measures to simplify transit through Lithuania, and explains the shortcomings of many measures that have been taken. EU technical assistance (through Tacis) has been of limited value. The paper describes this in some detail.

A section headed 'The weakening voice of Kaliningrad' provides a critical assessment of policies adopted by the present Oblast administration. The author offers suggestions on lessons that can be drawn from past mistakes. He suggests that there are grounds for cautious optimism, including the following:

● Russia is prepared to turn the Kaliningrad Oblast into a pilot project area, while the EU intends to include Kaliningrad in its Northern Dimension action plan.

● Lithuania is showing an increasing degree of pragmatism and recently took the lead in preparing joint Northern Dimension initiatives that have been presented recently to the European Commission.

● The Russian Government is starting consultations with the EU on Kaliningrad.

● Some high-ranking EU officials have mentioned the need for special arrangements for the Oblast (although others are reportedly against any exceptions to the rules).

● The issue of freedom of movement for residents in the Kaliningrad Oblast has been taken up by Mr Ole Espersen, the Commissioner of the Council for Baltic Sea States (CBSS) for Democratic Institutions and Human Rights, including the Rights of Persons belonging to Minorities.

The paper concludes with recommendations for the way forward, including a Constitutional Law for the Kaliningrad Oblast with the following elements:

● More involvement and responsibility for the Federal Government in regional matters that affect national interests. This should include the search for fruitful arrangements with the EU.

● More discretion for the Oblast authorities in economic and trade matters: in particular by giving increased room for manoeuvre in tax, tariff, banking regulations and, perhaps, customs duties.

● Gradual transfer of some units of the Russian MFA to Kaliningrad to make it an important centre of Russian, Baltic and European politics.

In conclusion, the author offers suggestions for improving the EU-Russia dialogue in respect of Kaliningrad.

Chapter 5 - Sylvia Gourova: 'EU-Kaliningrad: Future Aspirations'

Sylvia Gourova is a Deputy Mayor of Kaliningrad. She has previously represented the city authorities in Brussels. The paper, which is closely based on her keynote address to the conference on 29 March, places Kaliningrad in the context of recent developments in EU-Russia relations. It argues that there is a need for experts to start work on specific issues. These should be divided into (a) exclusively Russian issues (involving the Oblast and the Federal Government), and (b) issues falling within international competence, which will have to be settled between the EU and the Russian Federal Government.

The paper discusses transit of goods, and argues for preferential tariffs to offset the effect of Kaliningrad's isolation. It then examines the question of personal travel, and suggests that, when Lithuania has to introduce a visa regime, there could be preferential arrangements for Russians who have been living in Kaliningrad for five years or more. The paper welcomes the interest of the Government of Lithuania, and goes on to discuss problems of electricity supply after Lithuania is disconnected from the existing Russian power network. Finally, the paper suggests that there is a need to streamline customs procedures.

This paper is significant as providing the views of the most senior representative from Kaliningrad taking part in the 29 March conference.

Chapter 6 - Igor Leshukov: 'The Regional-Centre Divide: the Compatibility Conundrum'

Igor Leshukov is a former Russian diplomat, who now heads an independent think-tank in St Petersburg specialising in EU-related issues. The paper opens with a detailed and clear account of the structure of regional government in Russia under the 1993 Constitution. The balance of power between Oblasts and municipalities does not work well (there have been some acute political difficulties in Kaliningrad), and there are problems over budgetary transfers between the regions and the centre. The SEZ in Kaliningrad is financially beneficial to the Oblast. If it were terminated, the region would cease to be a net donor to the federal budget and would instead become a net recipient.

Against this background, the paper summarises the changes that Putin is making to strengthen centralised control and limit the independence of Governors. It then highlights the dilemmas that inadequacies in regional government pose for EU Governments.

The author explains why Kaliningrad is an especially tricky case. He refers to the historic sensitivities, 'a conquered piece of land,' and describes the Oblast as 'one of the most notorious regions in Russia in terms of lawlessness, corruption and criminality...a messy basket of national pride and maladministration...' The paper concludes by suggesting that Kaliningrad is so atypical that it cannot be regarded as a 'pilot' region for EU-Russian co-operation in any meaningful sense. What is needed is a concept agreed by the Federal Government for economic and social development, in effect a mission statement for Kaliningrad. Without this, any intensified European approach would be risky and involve high political costs.

This paper offers a trenchant analysis of Kaliningrad's difficulties, and is also of interest more generally in the context of regional-centre relations in Russia.

Chapter 7 - Vygaudas Usackas: 'Lithuania and Kaliningrad: Building a Partnership for the New Europe'

As Lithuanian Deputy Foreign Minister, Vygaudas Usackas has been active in exploring with the Russian Federal Government means of providing help to Kaliningrad. This is a lucid and important paper, which sets Lithuania's co-operation with Kaliningrad in the wider context. It describes various regional frameworks, including the Council of Baltic Sea States (CBSS), the EU's Northern Dimension, EU multilateral cross-border programmes ('Euroregions') and the United States Government's Northern European Initiative.

The paper turns to the process of Lithuania's and Poland's integration into the EU and the parallel process of deepening EU-Russian relations and the opportunities for expanding co-operation with Kaliningrad. It gives a clear account of his contacts with Kaliningrad, and suggests that there is a need both in Kaliningrad and Russia more generally for an information campaign to raise public awareness of EU issues.

The author concludes with a five-point programme of recommendations, and argues that the Kaliningrad region should be seen not as a problem but rather as an opportunity for introducing new forms of regional co-operation. 'In the light of ongoing political changes in Russia, Kaliningrad presents itself as an interesting test case of Russia's 'Europeanisation' vis-à-vis the processes of Euro-Atlantic integration.'

This optimistic conclusion provides an interesting contrast with the darker outlook of the preceding paper by Igor Leshukov.

Chapter 8 - Wojciech Zajaczkowski: 'Poland and the Kaliningrad Region: the Present and Future Prospects for Co-operation'

The author is a senior diplomat in the Polish Foreign Ministry. The paper offers a clear and practical explanation of Poland's policy towards Kaliningrad, which is firmly anchored in the broader context of Polish-Russian relations. One element of the institutional base of links with the Oblast is the Polish-Russian Commission for Co-operation between the North-Eastern Voivodships of the Republic of Poland and the Kaliningrad Region.

The paper describes steps to open up Kaliningrad in the early 1990s. At that time, a dilemma emerged over the identity of the region: was it to be the most westerly Russian military base or a region enjoying prosperity by playing the role of a bridge between the EU and the Russian Federation? The author comments that an observer will still gain the impression that there is no precise development strategy for the Oblast.

Nevertheless, enlargement of the EU will provide an opportunity to reverse these trends. The influence of Poland and other European countries should be directed at making Kaliningrad more open to economic and cultural co-operation, as well as to dialogue with Europe. Much will depend on the attitude of the central Russian authorities and the shape of the federative system of Russia. The paper goes on to list the bilateral and multilateral co-operation projects affecting Kaliningrad in which Poland is involved.

The paper explains Poland's plans (due to be implemented in 2001) to introduce visas for citizens of the Russian Federation visiting Poland. The intention is 'not to build a new iron curtain' but to put in order the mechanisms governing the movement of people. Poland will simultaneously expand its consular missions in Russia, including Kaliningrad, improve border crossings and ensure that visa charges are set at an affordable level.

Chapter 9 - Pertti Joenniemi: 'Kaliningrad, Borders and the Figure of Europe'

The author is a prominent academic expert on Kaliningrad, and is one of the co-authors of 'The Kaliningrad Puzzle'.

The author argues that Russia is faced by a dilemma: should Kaliningrad be a defensive outpost or an economic bridge? Increasingly Russia is prepared to treat Kaliningrad as a special case and is prepared to ask for special treatment for it. The Oblast remains an integral part of Russia, but has become increasingly a joint concern between Russia and the EU.

The EU is similarly pulled in two directions. Different priorities are created by (a) the EU's relationship with Russia as a whole and (b) the requirements of Kaliningrad, which is to a considerable degree exposed to the EU's policies and is part of the EU's 'near abroad'. On the one hand, the Partnership and Co-operation Agreement and the EU's Common Strategy on Russia of June 1999 both view Russia in undifferentiated terms and treat Kaliningrad as simply another Russian border. On the other hand, the EU's Northern Dimension rests on the premise that special policies are required in northern Europe.

Although the EU is taking steps to examine the problems created by Kaliningrad, it has not yet produced concrete policies. There is little comprehension within the EU that enlargement will bring in its wake a Russian enclave within the EU. The EU still acts as if Russia is something external and which it can either take or leave. It does not appreciate that, unless it modifies its policies, it will contribute to an increasing sense of isolation in Kaliningrad.

The author concludes by arguing that Kaliningrad calls for new thinking. 'The puzzle contrasts views of a Schengen-Europe with strictly defined borders with an alternative concept of Europe with a fuzzy eastern border – one that strives to open up the free movement of capital, services, goods and people. The border can be a sign of power to mark outer boundaries, ... or can provide space for a meeting ground that bridges distinctions between insiders and outsiders.'

This is probably the most radical and challenging paper in the collection. It offers a valuable analysis of the structure of the problem posed by Kaliningrad. However, the author does not offer detailed or precise policy proposals.

Some participants at the conference on 29 March did talk in specific terms of a possible removal of tariff barriers between the EU and Kaliningrad and freedom of travel – in effect proposing that Kaliningrad should be treated as if it were part of the EU. In practice, measures of this sort are unlikely to be acceptable either to the EU or to the Russian Government within the foreseeable future. The EU could not remove controls on its borders with Kaliningrad without exposing itself to major risks. It is equally hard to imagine that Russia would allow Kaliningrad to enjoy concessions which would involve the establishment of tariff barriers (going beyond those already created by the SEZ) and other controls between the Oblast and the rest of the country.

Chapter 10 - Stephen Dewar: 'Myths in the Baltic'

This is an authoritative and witty second paper by Stephen Dewar. The author speaks with detailed first hand knowledge. His astringent conclusions deflate wishful thinking and encourage a factual rather than a romantic approach.

The paper dissects some of the assumptions and assertions that are often made about Kaliningrad:

● It is a natural gateway between Russia and the West. Answer: not so in practice. Despite the tax concessions of the SEZ, Kaliningrad's isolation and the additional costs of transit militate against this.

● Potential Baltic Hong Kong. Answer: the dissimilarities are enormous.

● Ice-free port. Answer: yes, but the infrastructure of the port is poor, and the competing ports along the Baltic coast are more competitive, convenient and effective.

● Abundant natural resources, especially amber. Answer: true of amber, but this industry is dominated by crime and smuggling.

● Extensive arable land. Answer: this is true, but the problems in the foreseeable future are those of neglect and chronic under-investment. Current inadequacies in Russian legislation preclude foreign investment.

● SEZ is a means of stimulating investment. Answer: the beneficial effects are limited, and uncertainty about the future of the SEZ reduces its value.

● SEZ is a means of boosting international trade. Answer: imports have indeed grown, but this is the result of Kaliningrad's inability to develop internationally competitive industries. The paper concludes by examining in detail the operation of the SEZ and the effects of current tax concessions.

Although the author suggests that he is writing in a polemic vein, this is in fact one of the key pieces in this collection and deserves close attention.

Chapter 11 - Andrew Dolan: 'Kaliningrad and the European Union: the Clash of Expectations'

The author is an academic expert on Kaliningrad. His paper (a companion piece to the preceding chapter) is a call for political realism, drawing attention to common misperceptions and unjustified expectations on both sides.

The Kaliningrad administration does not appear to understand that derogation of the EU acquis, or concessions over visas, are out of the question. Similarly, well-meaning EU analysts sometimes overestimate the room for manoeuvre and underestimate just how sensitive the relationship is between Moscow and the regions.

The paper asks whether there is scope for an imaginative partnership between the Oblast and a future enlarged EU. It acknowledges that there may be opportunities for investment in Kaliningrad and help with structural reform and public administration.

However, Moscow will not allow Kaliningrad the autonomy it would need to become a magnet for business, and in any case the hard and uncomfortable truth is that the region is simply economically unattractive.

The message for the decision-makers in the Oblast is that they must themselves tackle internal reform. What has been achieved in Lithuania and Poland provides an example for Kaliningrad to follow.

Chapter 12 - Christopher Donnelly: 'Kaliningrad from a Security Perspective'

The author is a prominent analyst of the Russian armed forces and security policy issues. He offers a strategic overview, which rests on western security interests in the broadest sense.

The paper points out that, during the cold war, Kaliningrad was of strategic importance because of its geographic position and forward garrison. However, Russia is no longer seen as a threat, and Kaliningrad (whose active garrison now numbers some 18,000 men) has in large measure lost its military significance. The second thing to note is that there is no challenge to Kaliningrad's status as a subject of the Russian Federation.

Nevertheless, there is a strong interest in ensuring that the region does not become a political or economic problem area – in other words a hindrance to the improvement of Russia's relations with the West.

Kaliningrad's geographical situation is both a challenge and an opportunity. One important factor is how Russia develops the relationship between the centre and the regions. The dilemma is that geographic and economic logic plus the inclination of the local population are pushing the region into the West, while in Moscow there are concerns that Kaliningrad will be encircled and cut off as NATO and the EU expand. This requires the attention of western policy makers. EU enlargement (with the consequence of tighter control of borders affecting free movement of population and goods) could be even more problematical than NATO enlargement.

The problems associated with Kaliningrad include organised crime and drug trafficking. Economic problems affecting the Russian armed forces could also lead to weapons proliferation. Economic migration could also become a problem for Lithuania. These issues are most appropriately dealt with under the EU's Justice and Home Affairs umbrella.

As far as security is concerned, the western interest is first that Kaliningrad should become an example of co-operation between East and West; secondly, that it should develop a more efficient political and economic system and become more capable of resolving its own problems; and, thirdly, that Moscow should improve its relationship with the region, establishing a judicious balance between regional autonomy and effective enforcement of law and order.

Chapter 13 - Dag Hartelius: 'Kaliningrad – a European Challenge'

The author is the Director of the Department for Central and Eastern Europe at the Swedish Foreign Ministry. It is relevant that Sweden will hold the Presidency of the EU in the first six months of 2001, and will wish to take forward policy towards Kaliningrad and the EU's Northern Dimension more broadly.

The paper gives a balanced account of the problems and opportunities that Kaliningrad poses for the EU. Nowhere else will the consequences of EU enlargement for Russia be so deep or direct. Neither the EU nor Russia can afford to ignore the issue. An isolated or underdeveloped Kaliningrad would be harmful to the interests of both.

The issues that need to be addressed include implementation of the Schengen visa regime, border crossings and transit through Lithuania. Internal market regulations and the possibility of extending some of them to Kaliningrad will be a more difficult question. It will be important to find solutions, but it is not clear whether the EU should or could accept derogations from its core rules affecting imports and exports of goods and services. The answer may lie in regarding Kaliningrad as a testing ground for longer-term solutions for extending some new openings to the EU internal market to Russia as a whole.

At the same time, the Russian Government will have to consider what it can do unilaterally. Moscow will need to put legal and economic reform and an advanced anti-corruption programme on the fast track. The EU should give technical assistance, but only when a credible Russian initiative is under way. If the region is to become a pilot project for a new era of EU-Russian relations, it should at the same time become a fully fledged pilot project for the Northern Dimension, which provides the ideal platform for developing and managing specific projects. Meanwhile the EU should co-ordinate its support with that of the CBSS and also with Lithuania (which, in view of its existing activity, could be given a lead role in some areas) and Poland.

If the EU and Russia can succeed in managing EU-Kaliningrad relations in a practical and constructive way, this could become a model for wider EU-Russian relations. Expectations should be realistic. Kaliningrad is unlikely to revert to being a military fortress and is scarcely likely to become a Baltic Hong Kong, but it will remain a piece of Russia at the heart of Europe. What happens there is likely to have major consequences for northern Europe and the whole range of EU-Russian relations.

Chapter 14 – Stephen Dewar: 'What is to be done'

In this article, Stephen Dewar pulls the debate in the book together and, as a practitioner who is both dispassionate and committed to the region, offers ideas that will deserve close consideration in Brussels and EU capitals. There are also messages for the Russian Government and Presidential Administration and the authorities in Kaliningrad. The author examines the EU's interests in the region as a whole, and proposes the establishment of a 'Kaliningrad Equalisation and Development Fund'. It is fitting that the collection of papers should end with a paper so firmly based on a recognition that politics is the art of the possible.

----

[1] The Russian term for an administrative region. The majority of the 89 'subjects' of the Russian Federation are known as Oblasts.

[2] The Northern Dimension is discussed in the paper by René Nyberg (Chapter 1).

[3] There are reciprocal arrangements for Lithuanian nationals making short visits to the Kaliningrad Oblast.

[4] *The Kaliningrad Puzzle* by Pertti Joenniemi, Stephen Dewar and Lyndelle B. Fairlie, published by the Baltic Institute and the Åland Islands Peace Institute, February 2000.

SETTING THE SCENE

EU/RUSSIA RELATIONS

Chapter 1

The Baltic as an Interface between the EU and Russia

René Nyberg
Head of Division for Eastern Affairs,
Finnish Ministry of Foreign Affairs

Success stories and fault lines

'Trade is booming across the Baltic Sea. […] It is the biggest, most complicated, and most promising piece of the new Europe.'[1] These ringing words of *The Economist* two years ago are just as apposite today. The Baltic Sea and North Eastern Europe fringing it is the region where we can discern the geographical *finalité* of the European Union. Today Russia borders one member state of the Union – Finland, but in the foreseeable future the Union will gain four new members bordering Russia. These are Poland, Lithuania, Latvia and Estonia. Some day, hopefully, it will even gain a fifth new member sharing a border with Russia, i.e. Norway.

Even after the contraction of the space ruled by Moscow, north west is the direction where the Russian heartland is closest to the outside world. Paradoxically the loss of the outer and inner Soviet empires have made Russia a much more European state than the Soviet Union ever was. The European Union, and indeed Euroland, is only 1,200 km west of Moscow, a mere 200 km from St Petersburg, 'the Northern Capital' as it is again being affectionately called. Not since the days of Peter the Great some three hundred years ago has Russia been as purely Russian in the ethnic sense as she is today. Around eighty per cent of the population of the Russian Federation claim to be Russian.

The post-Soviet space, as the territory of the former Soviet Union is called in Russian parlance, can show very few success stories. The Baltic States - Estonia, Latvia and Lithuania - are the ones that come to mind, consolidated and firmly set on a path of European integration. But Russia herself is another success story not always recognised as such by the Russians themselves, or the West for that matter. Compared with the rest of the CIS states, against any criteria, Russia is a country of reforms and economic opportunity that attracts immigrants. Today, all of Russia's borders constitute growing fault lines for different reasons. Only on its border with the EU and its future member states is the gap growing to the disadvantage of Russia.

Despite a history of invasions from there, west is today the only benign direction for Moscow. West is also the direction of Russian exports that have during the past ten years - without exception - secured Russia a hefty annual trade surplus. The Russia of today is much more dependent on foreign trade than the Soviet Union ever was. According to a recent report of the Russian Council for Foreign and Defence Policy, *SVOP*, economic relations with the outside world affect the lives of one third of the Russian population.[2] Sixty per cent of Russian GDP is generated by foreign trade. This is an exceptionally high figure for such a large country. Forty per cent of her trade goes to the EU, and the share will rise to fifty per cent after the enlargement of the Union. Sixty per cent of all investments in Russia come from Europe. Russian gas will never heat - or cool - American homes. US trade with Russia is no larger than that of Finland.

The centre of Russian economic gravity lies clearly in the west. Russia has come to know the 'Rotterdam syndrome', being dependent on ports outside her sovereign control. The Baltic ports, non-Russian and Russian alike, are essential gateways for exports and imports. Attempts to resist interdependence, this most European of phenomena, echo Soviet autarkic thinking.

Claims of Russian success could easily be dismissed by, for example, a Ukrainian observer, who could point out that the real difference between the two largest countries in the post-Soviet sphere lies in hydrocarbons and minerals, exports of which foot all of Russia's bills, including the one for the war in Chechnya. This is a correct observation, to a point. But the same observation also captures the challenge to which Ukraine must respond. Both countries face economic and social ruin without a large-scale reconstruction of their whole society, from infrastructure to the social sphere. The essence of the chasm at the western border of Russia and Ukraine alike is the risk of being cut off from the dynamism of the enlarging EU and having to face self-inflicted isolation behind a growing normative divide.

The need for investments is understood by the Russian leadership. Unfortunately, as so often in Russia, even the creation of a climate conducive to investments is approached with a quick fix. The *SVOP* report speaks about the need to introduce privileges for foreign investors including the creation of special organs, ministries, state committees, etc. *SVOP* demands the creation of the means to protect the investments even by the use of force.[3] There is no reason to doubt the sincerity of these recommendations, but they do reveal a stunning lack of comprehension of the core problem – the absence of the rule of law. Privileges for foreign investors introduced by decree can just as easily be rescinded by decree.

The Russian market offers enormous opportunities. But trade with Russia is today not essential even for a next-door neighbour like Finland. Only four per cent of Finnish exports go to Russia. This is less than our exports to the three Baltic States taken together. The corresponding figure for Poland is five per cent. In the case of the UK we are talking of only 0.5 per cent. Even for Germany trade with Russia is less than two per cent of total exports. As things stand today Russia has only one export item which is vital for Europe – gas. But increasing output of gas will require huge investment, an issue discussed below.

Russia remains the challenge for the enlarging Union. The ongoing debate in Russia covers a wide range of alternatives, but after the inauguration of Vladimir Putin, it is clear that Russia will not opt for isolationism or try to turn her eyes towards the East in search of a Eurasian option that does not exist. As *SVOP* points out, a multipolar world is unattainable for Russia, herself a weak pole.[4] In other words, Russia has made her choice. That choice is trade and co-operation with the European Union and the West in general. It is a rational choice as it reflects the reality of the Russian economy.

Hegemonic demon

Most of the references to Russia as a new Weimar Republic seem mistaken. In a recent speech, the German Foreign Minister Joschka Fischer discussed the Weimar period and the 'hegemonic demon' of German politics in a way that also gives an observer of Russia food for thought. According to Joschka Fischer, Germany's 'ability for peace' (*Friedensfähigkeit*) in Europe is still today being assessed on the basis of her relationships with her largest neighbours, France and Poland.[5]

Russia is agonising about her lost glory. It is painful to admit that the Soviet Union lost the very peace it had achieved at such an enormous cost. The *SVOP* denies that Russia lost the Cold War, instead she lost the post-Cold War peace.[6]

Russian society is torn between its own rhetoric and the stark reality of the land. Henry Kissinger recently wondered whether Russia would try to resurrect the Russian Empire or search for security within her existing borders.[7] This is reminiscent of the historic advice that a poet gave the Swedish nation in 1811. After the loss of one third of the Swedish realm, i.e. Finland, to Russia in 1809, Sweden was dangerously weakened and faced a risk of partition by Denmark and Russia. The poet counselled the nation to 'reconquer Finland within Sweden's [new] borders'.[8]

As the German diplomat and historian Jürgen von Alten notes in his perceptive book *Weltgeschichte der Ostsee* (World History of the Baltic Sea), Finnish history has in many ways caught up with Swedish history. Sweden almost bled white in her conflicts with Russia.[9] By forsaking Finland in 1812, when he met Alexander I on lost Finnish soil in Turku, Jean Baptiste Bernadotte, the former *maréchal de France* and future King Charles XIV John of Sweden, ushered in an unprecedented period of stability and peace for Sweden and the Autonomous Grand Duchy of Finland alike. The union of Finland with Russia was basically a happy marriage before it was destroyed by attempts to curtail Finnish autonomy and russify the nation.

It is often painful to come to grips with one's past. *Vergangenheitsbewältigung* or rather the lack of it explains many problems - and not only in Russia. I am thinking of Austria, which has yet again been caught up by her own history. But without facing its own history a nation cannot face the future. The only surviving original of the secret additional protocol to the Molotov-Ribbentrop Pact of August 1939 did after all, despite repeated Soviet denials of its very existence, surface from the General Secretary's archive. I have seen it with my own eyes exhibited in Moscow with Stalin's signature written large in blue ink on a German military map.

Reconciliation

European post war history is a history of reconciliation. And its success is based on this very reconciliation. According to Joschka Fischer, the eastward enlargement of the EU, *Osterweiterung*, is an essential part of German reunification. Enlargement would not only constitute an act of historic justice and increase the stability of Germany, but it would, in the negative case, be a blow to the whole idea of European integration.

The future of European integration will also be affected by the ability of Russia to reconcile herself with her own past and with the past she shares with her neighbours.

Katyn remains the key to Russian-Polish relations. That the Finno-Russian drama eventually led to reconciliation was never preordained nor was it guaranteed. Even Gorbachev could never bring himself to admit that Russia had attacked. It was left to Yeltsin in 1992 to lay a wreath at the National War Memorial in Helsinki and pronounce the little words, 'I am sorry', words taken to heart by the Finnish nation.

It is from the vantage point of a reconciled neighbour of Russia that Finland watches with apprehension the recurring tensions in Baltic-Russian relations. Some of the rhetoric is evidently tactical in order to divert attention from real problems. Some of it addresses issues that are in the process of being settled under the relentless pressure created – not by Russian intervention – but rather by European integration.

The cause of friction between the Baltic States and Russia is political and historical despite its legalistic veneer and moralistic undertones. It is the wrong done to the Estonian, Latvian and Lithuanian nations through their forced incorporation into the Soviet Union in the summer of 1940.

To add insult to injury, the person who was ordered to recommend to the Supreme Soviet that it accept the application of the Estonian puppet government to join the 'family of Soviet peoples' was none other than Otto Vilgelmovich Kuusinen. He had failed to carry out Stalin's previous order to preside over the 'Popular Government of Finland' created after the Soviet attack in November 1939. Kuusinen was an ethnic Finn - a Quisling before Quisling - who survived Stalin and died in 1964 as a member of Khrushchev's presidium-cum-politburo and was buried in the Kremlin wall.

The basic cause of rancour is not the fate of the Russophone population of Latvia and Estonia, who are economically far better off than most Russians living in Russia or any other Russians in the diaspora in the post-Soviet sphere. It is Russia's difficulty in admitting yet another Winter War or Katyn despite the fact that Yeltsin and the Russian *intelligentsia* did so in the early days of democratic Russia. That is something that also many Balts, unfortunately, seem to have forgotten. Reconciliation is a two-way street.

Benign Nordic influence

Finland and Sweden share a deeply ingrained tradition of caution in their relations with Russia. Historically this is reminiscent of the Prussian experience lost after Bismarck. A reference could also be made to Atatürk. This basic disposition has, at times, forced the neighbours to align themselves with Russia, but today this tradition is at a premium in dealing with the Baltic Sea region, which has become the interface between the EU and Russia.

The Russian path to integration with Europe and the world is thorny and will be long. Unlike the Central European countries, Russia has so far not been able to profit from the closeness of her dynamic neighbours. Nokia has eight factories in China, none in Russia. Mathematicians are recruited from all over the world - India, China, Israel and Hungary - but strangely enough not very often from Russia. Electronic component firms wanting to establish themselves in St Petersburg, in order to profit from the considerable scientific muscle of the city, are frustrated by red tape. The city of Vyborg, the largest city in the Leningrad *Oblast* and Finland's second city before the war, has been degraded into a bazaar of cheap petrol and liquor, prostitution and pirate recordings. This very same fault line can be observed at the Estonian-Russian border, on the River Narva, across which the two fortresses built in the 16th Century by King Erik XIV of Sweden and Tsar Ivan III still face each other.

The Russian Government does not deny the benign influence of Finland and the other Nordic countries and especially that of the EU on the Baltic States. Nevertheless Russia is locked in unproductive polemics with both Latvia and Estonia. The relationship with Lithuania is better, although the Duma has to this very day failed to ratify the border treaty that the two countries have signed. In the case of Estonia an initialled border treaty is waiting to be signed. Despite the demarcation of the border with Latvia, Russia has not even agreed to initial the treaty. In the course of the negotiations Russia repeatedly pocketed concessions and asked for more.

Euro-ignorance and geoeconomics

For the first time, a genuine interest in the European Union can be seen in Russia. By far the most important outcome to date of the EU's Common Strategy on Russia was the decision by the Russian Government to respond with a Russian strategy for co-operation with the EU. This document was presented by then Prime Minister Putin at the EU-Russia Summit in Helsinki in October 1999.

Despite efforts to reassess Russia's place in the world the political elite is still plagued by what could be called 'euro-ignorance' and by an insufficient understanding of the whole process of integration. The role of Russia in European integration has never been really discussed in Moscow. Do we in the EU have a clearer picture? The Partnership and Co-operation Agreement (PCA) which forms the legal basis of EU-Russia relations sets a free trade agreement as one of the main goals. This is a tall order for both parties, comparable to the eastward enlargement of the Union.

The northward enlargement of the European Union through the accession of Finland and Sweden gave the Union a new look. The 1997 Finnish initiative on a Northern Dimension for the policies of the Union was an attempt to describe the changed situation of the expanding Union as a neighbour of Russia – an attempt to view the upcoming eastward enlargement from a Northern European standpoint.

It is by no means easy to influence the development of Russian political thinking. A vestige of the past is the continued prevalence of a view of the EU as a kind of free trade organisation operating in the shadow of NATO. Another is to recognise only the political character of the Union without understanding the dynamics of the deepening integration – the Single Market, EMU, etc.

Only very gradually and very hesitantly is Moscow coming to acknowledge the fact that the expanding EU is thoroughly and profoundly changing Europe. The deeply entrenched perception of NATO as the enemy colours every analysis. Geopolitics, or, to use von Alten's words, 'unproductive geopolitical thinking' still takes precedence over geoeconomics.[10]

Recently one of President-elect Putin's top economic advisers, Vladimir Mau, floated the idea that Russia should strive to fulfil the Maastricht and Copenhagen criteria, not in order to join the Union, but in order to be able to integrate with European structures.[11]

The following six events that have influenced Russia's perception of Europe and the world are instructive:

● Finland's membership of the European Union made Russia a geographical neighbour of the EU. At the same time, Finland extricated itself from the Russian sphere of influence to which it had been consigned under the Molotov-Ribbentrop Pact;

● The 1997 invitation to Estonia, as the first ex-republic of the Soviet Union, to enter into negotiations on accession to the EU, was registered with keen interest in Moscow;

● The introduction of the euro in 1999, and especially the decision of the Germans to give up the Deutschmark, had a profound impact and rocked the very foundations of the traditional geopolitical approach;

● The shock of Kosovo is still being felt and is once again complicating determination of the true weight of the European Union;

● The introduction of a European security and defence policy shows yet again that progressive European integration is in fact a moving target and does not fit neatly into traditional categories of thought;

● And, finally, China's steps towards membership of the WTO clearly demonstrate to Moscow how much more progress China has made in the area of economic reform.

Gas

The common agenda of the EU and Russia includes a number of vital issues like the environment – operational safety of nuclear reactors, nuclear waste, pollution of the Baltic – and energy – the Baltic Energy Ring and the North European Gas Pipeline.

Russia needs investments in every walk of life. The main sources of export revenue – gas and oil – are no exception. The problem was dramatically brought to the attention of the Russian people in a recent public clash between two CEOs and oligarchs, Anatoly Chubais of Unified Energy System (UES) and Rem Vyakhirev of Gazprom. The clash was ultimately mediated in front of a TV audience by President-elect Putin. Chubais' claim that Gazprom has neglected to invest in upstream production squares with the facts. In order to fulfil both its export commitments and satisfy its inland clients like UES, Gazprom has to invest in existing production fields, open up new fields and build new pipelines. All of this cannot possibly be done at the same time.

Western Siberia will remain for years to come the largest source of Russian gas. The strategic choice of Gazprom seems, however, to be to open up a new production site in the Barents Sea. The decision to defer the opening of production sites on the Yamal peninsula and instead go for offshore production in the Barents Sea also has implications for future pipeline routes. Instead of developing gas production only in Western Siberia and hence building a second so-called Yamal pipeline through

Belarus and Poland, Gazprom and the Russian Government are seriously looking at an alternative. Developing the Shtokmanovskoye field in the Barents Sea on the basis of a production-sharing agreement would require a second pipeline.

The North European Gas Pipeline, as the project is called, would be 1,000 km shorter than a second Yamal pipeline. The pipeline would not be burdened by transit fees or theft and would link directly with the European gas network.

The reasons are both economic and political. Shtokmanovskoye lies further to the north but does not otherwise require different technology or know-how than present offshore production in the North Sea. It is definitely a more hospitable environment than the permafrost of Yamal. As an offshore site it is also better suited for production sharing than Western Siberian fields would be.

On 21 April 2000 the Duma approved legislation providing for production in the Shtokmanovskoye field to be shared. The envisaged consortium would consist of two Russian companies, Gazprom and Rosshelf, each with a 25% stake, and four Western companies, Conoco, Fortum, Norsk Hydro and Total Fina, each with a 12.5% share.

In a message to the Baltic Sea States Summit in Kolding, Denmark, on 12-13 April 2000, President-elect Putin confirmed that Russia '... is open to co-operation and implementation of major investment projects, primarily in the fields of energy and infrastructure development. The construction of the North European Gas Pipeline and the Baltic Pipeline system, as well as shaping the Baltic Energy Ring, can provide a stable energy base for the whole of Europe, not only our region.'

On the basis of the feasibility studies conducted, it is evident that laying a pipeline on the bottom of the Baltic Sea is practicable from the technical, environmental, legal and economic points of view. The most likely landfall on the southern shore of the Baltic Sea seems to be the German city of Greifswald close to the Polish border, where the infrastructure of the largest decommissioned East German Nuclear Power Plant - Lubmin - offers a possibility to construct a gas-fired station.

There can be no doubt that energy offers the most important field of co-operation between the Union and Russia. The production-sharing agreement for Shtokmanovskoye is a telling example. Legislation approved by the Duma requires that the share of Russian technology and services in the investment projects should be 70%. In other words the opening of a large production field in the Barents Sea would mean boom and salvation for the entire shipbuilding and engineering sector in the Russian North West. These are the vistas that have convinced the Russian political and economic elite of the merits of the Northern Dimension.[12]

Kaliningrad

During the meeting of the EU Troika with Russia in June 1999, Russia floated a proposal to discuss the consequences of EU enlargement for Kaliningrad in the context of the PCA. This was quite a sensation and certainly took the Union by surprise. It was followed in September by Russia's very positively formulated response to the EU initiative on the Northern Dimension. Then Prime Minister Putin characterised Kaliningrad as a pilot region when he presented Russia's Strategy for the EU in Helsinki in October.

A lot of the credit goes to Lithuania. I am convinced that it was the astute and well-considered approach of the Lithuanian Government that convinced Moscow to revise its policy towards Kaliningrad. In a series of round table discussions from 1997 onward the subject of Kaliningrad was broached from the standpoint of both Moscow and Kaliningrad. The economic crisis of August 1998 and the approaching enlargement of the Union ultimately persuaded Russia not only to discuss Kaliningrad with the EU, but also to agree to a joint Lithuanian-Russian proposal for projects for Kaliningrad in the context of the Northern Dimension. With this, the EU's first and most important basic condition was met: that the problems of Kaliningrad be put on the table in Brussels only at Moscow's initiative.

Kaliningrad is in many respects the flashpoint of the Baltic Sea region and at the same time a microcosm of the problems of Russian society. If Kaliningrad is a pilot, it is also a test; a Russian exclave to become an EU enclave. With Kaliningrad finally on the EU-Russia agenda several red herrings are being chased by Russian and Western aficionados alike. The upcoming gubernatorial elections in November 2000 are already being felt in Kaliningrad. The most difficult and probably the most likely issue to create tension is the question of transit to and from Russia. This is no minor problem as it directly affects the Union's future external border regime.

Despite demands for special arrangements by the Russian authorities and well-meaning Western academic advice, there can be no derogation from the Schengen *acquis*. Notwithstanding the differences, the Finno-Russian border remains the only relevant comparison to the future common border of the Union with Russia in Kaliningrad. The integrity of the external border and the security of the Union cannot be vouched for with arrangements emanating from Soviet and post-Soviet practices where passports and visas are replaced by identification documents and special permits (*propuska*).

As a future member of the Union, Estonia has already decided to stop the so-called visa-free small border traffic between Narva and Ivangorod and in the South East (Petseri/Pechora). She now requires passports, but is ready to issue multiple entry visas without a fee for locals.

As the guardian of the only EU-Russia border, Finland claims that the existing border regime has proven its worth. It is both flexible and secure. It will be adapted to Schengen when Finland and the other members of the Nordic Passport Union start to implement Schengen rules in March 2001. It should come as no surprise that Finland will demand that all acceding countries sharing a common border with Russia adopt a border regime on a par with her own.

St Petersburg

Kaliningrad might be the immediate test, but St Petersburg is the key to a European future for Russia. Most western ideas and innovations that have entered Russia during the last 300 years have done so through St Petersburg. The end of communist rule saw a lot of energy set free in the city, but, *hèlas,* so far it has mostly been in the form of a steady brain drain to Moscow. It is stunning to realise how large the St Petersburg expat community is among the ruling elite of the country. President Putin has surrounded himself with people he knew and worked together with in Leningrad/St Petersburg.

St Petersburg still suffers from eighty years of neglect and ostracism and a recently acquired reputation for rampant crime. Instead of turning its attention to the wide open world, both near and far, the city has too long been fixated on Moscow.

St Petersburg has no future as the major arms maker it used to be during Soviet times. The city has yet to define its new role in Russia and in the Baltic Sea area. Under market conditions sustainable growth can only be achieved on the basis of real strengths.

St Petersburg is still the largest metropolis in the Baltic Sea area. The city is a gateway to the enlarging EU. It has the only major Russian port in the Baltic and a highly skilled labour force. Its scientific and cultural assets are considerable. St Petersburg, Russia's Northern Capital, has advantages that Russia cannot disregard in her evolving relationship with the European Union.

---

[1] The Economist, *Sea of Dreams,* 18 April 1998.
[2] *Rossiskaya Vneshnyaya Politika Pered Vyzovami XXI Veka* (Challenges of the 21st Century facing Russian Foreign Policy), March 2000, *Sovet Vneshnyei i Oboronitelnoi Politiki (SVOP),* Moscow, pre-print p.12.

[3] *SVOP*, p.19.

[4] *SVOP*, p. 16.

[5] Joschka Fischer: '*Gustav Stresemann - Außenminister als Außenseiter*', speech, 26 January 2000, Berlin.

[6] *SVOP*, p.11.

[7] *Die Welt am Sonntag,* 26 March 2000.

[8] Esaias Tegnér: *Svea* 1811 (...*inom Sverges gränser erövra Finland åter.*).

[9] Jürgen von Alten, *Die Weltgeschichte der Ostsee*, Berlin 1996 Siedler, p.164, footnote 50.

[10] von Alten, p. 125; See interview of the Russian Ambassador to the EU, V.N. Likhachov, *Nezavisimaya Gazeta*, 6 April 2000.

[11] *Kommersant Vlast,* 21 March 2000.

[12] Kauppalehti, *Fortumin jättihankkeet etenevät taas Venäjällä* (Fortum's giant projects in Russia advance again), 19 April 2000.

Chapter 2

EU/Russia Co-operation: The Moscow Perspective

Yuri Borko
President, Association of European Studies, Moscow

A comparison between the EU's Common Strategy and Russia's Strategy Paper

This paper looks at the prospects for EU-Russia co-operation as seen in Moscow. It looks, first and foremost, at the official policy formulated in the 'Medium-term Strategy for the Development of Relations between the Russian Federation and the European Union' (hereafter called the Strategy Paper) which was presented by the Russian government at the EU-Russia Summit in Helsinki on 29 October 1999. The Strategy Paper was the first statement of its kind proclaimed by the Russian government in the 1990s. Moreover, it still remains the only Russian strategy of its sort. As such, it deserves comment.

The core of the document is the idea of establishing an EU-Russia strategic partnership. According to the text:

'The strategy is aimed at the development and strengthening of a strategic partnership between Russia and the EU in European and world affairs and the prevention and settlement, through common efforts, of local conflicts in Europe with an emphasis on the supremacy of international law and non-use of force. It provides for the construction of a united Europe without dividing lines and the interrelated and balanced strengthening of the positions of Russia and the EU within an international community of the 21st century.'

Four points are worth mentioning:

1. This strategy is interlinked with the objective of 'mobilising the economic potential and managerial experience of the EU to promote the development of a socially oriented market economy in Russia based on fair competition principles and further construction of a democratic state governed by the rule of law.'

2. Moscow regards the strategic partnership as a goal to be achieved by settling some short and medium-term tasks and by establishing an adequate basis for the partnership. The main legal and organisational framework of this strategy remains the Partnership and Cooperation Agreement (PCA) between the Russian Federation, on the one hand, and the EU and its Member States, on the other hand. This was signed in 1994.

3. The Strategy Paper takes into consideration the goals and aims of the 'Common Strategy of the European Union on Russia' adopted at the European Council in Cologne on 4 June 1999. Preparation of the Russian document was begun in the context of the EU initiative. Moscow's aim appears to be to combine the benefits of both strategies.

4. Moscow underlines what partnership means in terms of mobilising the potential of EU and Russian support for the EU's efforts to achieve its goals, if and where their interests coincide. For instance, support could include: contributing to economic growth and a reduction in unemployment in EU Member States due to an economic revival in Russia and growing flows of mutual trade and investment; supplying the EU with fuels (gas and oil); integrating the potential in those fields of R&D where Russia has achieved unique results; Russian

participation in the development of various Trans-European infrastructure networks (transport, pipelines, electricity, electronic communications); co-operation in space; and participation in the eurozone.

The Strategy Paper defines several priorities for implementing the strategic partnership:

● 'To ensure pan-European security by the Europeans themselves without either the isolation of the United States and NATO or their dominance on the continent.'

● 'To work out Russia's position on the 'defence identity' of the EU with the Western European Union (WEU) to be included in it, as well as to develop political and military contacts with the WEU as an integral part of the EU, and to promote practical co-operation in the field of security (peace-making, crisis management, various aspects of arms limitation and reduction, etc.) which could counterbalance, inter alia, NATO-centrism in Europe.'

● The formation of a developed all-European economic and legal infrastructure as a reliable basis for trade, investment, sub-regional and trans-border co-operation; environmental protection; co-operation in science, education and public health; the fight against terrorism, the illegal trade in drugs and trans-national organised crime.

● Consultations and, if necessary, the co-ordination of positions in international organisations. Besides, Russia intends to apply the positive experience of European integration with a view to promoting both the development of integration processes within the Commonwealth of Independent States (CIS) and the involvement of the Newly Independent States (NIS) in political, economic, financial and humanitarian relations with the EU.

Last but not least, this strategy takes into account Russia's relations with the UN, OSCE, NATO, the Council of Europe, OECD, the World Bank and EBRD. It is because of this approach that the implementation of the strategy will be interlinked with the attitude taken by Russia towards these organisations.

Two questions need to be answered in the light of this analysis of the Strategy Paper:

● What are the similarities and differences between the strategies announced by both Russia and the EU?

● What are the prospects for implementation of the Strategy Paper?

The second question will be analysed after looking at the subsequent sections of the Strategy Paper which deal with some concrete areas of co-operation between the parties concerned.

Both parties have been inspired by the idea of co-operation with a view to strengthening security in Europe and beyond. Meanwhile, only the EU's Common Strategy underlines the correlation between security and stability, taking into consideration the very unstable situation in several post-communist countries. The Russian Strategy Paper does not mention this interdependence at all. At the same time, Moscow emphasises the idea that Europeans should guarantee European security themselves, without US and NATO dominance. The Russian foreign policy concept is free from the *idée fixe* of utilising so-called 'intra-imperialist contradictions'. The new approach is more pragmatic - to rely both on a more profound interdependence between Russia and Western Europe in terms of security and on an improved mutual understanding between them. This is clearly intended to counterbalance Western Europe's relationship with the US.

Both documents speak about Russia's transition to a market economy and democracy. The difference relates to the interpretations of correlation between this process and relations between the Partners. The EU's Common Strategy speaks about the EU's 'assistance' and 'contribution' to transition in Russia. Moscow prefers a different concept - 'utilisation' of the potential and experience of Western Europe. This is the difference between a donor and a recipient. There is also a hidden difference which, to my mind, seems to be more important. It is defined neither by the EU's Common Strategy nor by the Russian Strategy Paper, but it is well-known. From the point of view of Western European capitals, Russia's successful advancement towards the above-mentioned goals will be a very important prerequisite of stability and security in Europe as a whole. It is because of this, that the 'consolidation of democracy, the rule of law and public institutions in Russia' is placed first on the list of the principal objectives of the EU's Common Strategy. According to the Russian Strategy Paper, the systemic transformation within the country is defined not as a goal of partnership *with* the EU, but as the goal of the Russian strategy *towards* the EU. A very remarkable nuance!

Both strategies aim at developing intensive economic co-operation between the Parties. Meanwhile, there are some differences in this area as well. According to the EU's Common Strategy, the long-term goal of economic co-operation has to be 'integration of Russia into a common European economic and social area', which will be preceded by establishing an EU-Russian Free Trade Area. The Russian strategy envisages only the gradual creation of a free trade area and Russian access to 'the entire European economic space' which should not be at variance with Russian economic integration within the CIS. It is unclear, whether the Russian Strategy Paper does not proclaim the idea of integration into the European economic area because of the short time frame (10 years) which this document deals with, or whether Moscow continues to give priority to integration within the CIS. The second suggestion seems to be more likely. In any case, Russia intends to apply the positive experience of the EU with a view to promoting integration within the CIS and to develop co-ordination of the CIS participants' policies towards the EU.

What about Russia's membership of the EU over the long term? The EU's Common Strategy is silent. However, it is well-known that this idea is rejected by all EU Member States, and there are no signs that this position will change. In its turn, according to the Russian Strategy Paper, Moscow does not intend to make an official application for accession to the EU. The explanation is that 'Russia must preserve its freedom to define and implement its domestic and foreign policies, as well as preserving its status and the advantages of being a Eurasian state and the largest country in the CIS'.

Summarising this analysis of the similarities and differences between both strategies, one can conclude that they do not seem to be mutually incompatible in terms of strategic goals and principles. But they are of a contradictory character as far as some perceptions, approaches and concrete aims are concerned.

This thesis can be confirmed by a more detailed exposition of particular aspects of the Russian Strategy Paper.

Perspectives of political dialogue

The aspiration of Russia for the development of its dialogue with the EU is based on several factors:

● It results from the fact of the EU's transition to a Common Foreign and Security Policy (CFSP), together with the perspective of establishing a European Defence Policy. Moscow intends to set up direct links with the institutions which are responsible for CFSP as well as having regular contacts with the WEU. The proposed annual meetings between the Chairman of the Russian Council of Ministers and the President of the European Commission will also contribute to a more intensive political dialogue.

● The lessons of Kosovo also encourage the development of political dialogue. Kosovo is not specifically mentioned in the Russian Strategy Paper. However, this is not significant. The authors of this document bear in mind the EU-WEU decision to found its own military corps, which will be capable of carrying out peace-making operations in conflicts in Europe independent of - i.e. outside - the NATO framework. From this point of view, it is surely very significant that the Russian document speaks about co-operation with the EU 'in the prevention and peaceful settlement of conflicts *in the OSCE area*' (emphasis added).

●The evident trend of the EU towards a more independent foreign, security and defence policy is taken by Moscow as a reason for strengthening the role of the OSCE as the principal basis of European security. Taken within this context, the formulation quoted above is evidently a deliberate choice.

● Moscow seems to be anxious to avoid the traditional accusation that it is attempting to drive a wedge between the EU and the US. To oppose this, the Russian Strategy Paper underlines the idea of Russia's participation in the EU's dialogues with the other great powers and economic groupings. In particular, Moscow supports the proposal made by Finland to hold a trilateral Russia-EU-US summit.

● The most sensitive topic of dialogue with the EU, i.e. Russia-NATO relations, is hidden behind the text. The only reference to NATO dominance is worded very cautiously. It seems that Moscow will try to find a balance between two goals - to diminish NATO's influence in Europe and to put in order its relations with the Alliance. Being in a state of uncertainty about NATO's plans for further eastwards expansion, Moscow has chosen a reserved position and said nothing on this topic in its strategic declaration. Nevertheless, the choice of the Alliance will be of crucial importance for the future political dialogue between Russia and the EU.

Co-operation in trade and investment

A general concept of the Russian economic strategy towards the EU is expounded in the following terms: Russia 'will continue its efforts with a view to the further opening of the EU's market to Russian exports, abolition of residual trade discrimination, stimulation of European investment, securing Russian interests in the context of the EU enlargement and the process of transition to the euro, countering any attempts to hinder economic integration within the CIS, including by means of so-called 'special relations' [between the EU] and some CIS states'. To my mind, this is not the best part of the Strategy Paper, not only because of its aggressiveness, but mainly because of the deficit of constructive ideas. This shortcoming is corrected a bit in the following sections of the Strategy Paper which are dedicated to various fields of economic co-operation between Russia and the EU.

Meanwhile, co-operation in trade and investment is put as the top economic priority. This approach results from the fact that the EU is Russia's principal trading partner, and there are no signs that it will be replaced by any other country or regional association in the near future. The EU share in Russian external trade is 33-35% as against 20-21% for the CIS, 11-12% for the CEE countries, 7-8% for the US and 4-5% for China. Stable growth of trade with the EU is of crucial importance for Russia. However, now their bilateral trade is tending to stagnate. This includes Russian exports to the EU and Russian imports from the EU. In the long term, sustained growth of trade turnover between the two sides will depend on Russia's export potential, which is currently very limited because of the extremely low competitiveness of Russian industry, in particular in the manufacturing sector. In other words, the prospects for growth in trade are linked to the re-structuring and modernisation of Russian industry and the national economy as a whole. Foreign investment is a necessary pre-condition to achieve this goal, because it means not only finance but also new technologies and a new quality of management. The Russian Strategy Paper provides for various actions, on their own or together with the

EU, to promote a greater flow of foreign investment into Russia, including more favourable legislation and a more favourable general climate as well as adequate guarantees for doing business with Russia on the one hand, and the utilisation of financial instruments and programmes of the EU and the European Investment Bank (EIB) in particular, on the other.

All the other topics - the opening up of markets, residual discrimination, anti-dumping procedures, etc. - are of a complementary character, although they need to be negotiated and solved on the basis of mutual compromises.

Other areas of co-operation, to which Russia attaches importance include:

● Development of Trans-European Networks (TENs) in transport, pipelines, electricity supply and electronic communications. Russian participation in these networks is seen as a very important way of integrating with the European common economic space.

● Co-operation in research and development, in particular in the framework of a new special agreement, which was prepared but postponed for signing because of the war in Chechnya; the participation of Russian researchers in the EU's framework R & D programmes and similar trans-European programmes.

● Reinforcement of the legal basis of Russia-EU co-operation, rapprochement of economic legislation, technical standards and procedures of certification.

● Co-operation in the field of Justice and Home Affairs (JHA).

● Trans-border and regional cooperation. Generally speaking, it is this field of links and interactions that could contribute to softening and surmounting the dividing lines between the EU and Russia. In more concrete terms, Kaliningrad Oblast is the only region of Russia that is named in the Russian document. Taken in the context of the EU enlargement, this region is seen by Moscow as an active participant in both trans-border co-operation with Poland and Lithuania (future EU Member States) and also in the inter-regional co-operation in the Northern Dimension framework.

EU enlargement and Russia's priorities

There are some other Russian regions which are interested in developing trans-border co-operation, e.g. Murmansk, St Petersburg, Karelia and Pskov. However, the spectrum of problems generated by the EU's future enlargement is much wider. The Russian Strategy Paper avoids taking a specific line over Russia's attitude to EU enlargement. The inevitability of this process is taken for granted. According to some statements made by high-ranking officials, Russia does not oppose EU enlargement in principle. On a more practical level, the consequences of this process for Russia are seen as being mixed. Russia's response is to aim at maximising the economic benefits which are expected to result from EU enlargement, while at the same time preventing or compensating for the possible negative effects.

This detailed description of the main items of the Russian Strategy Paper leads to the conclusion that there is significant potential for a 'step by step' development in Russia-EU co-operation. The main components of this potential are taken into account. The questions are, whether the new Russian leadership will be ready to follow this strategy and whether it can rely upon public support.

Taking into consideration the key responsibilities of the Russian President in defining and implementing the internal and external policies in accordance with the Constitution, questions concerning President Vladimir Putin's foreign policy concept are important. Despite the absence of any special statements, his approach to relations between Russia and the West and Western Europe is more or less clear. He is in favour of a consistent, peaceful and gradual transition of the country to a market economy and democracy. He has underlined that 'our priority is to build a foreign policy in accordance with the national interests of the country', and that it is necessary to recognise the superiority of internal over external goals.[1] He has insisted on 'the consistent integration of the Russian economy into global economic structures' in order to reach the level of economic and social progress achieved by the advanced countries.[2] As far as the West, individual Western countries, the EU and NATO are concerned, Putin evidently intends to develop mutually beneficial co-operation between Russia and the most advanced countries, but under the condition of maintaining a firm defence of national interests.

What are the chances of the new President getting the necessary support within Russian society? In my opinion, they seem to be very good. There is a new generation of better educated, pragmatic and focused professionals in all areas of political, economic and intellectual activities. There is a new State Duma in which the communist opposition is in a minority. There is a very high level of electoral support for Putin. And last but not least, there is a prevalent pro-western orientation among Russian public opinion.

This final assertion needs to be confirmed because of the contrary belief of a great number of Europeans that 'anti-westernism' currently prevails in Russian society. The results of a poll carried out by the Institute of Sociological Analysis in Moscow in February 2000 are of considerable interest.[3] They relate to electoral preferences immediately before the Presidential election.

Table 1 (% of respondents)

Model of State	Model preferred by you	Expected model under Putin
Monarchic empire (Russia till 1917)	4	3
USSR model	22	6
Western model	39	38
Unique model	28	25
Difficult to define	8	29

Three conclusions can be derived from this table. First, the share of adherents of the Western model is at the top. Second, most of them expect that Putin will choose the Western model, whereas most adherents of the Soviet model do not believe that the new President will agree with their preference. Third, the share of expectations in favour of the Western model is larger than the sum of rest of the expectations.

Table 2 (% of respondents)

Pattern of regime	Regime you are in favour of	Expected model of Putin
Western liberal-democratic regime	51	45
Pinochet regime	11	17
China one-party regime	4	4
USSR one-party regime	18	5
Difficult to answer	16	29

This table leads to the conclusion that the share of people who are in favour of a regime based upon the market economy, rule of law and primacy of human rights is larger than that in favour of the Western model (see Table 1).

Table 3 (% of respondents inclined to vote for Putin)

	Regime you are in favour of				
	Western	Pinochet's	Chinese	Soviet	Under question
People for Putin	63	12	4	11	11

Two thirds of respondents, who intended to vote for Putin, linked their preference with the expectation of their future choice in favour of a Western model of society.

This part of the analysis can be summarised as follows:

Today the pro-western preferences of Russian society as a whole are stronger than those of the political and intellectual elites.

Moreover, if Putin implements the above-mentioned course of strategic partnership with the European Union, his policy will be supported by half the population as against about 30% of his adversaries. In other words, the political pre-conditions for implementing this course of action are more favourable than in the 1990s, except perhaps for a very short period of common euphoria immediately after the demise of communism in the USSR.

These conclusions will be helped by favourable economic factors, i.e. in particular the new stabilisation following the financial crisis in August 1998.

There is no automatic link between these favourable conditions and the future course of events. Any prognosis of the likelihood of implementation of the Russian Strategy Paper must be cautious. The obstacles are evident and numerous. Some of them are being reproduced because of various internal trends which are well-known and need not be mentioned here, except for one. If Russia drifts towards a severe authoritarian regime which could result in the wide-spread violation of human rights, the Strategy Paper will be unlikely to be implemented. Some others, on the contrary, are of external origin. Most of them could be solved on the basis of mutual compromise. The event which could have the most serious consequences for the future of Russia's relations with the West in general and for Russia-EU relations in particular would be a new eastwards expansion of NATO. To my mind, Moscow will oppose this scenario drastically as long as it feels itself to be in a position of weakness.

The best means of advancing towards a strategic partnership seems to be the well-tried 'step by step' approach that has been followed successfully by the EC/EU for 50 years. The best means of implementing this policy will be to develop concrete programmes and projects with clear goals and tangible results. In this context, plans for including Kaliningrad into the network of trans-border and regional co-operation in the Baltic region will be of particular significance.

---

[1] Vladimir Putin, An open letter to Russian voters, *Izvestiya*, 25 February 2000, page 4.

[2] Vladimir Putin, Russia on the eve of the millennium, *Nezavisimaya Gazeta*, 30 December 1999, page 3.

[3] Kutkovets T. and Kliamkin I., What does Russia expect from Putin?, *Moscow News*, No. 9, 7-13 March 2000, pages 8-9.

KALININGRAD OBLAST

Chapter 3

Kaliningrad:
Key Economic Issues

Stephen Dewar[1]

Independent economic consultant,
Moscow

This chapter examines some important trends and developments in the nearest neighbours of Kaliningrad – the EU accession countries of Poland, Lithuania and the other Baltic States – and tries to show their significance for the future of Kaliningrad.

First we look at important trends in international trade relationships around the eastern end of the Baltic Sea. Then we examine how Kaliningrad is affected by these trends and, in particular, the state of Kaliningrad's transport infrastructure and services. Next, a brief overview is given of Kaliningrad's own trade relationships and patterns.

Regrettably, the findings of this overall review are somewhat gloomy. The final section, therefore, makes some brief proposals as to what could – and should – be done to prevent the possible development of a significant social and economic crisis, with the political implications that such a scenario implies. A more thorough assessment of what should be done is offered in Chapter 14.

Stephen Dewar

International trade trends

As one would expect, the last decade has seen a significant shift in international trade patterns in the Baltic region. Poland and the Baltic States are increasing their share of trade with the EU while, conversely, their relative trade with Russia and the Newly Independent States (NIS) is decreasing.[2] This reflects the dissolution of the Former Soviet Union (FSU) and the Council for Mutual Economic Assistance (CMEA), on the one hand, and the growing accessibility of EU markets on the other. The continuing failure of the Russian economy to restructure effectively, worsened by the August 1998 crisis, is a significant additional contributory factor. However, the fact that the Baltic States and Poland are EU accession states – progressing towards economic integration with the EU - is the principal driving force.

This sort of change is not unusual in regions where economies are moving towards membership of a regional trading block, for instance (outside Europe) in the North American Free Trade Area (NAFTA – comprising Canada, the United States and Mexico). The 'new' partners in the block become relatively more important, while the 'old' partners outside the block decline in relative importance. [3] Indeed, it would be surprising if this was not the case.

A few examples will help to illustrate this point.[4] Before looking at these, however, a word of warning to the reader. If you find strings of figures tedious, no harm will be done by skipping over them – subject to accepting the conclusions drawn on faith! Between 1993 and 1998 Estonia saw the share of exports to Russia fall from 22.6% to 13.4%. In 1993 Russia had been Estonia's most important export market, but by 1998 had dropped to third place, with Finland and Sweden taking first and second place. Although 1998 saw a fall in exports to Russia compared with 1997, as one would expect in the aftermath of the Russian crisis of 1998, exports to Russia had been losing market share throughout the entire period. Similarly, imports from Russia accounted for 17.2% of Estonia's total in 1993, but only 11.1% in 1998.

In Latvia's case, in 1999 the EU supplied 54.5% of total imports, compared with 11.5% in 1993. By contrast, the share taken by the Commonwealth of Independent States (CIS) countries as a whole fell from 38.5% to 15.0% over the same period.

For Lithuania (see Table 1) provisional figures for 1999 show exports to the EU now exceeding half the total (50.1%) compared with 16.9% in 1993, with exports to Russia falling dramatically from 33.1% to only 6.8% over the same period. Imports from the EU accounted for 46.5% in 1999 (18.7% in 1993), with Russia accounting for 20.2% in 1999, down from 53.7% in 1993.

Table 1

Patterns of trade between Poland (1992 to 1997), Lithuania (1993 to 1999) and selected markets

LITHUANIA

	Exports as % of total to:				Imports as % of total from:			
	Poland	Latvia	Russia	EU	Poland	Latvia	Russia	EU
1993	7.00	7.30	33.10	16.90	2.20	1.50	53.70	18.70
1994	5.00	8.40	28.20	25.80	4.00	2.70	39.30	26.40
1995	3.90	7.10	20.40	36.40	4.20	3.20	31.20	37.10
1996	3.20	9.20	24.00	32.90	5.10	3.30	25.90	42.40
1997	2.30	8.60	24.50	32.50	4.90	3.40	24.30	46.50
1998	3.00	11.10	16.50	38.00	5.50	1.80	21.20	47.20
1999	4.50	12.70	6.80	50.10	5.70	2.00	20.20	46.50

Note: Figures for 1999 are provisional

POLAND

	Exports as % of total to:				Imports as % of total from:			
	Lithuania	Germany	Russia	EU	Lithuania	Germany	Russia	EU
1992	0.30	31.40	5.50	58.00	0.40	23.90	8.50	53.20
1993	0.30	38.30	4.60	63.20	0.50	28.00	6.80	57.20
1994	0.70	35.70	5.40	62.70	0.40	27.40	6.80	57.50
1995	0.80	38.30	5.60	70.00	0.20	26.60	6.70	64.60
1996	0.90	34.40	6.80	66.30	0.30	24.70	6.80	64.00
1997	1.30	32.90	8.40	64.00	0.30	24.10	6.30	63.80

Source: Hedegaard, Lars and Lindstrom, Bjame (eds.) *The North European and Baltic Integration Yearbook, 1999*, Springer and Nordic Centre for Spatial Development, Berlin, 2000.

Throughout all three Baltic states, therefore, Russia's relative importance as a trading partner has fallen dramatically during the 1990s, while that of the EU has risen equally dramatically. More interesting than this, however, is the pattern of trade relationships that is developing within Kaliningrad's two Baltic Sea neighbours – Poland and Lithuania.

The key trends that the figures show in Table 1 are more easily perceived in the charts on the next three pages.[5]

What is striking is the very low level of trade between Poland and Lithuania – considerably less than one would expect between two direct neighbours.[6] Between 1993 and 1999 the relative importance of Poland as an export market for Lithuania has shrunk from 7% to 4.5% while, over the same period, Latvia – a much smaller economy – has grown from more or less the same starting point, 7.3%, to 12.7% (see Chart 1).

Chart 1
Lithuania: share of total exports to selected markets,
1993 - 1999

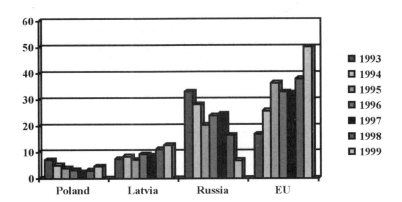

Looked at from Poland's perspective, the share that Lithuania contributes to Polish imports has declined from a tiny 0.4% to an even smaller 0.3% (Chart 4). Even though Lithuania has grown in significance for Poland as an export market, the figures are also very small – from 0.3% in 1992 to 1.3% in 1997 (Chart 3).

It is also notable that Poland's dependence on the Russian market has been fairly low throughout the 1990s while Lithuania's, although declining, has until recently been significantly greater – 20.2% for imports in 1999, although only 6.8% for exports, this latter figure clearly reflecting the 1998 Russian crisis.

Chart 2
Lithuania: share of total imports from selected markets, 1993 - 1999

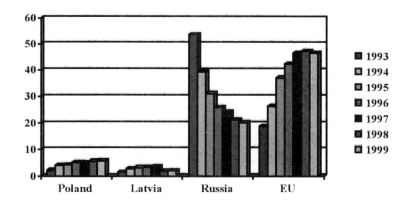

It is unusual to find this low level of trade between these two neighbours, Poland and Lithuania, particularly as both countries are turning away from Russia and the NIS towards the enlarging EU. *A priori*, one would expect there to be a growing level of interdependence, especially as this is so in other areas of co-operation, such as political and security matters. This suggests that the Polish-Lithuanian border denotes some kind of economic demarcation line within the Baltic Sea Region and within the enlarging EU.

Chart 3
Poland: Share of total exports to selected markets,
1992 - 1997

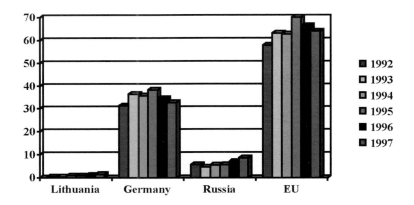

Chart 4
Poland: Share of total imports from selected markets,
1992 - 1997

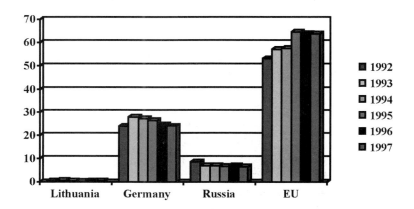

Nor is this some accidental feature solely affecting these two countries. Poland's trade relations with Latvia and Estonia are also very slight, and vice versa. In trade terms, there is very little 'connectedness' or integration between Poland and the three Baltic States. The former, in effect, is more or less 'ignoring' its northern neighbours, while the latter are 'leap-frogging' Poland in developing their western-oriented links, with Estonia strongly building up its relationships with the Nordic countries – Sweden and Finland having pushed Russia out of first place in importance.

In short, it is as if there are two major flows of trade developing around the Poland-Lithuanian economic space – each of them being predominantly *away* from the area where Kaliningrad happens to be located – to the north from Lithuania and to the west from Poland.

In this situation, the question naturally springs to mind: where does this leave Kaliningrad?

Kaliningrad: a thoroughfare or a *cul-de-sac*?

Kaliningrad is often described as a 'gateway' between the Russian mainland and the West. There is no significant evidence to suggest that this role has ever been fulfilled (see Chapter 10). Apart from anything else, Kaliningrad is separated from the Russian mainland by a minimum of two countries, regardless of which overland route one takes (Lithuania-Belarus; Lithuania-Latvia; Poland-Belarus). Furthermore, Kaliningrad port has never handled more than 4 or 5% of total cargo going through the Baltic ports from St Petersburg down to Kaliningrad (see Chart 5 below[7]). Taking account of Finnish ports and Gdansk reduces this share even further. Latvia, for example, handles considerably more inbound and outbound Russian cargo than Kaliningrad, although it is the case that Kaliningrad handles a significant amount of traffic to and from Belarus.

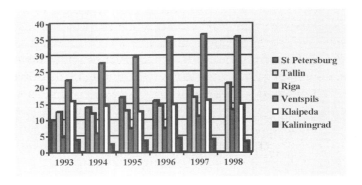

Chart 5
Turnover of cargo volumes through selected Baltic Sea ports, 1993 - 1998, MT

St Petersburg
Tallin
Riga
Ventspils
Klaipeda
Kaliningrad

1993   1994   1995   1996   1997   1998

Sources: Hidrosfera - Klaipeda Port Services; Tacis EDRUS Project; TransRail West

However, a more plausible gateway – or 'conduit' – role could be envisaged for trade passing between the Baltics and Poland. But, as we have seen earlier, there is very little trade directly between Poland and Lithuania, and even less between Poland and the other two states while, in any case, there is a direct frontier between Poland and Lithuania – so there is no need for most such trade to pass through Kaliningrad at all. This could change, perhaps, if Kaliningrad offered superior transport infrastructure and services on some key routes, especially between north-west Poland (Gdansk catchment area) and either Vilnius or Kaunas, as well as further on north to Riga and Tallinn, or the other way round.

However, the transport arrangements would have to be very advanced and competitive to compensate for traffic having to pass through the additional customs clearance and other formalities necessitated by transit through this part of Russia. And this simply is not the case. Border delays and customs procedures are notorious sources of delay in Kaliningrad. In addition, as Poland and the Baltics get closer and closer to eventual EU membership, it would be logically absurd to route trade unnecessarily through a non-member territory.

Furthermore, the physical transport infrastructure is falling behind. Kaliningrad has stretches of two TENs[8] passing through it – routes I A and IX B & D. However, in both cases these are spurs off the main routes for I and IX, not the principal trunk systems themselves. If they are not brought up to the desired standards, it will not harm any other country's economic and transport interests significantly, with the possible exception of Gdansk. It follows that Kaliningrad suffers a double disadvantage: it does not have a competitive transport infrastructure to service transit traffic between Poland and the Baltic States, and countries beyond these axes, and furthermore its transport infrastructure is not essential to the region as a whole. Kaliningrad can easily be by-passed without a significant effect on the neighbouring economies.

What is more, each country is responsible for raising the funds from International Financial Institutions (IFIs) and other sources to finance its own stretches of these TENs. This is exceptionally expensive.[9] In Russia, priority has been given to date to the major arteries (e.g. the Russian components of the Helsinki-St Petersburg-Moscow-Kiev legs of route IX, Moscow-Minsk-Warsaw on II) and there appears to be little if any funding available for the Kaliningrad spurs.

One possible option might be for Kaliningrad to offer an 'airbridge' between goods emanating from these countries and mainland Russia. This would seem a plausible idea in that Kaliningrad's isolation could actually work in its favour, simply by virtue of being the nearest part of Russia to Poland and Lithuania and much of central and eastern Europe. Goods cleared through Russian Customs in Kaliningrad could then be air-freighted directly into the Russian mainland. However, Kaliningrad's air services are deplorable. As with many other 'mini-Aeroflots', especially in the wake of the August 1998 crisis, Kaliningrad Air Enterprises (KLN) is in serious financial difficulties. Its fleet – all passenger aircraft, which comprised two long-haul Tu-154s and ten medium-haul Tu-134s in 1996, has been cut by half to one Tu-154 and five Tu-134s. The others have been arrested or are inoperable, with KLN unable to raise the funding to pay for repairs and necessary maintenance. This is hardly a solid basis to start a major air cargo service.

Furthermore, there are totally inadequate physical facilities to support warehousing and cargo handling operations at the airport.

Major investment, together with ensuring a viable service, are essential prerequisites for fulfilling this approach. Furthermore, it is also essential that there should be good international scheduled passenger services in and out of Kaliningrad. The map below shows how far from this ideal lies the reality. The lines between the major cities around the Baltic Sea show existing scheduled passenger air services, with the thickness of the lines approximately related to the number of flights per day.[10] What is immediately apparent is that the three Baltic States are closely connected – one can fly from any one of the three capital cities to both of the other two. Equally the Nordic countries have highly developed point-to-point services. There are also good services interlinking the Nordic states with the Baltics, while it is reasonably easy to fly to Minsk in Belarus. Furthermore, one can get to Poland directly from Minsk, Vilnius, Helsinki, Stockholm and Copenhagen.

Unfortunately, there is only one direct air link between Kaliningrad and a foreign country – Copenhagen, Denmark – and that operates once a day for six days a week only (see dotted line on map). There are no direct flights linking Kaliningrad to Poland, Lithuania, Belarus, Latvia, Estonia or other countries. To some extent this may be a vicious circle: it could be that these international services do not exist because there is no demand for them sufficient to make the provision of these services commercially viable. But since business people cannot easily get in and out of Kaliningrad – developing trade, investment and other commercial links and hence generating the need for more travel services - this may help to explain why the demand does not exist in the first place. Better air services will grow with the development of international economic and business relationships, but these relationships are being held back by the absence of the air services. This is a complex and expensive problem to solve, but it must be addressed as a matter of urgency.

In short, therefore, Kaliningrad is located on a sort of economic fault-line between Poland and Lithuania, where the main trade routes are moving *away* from this point, not towards and through it; nor can Kaliningrad hope realistically to capture a significant share of such north-south traffic as does exist – there is a common Polish-Lithuanian border which eventually will be an internal EU crossing point, while Kaliningrad's transport infrastructure and services are likely to become increasingly relatively unattractive to transit shippers. Finally, it is very difficult to get in and out of Kaliningrad from neighbouring countries.

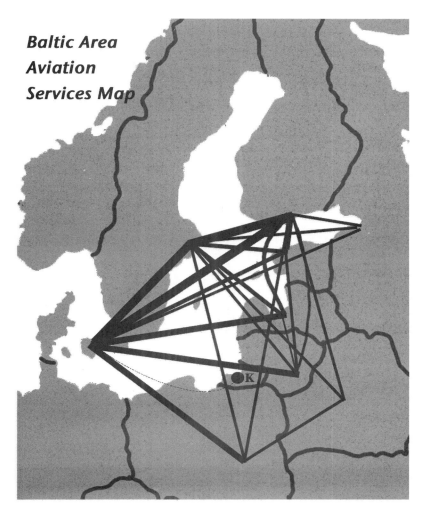

Baltic Area Aviation Services Map

Sample day's flights

	TLL	RIX	VNO	KGD	WAW	CPH	HEL	STO	LED	MSQ
Tallin		2	2	0	0	3	9	4	0	1
Riga	2		1	0	0	5	3	3	0	0
Vilnius	2	1		0	2	4	3	3	0	0
Kaliningrad	0	0	0		0	1	0	2	0	0
Warsaw	0	0	2	0		4	2	2	0	1
Copenhagen	3	5	4	1	4		7	23	1	0
Helsinki	9	3	2	0	2	7		21	2	0
Stockholm	4	3	2	0	2	23	21		2	1
St. Petersburg	0	0	0	0	0	1	2	2		0
Minsk	1	0	0	0	1	0	0	1	0	

The main conclusion of the discussion so far seems to be, therefore, that Kaliningrad is of no particular value to anybody else in the immediate Baltic Region, and there is no obvious prospect for this situation to improve. Kaliningrad is not a gateway or a crossroads; it is closer to a dead-end.

What can Kaliningrad do?

A plausible development strategy for Kaliningrad could have been to exploit her location to attract transit traffic in the increasingly dynamic Baltic economic space, offer added-value services initially related to transport, and gradually build up the region as a low-cost, efficient and geographically convenient location for domestic and foreign direct investment.

Indeed, to a considerable degree this appears to have been the actual strategy that was followed, supported by the FEZ/SEZ. Unfortunately, the present state of Kaliningrad's economy – especially when compared with neighbouring economies – is sad testimony to the failure of this approach. The discussion offered throughout this chapter attempts to identify some of the major reasons why this has been so – poor and uncompetitive transport infrastructure and the absence of burgeoning international trade in the immediate area. They are not the only reasons, of course – the general inhospitality of the investment climate in Russia and the increasing media portrayal of Kaliningrad, both in Russia and abroad, as a territory particularly afflicted by corruption are two further and particularly striking factors.[11]

However, the main arguments presented here suggest that, even without these other problems, Kaliningrad would still be confronting a serious challenge. A measure of this is the increasingly unfavourable development of Kaliningrad's own international trade – and what appear to be highly volatile patterns of trade relationships within the aggregate picture. First, there is the overall trend. Kaliningrad leaders frequently cite the rapid growth of international trade as a success of the SEZ. In fact, the performance is a severe indictment of the failure of the economy to develop successfully, as the charts below vividly illustrates (see also Chapter 10).

If Kaliningrad were an independent state it would be suffering a severe structural balance of payments crisis, now approaching an annual deficit of a billion dollars. This is unsustainable. The more or less flat level of annual exports indicates failure to develop competitive businesses and industries.

Within this overall picture there is a highly fluctuating set of relationships, as Charts 7 and 8 illustrate. The Nordic states (Denmark, Finland, Norway and Sweden) account for less than 5% of Kaliningrad's exports and a little over 5% of imports. Latvia and to a more marked extent Estonia hardly figure at all, which is surprising given their geographic proximity – but

Chart 6
Kaliningrad's International trade performance
1992, 1995 - 1998

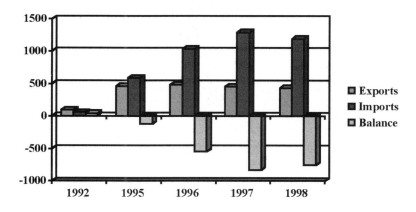

Source: Kaliningrad Region State Committee on Statistics

perhaps less surprising in terms of poor transport communications with these two states.

Poland is easily the most important export market, followed by Germany and Lithuania. The same three countries are the top three sources of imports to Kaliningrad around the Baltic Sea, accounting for over 57% of total imports in 1997. The dominance of these countries is not remarkable, but the violent fluctuations in relative shares from year to year indicates a lack of firm foundations in trade relations.

This volatility may be more apparent than real – for instance, due perhaps to inadequacies in data collection and analysis. It may also be due to disproportionate impacts from large individual transactions. Grey and black economy trade, which is generally acknowledged to be large in Kaliningrad, as well as possibly inaccurate reporting of legitimate shuttle-trading activities, further contribute to the statistical uncertainty. Finally, it is extremely difficult to distinguish those goods that are shipped onwards to the Russian mainland, or re-exported, from those that are consumed locally and, conversely, to identify those exports which are manufactured locally as opposed to being brought in from Russia or, indeed, Belarus, given that the latter country has some form of customs union status with Russia.

Chart 7
Percentage shares of Kaliningrad's total imports from selected markets, 1993 – 1997

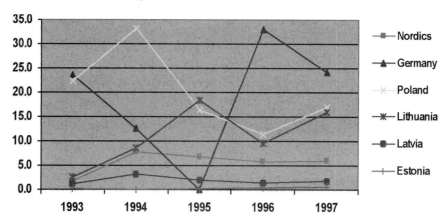

Chart 8
Percentage shares of Kaliningrad's total exports to selected markets, 1993 – 1997

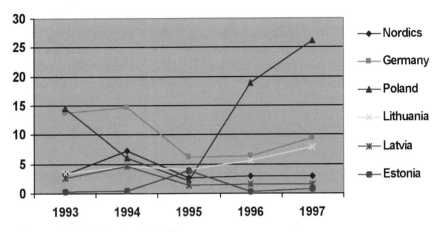

Source: NEBI Yearbook 1999

Having said this, these are the only statistics available. So while necessarily exercising caution over their reliability, one is confronted with the choice of using this data as some sort of indicator or simply giving up. It seems more prudent to accept the probability that there is no firm structural basis to Kaliningrad's trade relations with other states, suggesting a considerable degree of economic under-development. This would at least be consistent with what one might expect from the undisputed view that the regional economy is still in overall decline, despite a few success stories here and there at individual enterprise level.

The actual composition of Kaliningrad's trade is also somewhat unusual. On the import side, in 1997, 9.7% of total imports were accounted for by cigarettes[12] – over $100 million, or over $100 for every man, woman and child, at wholesale, duty-free prices.[13] Although it is perfectly possible that Kaliningrad residents smoke more on average than, say, people in many western countries, it is not credible that all these cigarettes were consumed within Kaliningrad. Clearly, much of this trade goes elsewhere, either legally or, as increasing anecdotal and media accounts suggest, into the criminal economy.[14]

Most of the rest of the imports are consumer goods (food, alcohol and home appliances) and other finished products (office equipment, vehicles) or industrial inputs (building materials).

Conversely, over six% of exports were fertilisers, which were manufactured elsewhere in Russia and Belarus. In short, therefore, it is very hard to get a clear picture of what exactly is going on in Kaliningrad, but the likelihood is that a great deal more is being imported than exported, even if much of the trade originates or ends up outside Kaliningrad.

In different vein, four of the main exports sectors for Kaliningrad – involving goods that are actually produced or manufactured there – are oil (22% by value in 1997), ships/boats (10%), fish and crustaceans (6%) and cellulose (5%).[15]

Crude oil – a mainstay of overall Russian exports – is subject to unpredictable price fluctuations. Currently, prices are high – but they could easily fall back. The high relative contribution of ships and boats (which on the surface suggests an internationally competitive ship-building sector) is more likely to have come from the sale of ships from Kaliningrad's fishing fleet.[16] Cellulose is a product of the declining paper and pulp industry. This was very important during the Soviet period, but is in terminal decline today. Most of the raw material (wood) is freighted in from very long distances away (Siberia), which makes it uneconomic. Furthermore, the technologies employed in the plants are obsolete and major sources of pollution. It is realistic to expect further decline in this sector.

Fish products have potential for growth and development. However, exports to EU states, including the neighbouring accession states in due course, may be adversely affected by adoption of Single Market standards in these markets and the need for meeting stringent certification requirements. There is no local source of authoritative information on what such standards may be, nor on how to adapt processing technologies to meet them.

The Kaliningrad economy resembles that of a typical less developed country (LDC), with over-reliance on commodities and primary materials for exports and a critical dependence on imports to meet virtually all consumer and industry needs. Although this is to some extent the same situation as confronted by Russia as a whole, the level of import dependence (80% for food, for energy, and so forth) is exceptionally high.

If Kaliningrad's future is to be a continuation of the experience of the last few years, it will be a depressing prospect for the unfortunate residents, who will see further declines in economic, social, environmental and other conditions, and increasingly worrying for the neighbours, who will be affected by growing cross-border crime, communicable diseases, pollution and other destabilising influences.

If Kaliningrad's future is to be a successful one, radical changes must be introduced. From Moscow and Brussels are coming encouraging signs that support for appropriate new approaches and policies could be forthcoming, as other contributors to this book have recounted. But what exactly should Kaliningrad do?

Kaliningrad has no alternative but to engage fully in international trade and investment activities. This is easy to say, but difficult to achieve in practice, given the structural problems that exist – as this chapter has tried to illustrate. An action plan for the future needs to be compiled, as recommended in the European Commission's draft Northern Dimension Action Plan:

> 'This process [of development of a joint EU-Russia initiative] could be backed up by a EU study providing an overview of the social and economic problems facing Kaliningrad at present, the support already provided to the region *and the necessary steps in order to mitigate its enclave status.*' [Emphasis in italics added].[17]

In advance of such a study being carried out, there are some guidelines and principles that could be heeded:

● Kaliningrad's economy does not at present have the potential to develop successfully.

● Foreign and Russian investment are therefore essential for transformation.

● The investment environment in Kaliningrad must be improved. While this is largely affected by the overall investment environment in Russia, there are still numerous regional and local initiatives that could be taken to make Kaliningrad more attractive *relative to other Russian regions.*

● A key role could be played by the SEZ, subject to considerable changes in its application and with the support of the Federal Government (both of these assumptions are very big ones), but the SEZ would have to become an *instrument* of policy not, as hitherto, a policy in itself. In turn, this implies the need to develop coherent and effective economic development policies.

● The potential advantages of Kaliningrad being part of Russia need to be turned into a set of concrete advantages that can be marketed to potential investors. Such advantages could include cheap labour, air-bridge connections to the Russian mainland, efficient Customs clearance procedures, advance factories, and much more – but they must be identified and developed.

● Conversely, major disadvantages must be dealt with – lack of international passenger air services, poor transport infrastructure, impending energy problems, and so forth.

● The lead in dealing with these issues must be taken by the Russian side but, as far as is practicable, should be supported by the EU. This support should include assistance with obtaining funding for essential capital projects.

● A special role can be played by Lithuania, which has already demonstrated a strong and serious commitment to mutually beneficial co-operation with Kaliningrad.

These are just a selection of key suggestions, which I consider to be particularly important. However, in Chapter 14 I try to offer a fuller and more detailed prescription for what could and should be done. For now, however, it must be recognised that nothing positive is likely to occur without the development of imaginative and innovative policies, and the full commitment and hard work by all concerned parties. This may turn out to be the hardest challenge of them all.

Statistical Annex

This annex gives the statistical data used to compile the charts in the text. The sources are shown under the charts themselves and are not repeated here.

Charts 1, 2, 3 and 4. Data from Table 1.

Chart 5, cargo volumes through selected Baltic ports.

	Millions of tonnes					
	1993	1994	1995	1996	1997	1998
St Petersburg	10	14	17.1	16	20.59	
Tallinn	12.5	12	13	14.5	17.1	21.4
Riga	4.7	5.9	7.4	7.4	11.21	13.3
Ventspils	22.4	27.7	29.6	35.7	36.77	36
Klaipeda	15.9	14.5	12.7	14.8	16.12	15
Kaliningrad	**3.8**	**2.5**	**3.5**	**4.4**	**4**	**3.4**

Chart 6, Kaliningrad international trade figures.

(1) Year	(2) Exports	(3) Imports	(4) Balance, +/(-)	(4) as % of (2)+(3), +/(-)
1992	91.4	54.0	37.4	25.7
1995	459.4	585.1	(125.7)	(12.0)
1996	480.8	1030.0	(549.2)	(36.4)
1997	452.0	1285.6	(833.6)	(48.0)
1998	429.3	1187.9	(758.6)	(46.9)

Chart 7, Kaliningrad's imports from selected markets in%ages of total imports.

	1993	1994	1995	1996	1997
Nordics	1.8	7.8	6.9	5.8	6
Germany	23.7	12.7	0.1	33	24.2
Poland	22.4	33.3	16.4	11.4	17
Lithuania	2.6	8.6	18.5	9.6	16
Latvia	1.3	3.2	2	1.4	1.8
Estonia	0.3	0.1	0.2	0.4	0.6

Chart 8, Kaliningrad's exports to selected markets in%ages of total exports.

	1993	1994	1995	1996	1997
Nordics	3.2	7.2	2.6	3	2.9
Germany	13.7	14.7	6.2	6.4	9.4
Poland	14.6	6	2.2	18.9	26.1
Lithuania	3.4	4.6	4	5.6	7.9
Latvia	2.6	4.7	1.4	1.5	1.5
Estonia	0.3	0.5	3.8	0.3	0.7

---

[1] For four years, during 1996 to the end of 1999, Stephen Dewar worked in Kaliningrad on economic and regional development issues.

[2] It is the *relative* share of trade that is decreasing, not necessarily the *absolute* value of exports and imports.

[3] This generalisation applies principally to merchandise trade. Trade in 'invisibles', such as financial services, does not necessarily conform to this pattern. Certain strategic resources (oil and gas, for example) can also be important exceptions.

[4] All figures quoted in the following paragraphs are taken from the relevant national statistical offices' websites, except where stated otherwise. These can be accessed through, for example, the IMF website at http://www.imf.org.

[5] The data used for compiling Charts 1 to 4 are taken from Table 1.

[6] For example, over 80% of Mexico's exports go to the United States. Since the United States is the largest importer in the world, it is hardly surprising that it should be so important to Mexico – as it is to other exporters. However, the *relative* importance of the US is, at least in largish part, due to proximity.

[7] Figures used for compiling Chart 5 are given in the statistical annex.

[8] Trans European Networks – the system of road and rail routes, linking Scandinavia and Finland with Russia, the Baltics, Belarus, Ukraine, and on to Poland and the rest of Eastern, Central, Southern and Western Europe.

[9] Not just expensive, but complex. For instance, Poland has recently announced that it expects to complete financing arrangements soon, involving raising Euro 622 million to fund the construction of a toll motorway linking Konin in central Poland with Poznan, the largest city in the western part of the country. This will greatly reduce driving time between Warsaw and Berlin. The financing package will be made up of a zero-coupon Government-guaranteed international and domestic bond issue worth euro 273 million, and an international 17-year loan for euro 280 million arranged by western commercial banks in consortium. Euro 50 million will be offered to domestic investors through a consortium of Polish banks, the balance will be offered abroad by a consortium of western financial institutions, (*Financial Times*, 28 March 2000).

[10] The day in question was Monday 20th March 2000 – the day this map was prepared.

[11] The Moscow-based English language, daily newspaper, *The Moscow Times*, has, since July 2000, been carrying a weekly column (every Saturday) called 'Letter from the Enclave' which regularly reports on cases of alleged corruption and criminality in the region. This newspaper is widely available and read around the world, through its free Internet service.

[12] Source: Kaliningrad Regional State Committee on Statistics, *Social and Economic Situation in Kaliningrad Region, 1997*, Kaliningrad, 1998.

[13] It should come as no surprise, therefore, that cigarettes were one of 35 product groups that were subjected to import quotas in September 1998. These quotas – covering food products to building materials, along with much else - were introduced by the Regional Administration, with the formal legal support of the Federal Government, as a measure to protect domestic producers. Licences under the SEZ concessions to import such

goods without duties up to the quota limits are auctioned by the Regional Administration, which keeps the auction proceeds. The quotas for cigarettes in each of 1999 and 2000 have been set at a generous 2.5 billion units.

[14] Since late 1999 local media have reported several contract murders of people believed to have been prominently involved in the cigarette-trading sector.

[15] Source, Kaliningrad State Committee for Statistics. Figures for 1997.

[16] See PROMETEE, *Kaliningrad Economy*, Tacis, 1998.

[17] European Commission, 28 February 2000, *Commission Working Document: Action Plan for the Northern Dimension in the external and cross-border policies of the European Union 2000-2003*, page 28, Brussels.

Chapter 4

Kaliningrad Oblast: Towards a European Dimension

Alexander Songal
Deputy Head of Analytical Department,
Kaliningrad Regional Duma

Negative paradigm

One of the sad discoveries that slowly dawned on the inhabitants of the Kaliningrad Region, as the newly found openness has been unfolding, is the smallness of the Oblast. Not just in geographic terms – it is becoming more and more evident that it has never been high on the list of priorities either in Russian, or in European politics, let alone on the world scene. A small part of Russia with no war or widespread famine is too far away from real, positive interests even for some Baltic neighbours (e.g., Finland, Latvia and, increasingly, Poland).

Traditional security concerns have become ever less important. However, new problems have arisen mainly due to the rapidly changing Baltic and European environment and the lack of a clear perspective for Kaliningrad Oblast in the context of these changes. The Kaliningrad paradigm has been dominated by threats rather than opportunities:

● For Moscow – the growing unease that there could be an increasing tendency in Kaliningrad towards separatism.

● For the EU – the threats of crime, pollution and economic collapse.

● For the Kaliningrad population – the threats of increasing isolation, restrictions on freedom of movement, and a worsening economic environment.

Seemingly, there is now a consensus among most experts as to how the problem should be best dealt with - broadly along the lines of looking for some sort of joint approach by the EU and Russia in the first place, and by Kaliningrad expressing more clearly its needs and aspirations. Nice 'brand names' are being used to describe the framework within which action should be taken: 'Northern Dimension' and 'Pilot Russian Region for Co-operation between Russia and the European Union in the Twenty First Century'. Are we talking about things going in the same direction? It is difficult to be sure at this stage: the Northern Dimension is slowly ageing without having accumulated any noticeable flesh on its attractively shining skeleton, and the 'Pilot Region' has yet to prove to be anything at all.

Any attempt to find the right answers and to reverse this negative Kaliningrad paradigm might warrant a brief look back at previous attempts by Russia and Kaliningrad to cope with the everyday problems of its existence within the circle formed by foreign borders and the sea.

First steps to gateway function

Although hard security issues have been diminishing in significance, it was around those problems that the European Dimension of Kaliningrad Oblast started to emerge:

- Concentration of troops in the Oblast on their way to the mainland;

- Transit problems for the military and for the civilians;

- Territorial claims by extremists, against the background of changing borders on the former territory of the USSR;

- Sovereignty concerns;

- Dealing with the past.

Of all the above, by far the most immediate and acute was the freedom of movement. Initiatives and actions by Kaliningrad and Russian authorities at those early stages of the post-Soviet era, although negatively motivated, objectively contributed strongly and decisively towards opening up the Kaliningrad Oblast. Negotiated compromise solutions were found for the transit problems.

Today some pictures from the very recent past seem to have an almost surrealistic flavour: a Russian border guard with a rake making sure that every tyre print is immediately wiped off to preserve the border intact; a Lithuanian customs official collecting 'protection money' from *babushkas* on a transit train; the Russian military threat as the main topic of heated debates at international conferences and meetings on the Baltic.

A very symptomatic feature of those times was that the Kaliningrad 'transit discourse' contained mostly a military connotation.

The first major breakthrough was provided by a special consultation and co-operation framework with Poland (*Russian-Polish Council on Co-operation of Regions of North-Western Poland with the Kaliningrad Oblast*) and the *Special Protocol to the Interim Russian-Lithuanian Agreement on Mutual Trips of Citizens* which entered into force in 1995. This latter document was born out of the initiative of the Kaliningrad regional authorities - first after hard negotiations which we had to conduct as the Oblast's representatives with the Federal Centre, followed later on by a somewhat easier agreement between Vilnius and Moscow.

Practical steps to improve the border and road infrastructure were being taken at the same time: necessary agreements were signed by Russia with Poland and Lithuania to open in Kaliningrad international border-crossings - road, rail and sea ones. In a very short period of time from 1992 to 1995 the Russian Government invested more than 100 million USD in the construction of border-crossings in the Oblast. Maybe because communication had been virtually non-existent with Poland, the first border-crossings there were of a better standard than those in the direction of Lithuania.

An international sector was opened at Kaliningrad airport, a European gauge railway from the Polish border to the city was restored and the Russian part of the Kaliningrad-Elblag motorway was reconstructed in the nick of time (symbolically it has never been met by an equal effort from the other part). With all these dynamic developments, by 1993-1994 one might think that the region was at a basic level prepared to start fulfilling a bridge function between mainland Russia and the countries of the Baltic Sea region.

Special arrangements for a unique Oblast

It would be right to assume that the Federal Centre does not have a consistent and coherent strategy towards the Kaliningrad Oblast with regard to its neighbours and the EU. But it is wrong to say that that such a strategy does not exist at all.

The territory of Kaliningrad region was first proclaimed a Free Economic Zone (FEZ) among 14 other regions of Russia in 1990. It was then a sort of a weapon in the tug of war for power between the leaderships of the Soviet Union and the Russian Federation (Matochkin Y., *At a Sharp Bend*, 1999, p.15). There followed the well-documented history of the FEZ which was proclaimed and cancelled, and eventually survived in the form of a Special Economic Zone (SEZ). Seemingly well protected by a State Law it remains one of the favourite targets for every new Russian Government, joined last year by the IMF. Currently a new campaign is in progress in the State Duma. As in previous cases, the Kaliningrad Oblast is treated in the same way as every other constituent entity of Federation – privileges are being cancelled in bulk.

It is not surprising that under these circumstances the SEZ has never lived up to expectations. Having contributed to a huge growth in imports it has not provided a reliable and stable framework for attracting investment as was originally intended. Still it remains the main brand name for the Oblast, a good starting point for developing a more coherent and economically viable set of rules. It sends a clear signal to the outside world that Moscow is continuing on the path of looking for a positive development of Kaliningrad, and also intends to benefit from its situation.

Although the most visible sign of the region's uniqueness recognised by the Federal Centre, the SEZ is not the only one.

In October 1994 the Security Council of the Russian Federation approved a document entitled *A Concept of the Federal Policy with regard to the Kaliningrad Region of the Russian Federation*. The Security Council supported the version, originally proposed by the Oblast authorities, of putting an end to the debate between the then Governor Y. Matochkin and the then powerful vice-premier of the Russian Government, Sergei Shakrai. The latter was a strong proponent of Kaliningrad being preserved as a military stronghold above anything else. It is difficult to estimate how widely this document is used now by different Federal bodies: apparently not much. Maybe it is because this author scribbled down its first outline, but it still looks as a well-balanced concept, laying an emphasis on the ways successfully to develop the economy of the region, explicitly mentioning the importance of international co-operation, including the EU programmes.

Another initiative that is worth mentioning as potentially a very important instrument, in providing, among other things, more stability in the contacts of the Oblast with the outside world, was Matochkin's proposal to create a special body within the Federal Government for dealing specifically with

Kaliningrad issues. This proposal was strongly backed by a meeting of Russian Ambassadors in countries around the Baltic Sea in May 1995 in Kaliningrad, and a governmental committee was created with the task of co-ordinating activities relating to the Kaliningrad Oblast. Headed at the outset in 1996 by the vice-premier Alexei Bolshakov, the Committee has never properly fulfilled its role, partly due to the instability of the Cabinet, but also because of the apparent lack of interest on the part of the current administration.

Among other innovative arrangements which are valuable for insuring a satisfactory functioning of the Oblast in its new environment, one should mention the special authority granted to the Governor of the Kaliningrad Oblast for dealing directly with the Polish and the Lithuanian Governments on the issues of regional co-operation; the right granted to the Oblast to conclude agreements with ministries of third countries; and participation in the Euroregions. Our proposal to Foreign Minister Kozyrev to introduce a position of special 'curator' for the Kaliningrad Oblast within the ministry proved to be a viable idea, which helped the region considerably in preparing government documents or resolving international issues.

The willingness of the Russian Government to support the opening in Kaliningrad of Polish and Lithuanian consulates, honorary consulates from Sweden, Denmark and Iceland, as well as the Mission of the Russian Ministry of Foreign Affairs (MFA) may be also seen as a sign of a general trend on the part of Moscow to contribute to the openness of the Oblast.

Kaliningrad Oblast in its turn has opened trade missions in Vilnius and Gdansk. Special regional legislation has been adopted to ensure their status and support from the regional budget. This arrangement also provides for a certain degree of accountability before the regional authorities.

Kaliningrad City also opened representations first in Bremerhaven and later in Brussels, though these have since closed.

Tacis in Kaliningrad

Priority status granted to the Oblast for realising Tacis projects in 1994 in fact was not much different from that given to a number of other regions of Russia, which obtained the same treatment by virtue of presenting competitive project proposals to the Tacis Co-ordination Unit in Moscow (for regions of North West Russia only 50 MECU were assigned). Political clout in Moscow was sometimes quite essential. We went through several phases of the 'approved/rejected' game, in the course of which the Governor Matochkin contacted various Federal officials. A small lobbying operation was mounted in Brussels with the help of the Russian Mission there, and with the kind advice and support of Ottokar Hahn and Sigrid Selz – then officials at the European Commission and the German Mission in Brussels accordingly. Critically important was the work of one of Governor Matochkin's advisers, the late Dr. E. Müller-Hermann. He was one of those influential former East Prussians, who till the last days of his life, without prejudice or rancour, made all his wisdom and experience available to Kaliningrad to help it find a European dimension of its own. He was also among those who provided a bridge from almost total oblivion of the region to its new openness.

At the very last stage of the decision-making process, almost half of the finance originally allocated to the Kaliningrad package was apparently diverted to Murmansk.

Finally, after a visit to Kaliningrad by Dr. Michael Emerson, Head of the EC Delegation in Moscow, a package of projects was devised for 8.1 MECU (slightly increased later on) aimed at the following areas of FEZ development:

● Transportation;
● Fishing industry;
● Energy supply;
● Support for privatised companies;
● Development of the educational potential of Kaliningrad State University;

● Support to the Oblast in the framework of the development of a FEZ.

Results of the programme were a mixed bag. Difficulties of an objective character appeared partly in connection with the drawbacks of Tacis at that period of time which are widely recognised now: stringent limitations on 'material' expenses, insufficient participation of Russian experts at the implementation stage as well as during the appraisal phase and complicated bureaucratic procedures. On the other hand, poor understanding of these rules by Russian beneficiaries often led to conflicts which in their extreme manifestations could be described by two phrases: 'Give us the promised money, we know better how to use it' or 'Write anything you like in your reports, provided it does not interfere with our work –your heaps of paper are of no use anyway'.

In other cases, where Russian participants had a well-formulated need for expert support, the results were much better.

Two of the most conflict-ridden projects were the 'Nuffield-Russia' reform agricultural programme (outside the main package) and 'Creating a Centre of Support for Privatised Companies'. In the first project the ambitious goal of creating a model farm and a Scottish-type college on 6.5 thousand hectares belonging to the Russian Agricultural Academy of Science could not be achieved, mainly because the Academy was unable to meet the conditions of the agreement, and was possibly concerned that it would lose control over operations on the farm, but partially also due to the energetic position of British farmers, who perhaps pushed too hard to get the results. More successful was the modified second part of the project aimed at training and consulting farmers and other agricultural/food sector professionals.

The roots of the conflict in the second of the above-mentioned cases were quite similar. This time, officials of the Regional Property Committee felt that they did not have enough control over key aspects of the project. In spite of organisational problems this project ended relatively well, with a small Russian consulting company continuing its operation after the end of EU financing.

In the opinion of local observers, and confirmed by representatives of the Monitoring Programme, the best results were obtained from the Programme of Energy Supply for Kaliningrad Oblast which has provided a business-plan for a newly-planned power station, project documents for an underground gas storage, and a scheme for energy supply for the town of Gusev. Fairly successful also were the projects in the field of transportation and support for the University of Kaliningrad.

Technical aid to the fishing industry was widely perceived in Kaliningrad to have been a failure – a classic case of thousands of pages of rather useless analysis and recommendations. Not because those were professionally weak or irrelevant, simply there was nobody prepared to take them.

It is more difficult to estimate the effectiveness of probably the key project aimed at supporting the SEZ. It started in January 1997 and finished in December 1998. The regional administration presently seems to be unable or unwilling to digest or properly apply the proposed measures. Although a Regional Development Agency was opened as recommended, it does not seem to have enough support or status to be even noticeable on the regional scene.

Thus, on the positive side, regarding the Tacis presence in Kaliningrad, one might mention:

● Expert analysis and perspective plans for some of the key sectors of the Oblast economy;

● Specific business-plans;

● Experience of joint work with western professionals;

● Training of a significant number of Kaliningrad specialists abroad;

● Increased educational potential of Kaliningrad University;

● Agricultural, computer and other equipment, software supplied as part of the projects;

● Intensified contacts between Kaliningrad and foreign companies.

On the negative side, beside the factors already mentioned, there was rather weak co-ordination of projects between the EC officials and the Oblast authorities.

The weakening voice of Kaliningrad

'Kaliningrad itself has displayed limited abilities to manoeuvre towards the more process-oriented challenges. The skills needed to utilise the new opportunities have turned out to be modest'. It is difficult to argue with this diagnosis of Joenniemi & Prawitz (1996, p241). Nevertheless, in my opinion, the period from 1996 to 2000 has shown quite clearly the significance of the internal situation in the Oblast, as well as the importance of regional initiatives for the process of adapting the Oblast to the changing environment. More precisely, the tendency towards isolationism and the absence of any positive 'European' initiative from the present administration has contributed a lot to the perception of the issue as one of a latent crisis.

As in 1991-1993, potential transit problems are the main incentive for the Oblast administration to start bothering again about the EU enlargement.

It is widely perceived locally that, over the last few years, the overall situation has deteriorated significantly with the result that:

● There appears to be no coherent strategy for the Region's development. In particular, there is a lack of any positive initiatives aimed at bringing the SEZ regulations into line with the current internal and external situation.

● Control remains over-centralised. There is a need for greater diversification of power and involvement of different groups in the process of running the Oblast.

● Foreign direct investment (FDI) has been discouraged by stringent controls, which have created an environment with little transparency. The position has been exacerbated by frequent changes to the rules of the game (e.g. the introduction of quotas on duty-free import privileges instead of measures to improve the operation of the SEZ). Some commentators have made allegations of corruption.

● Co-operation in the Baltic Sea area in general, and with neighbouring territories in particular, has been drastically curtailed.

● The civil service in the Oblast has not been given the attention and support that it deserves. Training has been neglected.

● There have been constant disagreements between the Oblast Administration, the Duma and the City authorities.

For more than two years (starting from the autumn of 1996), the topic of the EU enlargement impact on the Kaliningrad Oblast has next to disappeared from the agenda of the region's executive authorities. Involvement of the Kaliningrad Oblast Duma's Chairman, Mr. Ustyugov, in the parliamentary activities of the Council of Europe and his efforts to attract attention to the Kaliningrad issue in Strasbourg have not been enough to reverse this negative trend.

It is hardly surprising that attempts to revive the European component in the regional politics in 1998-1999 ended in a very symptomatic manner. A plan presented to the present Governor Mr Gorbenko by the Representation of the Russian Foreign Ministry, where this author was employed during that period, included a number of specific steps. They were mostly aimed at establishing some sort of a formal dialogue framework on the Kaliningrad issue between all interested parties, as well as providing a scheme for expert appraisal and information exchange based directly in Kaliningrad. Using instruments of the Partnership and Co-operation Agreement (PCA) was also proposed.

The only thing that seemed to be really attractive to all parties was some sort of public relations presentation of the Oblast in Brussels. However, this project fell apart over an attempt to send a working group from Kaliningrad to Brussels (with Tacis support). The group was meant to be representative, and to include senior officials from the Regional and City administration, the Duma and the MFA. However, it proved impossible to reach agreement with all concerned over a choice of representatives.

A year later, in February 2000, the Russian MFA finally made the first publicly announced practical step to introduce the issue of Kaliningrad into the Russia-EU dialogue. A fact-finding mission by a team of experts headed by the Deputy Foreign Minister of Russia, Mr Ivan Ivanov, started preparing the Russian position by consultations with Kaliningrad. As stated by one of the local newspapers, Ivan Ivanov left Kaliningrad with an empty case. A director of one of the companies participating in a meeting with the Minister said, 'we do not have any problems with the EU, we have problems with Moscow'. The worlds of a typical Kaliningrad businessman and that of a high-ranking diplomat are not easily compatible.

First and foremost, there is too little information readily available in the Oblast for people to relate directly EU enlargement with their natural desire to have favourable economic and trade conditions as well as free communication with the rest of Russia and their partners in neighbouring countries. Second, no ready-made recipe exists for Kaliningrad's problems, whose resolution remains in the domain of international politics. Analogies with apparently similar cases of former East Prussia, Hong Kong, West Berlin, Alaska etc., all prove to be a bit of a fallacy – each time the concrete situation and relations between the parties involved are much more important than geography.

In the mean time the neighbours are increasingly involved in a dynamic process of trying to take on board the *acquis communautaire* and getting access to ever-growing volumes of EU funds, leaving Kaliningrad as a passive observer of these changes.

Lessons that might be learnt

1. The above analysis seems to prove that the Federal Government of Russia and the regional authorities have undertaken a number of untraditional measures to help the Kaliningrad Oblast cope with the changing external environment. Most of those measures objectively contributed to the openness of the region, which in turn helped to avoid the worst isolationist scenarios. The recent history has also made clear that the declared strategy will inevitably be undermined unless it is backed by coherent and dynamic instruments with a strong federal involvement.

2. There has been some interest from the EU and limited expert support within the Tacis scheme - though little different from other Russian regions which were chosen for EU technical assistance. No specific measures have been proposed by the EU to compensate Kaliningrad for the deteriorating transit and trade environment. Not enough information about EU-related changes in the neighbouring countries (Poland and Lithuania in the first place) which affect the Kaliningrad Oblast has been made available in the region.

3. Neither Moscow nor Brussels have any strong political incentive to do anything energetic about the issue.

4. If the last decade has proven something beyond doubt, it is a fact that things in and around Kaliningrad Oblast cannot change naturally for the better. An artificially devised world being created around this small spot on the map makes it a must to start applying the same kind of logic and procedure to Kaliningrad. All other scenarios are 'lose-lose' solutions', if

an attempt is made to apply a long-term rather than a short-term perspective.

5. Both Moscow and Brussels would prefer to talk about Kaliningrad without involving the Kaliningrad authorities too much. Moscow – apprehensive of giving more status to the Oblast than it probably should have, especially since it has no previous experience of running a similar kind of territory at any point in its previous history. Brussels is understandably very cautious of dealing with a part of a sovereign state.

6. Kaliningrad cannot cope on its own for a variety of reasons, lack of sufficient expertise being crucial.

7. The role of the Oblast administration can be very significant – probably more than anywhere else in Russia. Transparency and fair play are conditions *sine qua non* for any hope of a prosperous future.

8. About the only area where Kaliningrad can, with a fair degree of irony, be branded a 'success story' is the one of politicians' and experts' brain games where it has become almost a perfect subject, and that of humanitarian aid, of which noticeable amounts have been attracted into the region.

A chance to start moving in the right direction

At the time of writing there are grounds for cautious optimism:

● Russia is prepared to turn Kaliningrad Oblast into a pilot project area and the EU intends to include Kaliningrad into its Northern Dimension action plan. Hopefully those two will meet somewhere not too far to the North.

●Lithuania is showing an increasing degree of pragmatism and recently took the lead in preparing joint Northern Dimension initiatives that have been recently presented to the European Commission.

● The Russian Government is starting consultations with the EU on Kaliningrad.

● Some high-ranking EU officials are mentioning the need for special arrangements for the Oblast (whilst some others are reportedly against any exceptions to the rules).

● The issue of freedom of movement for residents in the Kaliningrad Oblast has been taken up by Mr Ole Espersen, the Commissioner of the Council for Baltic Sea States (CBSS) for Democratic Institutions and Human Rights, including the Rights of Persons belonging to Minorities. He has prepared a report on this subject. The CBSS Secretariat last year joined forces with the Council of Europe to start consultations, including with the European Commission, on ways to ensure a favourable cross-border regime for Kaliningrad Oblast.

Hence an optimistic scenario for Kaliningrad seems to be more likely these days. Here are some directions, which in my view could substantiate this optimism.

1. It is highly desirable that the *Concept of the Federal Policy with regard to the Kaliningrad Region of Russian Federation* and those parts of the SEZ legislation which proved to be positive should be extended, supplemented and further elaborated into a Constitutional Law on the Kaliningrad Oblast. Cornerstones of such a law could be laid down along the following lines:

● More involvement and responsibility for the Federal Centre in those matters of the region which are in the sphere of national interests, searching for arrangements with the EU being one of those.

● More discretion to the Oblast authorities in economic and trade matters: in particular by giving increased room for manoeuvre in tax, tariff, banking regulations and, perhaps, customs duties. A parliamentary way of forming a regional government could be experimented with to help the development of civil society.

● Gradual transfer of some units of the Russian MFA to Kaliningrad to make it an important centre of Russian, Baltic and European politics.

2. If the goal is set to provide some sort of development prospect for Kaliningrad Oblast, it would be very appropriate for both Russia and the EU to establish a permanent framework for a day-to-day dialogue and an information exchange on the issue. As elements of such a framework the following steps could be recommended:

● Appointing a Russian Government official to deal with EU-related issues in Kaliningrad.

● Opening in Kaliningrad a subsidiary of the EC Delegation in Moscow.

● Participation of Kaliningrad representatives in PCA committees where appropriate.

3. As no detailed assessment of the trade and economic situation in the region exists which could form a basis for any serious EU-Russia action plan, starting a joint programme of this kind is an urgent requirement. Such a joint programme (Tacis+Phare+Russian contribution) could help to estimate the specific impact upon Kaliningrad Oblast of EU-related changes in Lithuania and Poland in the various areas of economics, civil society building, etc. Another welcome outcome would be arriving at a common EU-Russian set of criteria for the situation appraisal.

4. Drawing up a joint EU-Russia Action Plan might be considered.

5. Last but not least, arrangements to ensure freedom of movement of people and goods for Kaliningrad are in the domain of basic human rights and should be negotiated in parallel.

Signing a Kaliningrad Protocol to the PCA in this author's view is not a precondition or an absolute necessity for positive action to begin. It could come later on as a natural development or alternatively would be not needed at all.

Without concrete action aimed at improving the economic prospects of Kaliningrad, the issue is destined to remain a mind game with all its scenarios, moves, probabilities and if/then assumptions. The simple answers, sought for at the end of the game, will be basically shaping up as those of a humanitarian nature: will there be freedom of movement for people and goods? Will they cope economically? Again, without a jointly agreed purposeful effort, few would doubt that the answer is 'No'. Humanitarian aid and promises of Federal Centre support, unaffordable at the moment, are a road to nowhere - just like the Russian part of the Kaliningrad-Elblag motorway.

In this search for a negotiated arrangement, the best alternative to such a solution for Moscow and Brussels is to see Kaliningrad sink into isolation and poverty quietly and decently without making too much fuss about the strange fate of this area, apparently doomed to exist within all kinds of peculiar political configurations. For the residents of the Oblast, no better alternative to a negotiated arrangement seems to exist at all.

References

Daschitschew W, *Freie Wirtschaftszone 'Jantar': Chancen und Risken, Königsberg/Kaliningrad unter Europäischen Perspectiven*, H.M. Hausschild, Bremen 1994, p 55-65.
Joenniemi P, Dewar S, Fairlie L.D, *The Kaliningrad Puzzle*, Baltic Institute of Sweden and the Äland Islands Peace Institute, 2000.
Jonniemi P and Prawitz J, *A Double Periphery*, European Amber Region, Ashgate, Suffolk, 1998, p 226-261.
Kwizinskij Y, *Kaliningrad – ein Prufstein fur die Zukunft des neuen Europas?, Königsberg/Kaliningrad unter Europäischen Perspectiven'*, H.M. Hausschild, Bremen 1994, p 55-65.
Matochkin Y., *At a Sharp Bend*, Jantarny Skaz, Kaliningrad, 1999.
Müller-Hermann E, *Königsberg/Kaliningrad unter Europäischen Perspectiven*, Einleitung, H.M. Hausschild, Bremen 1994, p 7-23.

Chapter 5

EU/Kaliningrad: Future Aspirations

Sylvia Gourova[1]
Deputy Mayor of Kaliningrad

For centuries, poets and thinkers have dreamt of a United Europe. We are now both witnesses and participants in a process of European integration that is without precedent. This reflects the ideas of Victor Hugo, who argued for a United States of Europe in 1849, and proposals advanced in the 1920s for the establishment of a Pan-European Union.

These ideas could not be implemented because of the world economic depression in the 1930s and the Second World War. However, starting with the Treaty of Rome in 1957 (leading eventually to the Treaties of Maastricht, Amsterdam and Nice), European countries have taken gradual steps towards integration. This process of evolution has been remarkable. During the first decade of its existence, the Common Market (as it came to be known) functioned primarily as a free trade zone, using only the simplest mechanisms to introduce preferential measures within common customs borders. These included exemption from fees and duties and the introduction of a unified tariff for trade with third countries. Later, EU member countries began a gradual harmonisation of their economic legislation in order to create a unified legal area for common economic and commercial activity within the EU.

Since 1989, the European Union has had a real opportunity to unite the whole continent of Europe. Under the Phare programme, first Poland and Hungary and subsequently most countries in Central and Eastern Europe have been given technical assistance. Every year the EU allocates about 1.5 billion euro, mainly in the form of investment subsidies, to these countries. Now, the countries that are applying for EU membership are making massive adjustments in order to adapt to the *acquis communautaire* and are also preparing to join the EU's Common Foreign and Defence Policy (CFSP) and European Security and Defence Policy (ESDP).

There is no doubt that the forthcoming EU enlargement will be an extremely complicated process. Instead of 15 members there will be 26, the geographical area of the EU will increase by 34%, and its population by 29%. Most importantly, the power of the EU to make decisions with world-wide consequences will increase significantly.

These changes, which are of global importance, will inevitably affect the political and economic interests of other European countries, not least the Russian Federation. But perhaps the greatest impact will be on the westernmost and smallest region of Russia - namely the Kaliningrad Region, which I represent. We are convinced that the creation of a united Europe must, from the very beginning, take into account the interests of all the countries and nations affected by it, and should not involve negative consequences for them.

In this connection, I should like to thank the organisers and participants of this conference for their readiness to listen and to consider the views that I am putting forward on behalf of the authorities of the City of Kaliningrad. I am confident that the recommendations of this conference will be taken into consideration during future discussions between the Government of the Russian Federation and leaders of the EU.

Issues of this kind are not usually the responsibility of the municipal authorities in other Russian cities. But the Kaliningrad Region is unique in having the status of an exclave, and the City of Kaliningrad, as well as the Regional (i.e. Oblast) authorities, are automatically involved in discussion of the key policy questions, because of the very close interrelationship between internal and external problems.

Our proposals on Kaliningrad are based on the documents that define the general rules and principles of the relationship between Russia and the EU. These are The Common Strategy of the EU on Russia, adopted at the Cologne Summit in June 1999, and the 'Medium Term Strategy for Development of Relations between the Russian Federation and the EU' which Vladimir Putin (at that time Prime Minister) presented to the EU/Russia Summit in Helsinki in October 1999. Both documents aim to produce concrete results and to fulfil international legal obligations, and both adopt a pragmatic approach to solving existing problems. They are directed towards co-operation and partnership in this era of globalisation in world politics and economics.

The Russian document sets out ten priorities in the development and strengthening of the relationship between Russia and the EU. A detailed analysis of all ten Chapters is not within the scope of this paper, but I should like to draw attention in particular to Chapter 1 which deals with the overall framework of the EU - Russia relationship and to Chapters 5 and 8, which refer to the Kaliningrad Region.

Chapter 1 underlines the **strategic character** of the partnership between the EU and Russia. In diplomatic practice, it is quite common to define the term 'strategic partnership' as co-operation based on a balance of mutual interests and a high level of trust and mutual responsibility, aimed at establishing and developing a common European economic and legal infrastructure. This is an excellent foundation for joint efforts to remove the threat that the Kaliningrad Oblast might become economically isolated from the rest of the Russian Federation.

Chapter 5 is devoted to the safeguarding of **the interests of Russia in the process of EU enlargement.** In general, Russia considers this process as being positive and based on the objective realities of political and economic development. However, as enlargement involves the interests of other countries including Russia, it is essential to establish without delay the basis for civilised legal settlement of any existing or future problems.

Finally, **Item 3** of **Chapter 8** refers to the protection of **the interests of the Kaliningrad Region as a subject of the Russian Federation.** The document seeks the definition of an 'optimal economic, energy and transport specialisation for the region', and the creation of all necessary conditions for its functioning and development as an integral part of the Russian Federation. The Russian Government believes that the Kaliningrad Region could become 'a pilot region of the Russian Federation in terms of Russia - EU co-operation in the 21st century'.

So today, in the light of this, there is a genuine legal basis for the preparation of all necessary documents and measures to ensure the normal development of the region in its future unique situation.

We are very satisfied with the readiness both of the EU and of our neighbouring countries, Lithuania and Poland (which are both applicants for EU membership), to start an open, constructive dialogue to minimise the possible negative consequences for Kaliningrad. All that I have said above shows that there is at present a full understanding of the problem of Kaliningrad at all levels, a realisation of the complexity and unique depth of this situation, and the commitment of all parties involved to begin solving the problem.

On the basis of all these considerations, the Kaliningrad City Administration is convinced that the time for diplomatic discussion has come to an end, and that experts should now begin work on specific issues.

We in the Kaliningrad City Administration believe that it is our own responsibility to carry out the larger part of the next phase of preparations. The steps that need to be taken in the near future can be divided into two groups:

First, specific *Russian* activities:- i.e. regional initiatives and proposals to the Federal Government, and the decisions of the Government based on them;

Second, measures falling within *international* competence which will have to be settled between the EU leadership and the Government of the Russian Federation. However, we are absolutely convinced that our local experts should also be involved in the preparation of these latter decisions.

While we shall, of course, keep the European context in mind while preparing the first group of measures, I should now like to consider in more detail the problems that we shall have to tackle together with our European partners.

I should like to emphasise that I do not claim to be giving a detailed analysis of the situation. That is a task for experts in different areas. I am rather mapping out some general terms of reference for future joint work, and the Kaliningrad City Administration's vision of the first steps in that direction.

The Kaliningrad City Administration considers that the most vital issue is the provision of reliable links with the 'mainland' of Russia. It will be equally important to ensure the free movement of people and goods through EU countries.

The best solution to the first question would be an agreement on preferential tariffs for goods transported to or from the Kaliningrad region. We wish at the very least to ensure that transit of goods to or from Kaliningrad is not liable to any discriminatory sanctions. Our experience shows that it is difficult and time-consuming to introduce changes into existing agreements. The present position over the transit of cargoes to or from Kaliningrad through Lithuania may serve as a good example.

The agreements regulating this process were adopted in the early 1990s. At that time the approach of the Lithuanian Government was not completely friendly – an attitude which was reflected in the relevant documents. Consequently, today, although this attitude has changed and a Russian-Lithuanian Working Group has been set up to settle this issue, the reduced transit tariff for Kaliningrad cargoes through Lithuania remains at 0.24, while that through Belarus is only 0.136. This could be characterised as discrimination, although there is understanding and readiness on the part of Lithuania to change the situation. We were persuaded of this during the visit of the Mayor of Kaliningrad, Yuri Savenko, to Vilnius.

This issue remains under discussion. The last meeting of the Working Group was held on 21-22 February 2000 in Klaipeda. But progress is still too slow, and the cost of the cargoes entering Kaliningrad, including those (such as fuel) which are vital for providing municipal services in Kaliningrad, is unfairly high because of the high transport component. We should like to avoid similar problems in future, and we believe that the joint search for mutually beneficial mechanisms could help in this.

The second most important problem for regional development, in the opinion of the Kaliningrad City Administration, is that of visas. The residents of the Kaliningrad Region enjoy the right of visa-free entry to Lithuania and Poland. It is evident to us that the situation will change after these countries join the EU, and that they will have to introduce a visa regime. But the City Administration believes that our European partners, and, above all, our neighbouring countries, understand and support the idea of giving some privileges to the citizens of our region over visa arrangements. The nature of these privileges could be jointly defined with our neighbours, bearing in mind the interests of the residents of the Kaliningrad Region and the concern of our neighbours about possible illegal immigration into their countries through Kaliningrad.

Experience in different countries offers different solutions, and we are ready to make our own input into this procedure. We suggest that the following question should be added to the visa application form - duration of residence in the Kaliningrad Region. We suggest that greater privileges be given to those who have been living here for more than five years. The most important benefit of such an arrangement would be that our citizens could visit EU-member countries freely, without excessive bureaucratic obstacles.

The financial aspect is also very important. At the moment, visas are relatively expensive because of high fees. When deciding the cost of visas, therefore, we hope that our partners can take into account that an average Kaliningrad resident crosses the border 14 times more often than an average citizen in the rest of Russia. This problem could be solved by offering multi-entry visas to Kaliningrad residents valid for a period of, for example, up to three years, but allowing a strictly limited period of stay in EU countries on the occasion of each visit. If another model is adopted, the level of the fee, which is a very important consideration for Russians, should be adjusted accordingly.

On the eve of the Tenth Anniversary of the Restoration of the Independence of the Republic of Lithuania, Kaliningrad hosted a visit by an official Lithuanian delegation headed by the Deputy Minister of Foreign Affairs, Vygaudas Usackas. The citizens of Kaliningrad were very pleased when Mr Usackas declared that the principle of good relations with neighbouring countries was a priority in the international policy of his country, and that the Lithuanians were 'concerned to avoid barriers in their relationship with Kaliningrad after Lithuania joins the EU and NATO'. This constructive attitude is very encouraging, and gives us hope that the third problem of greatest concern to the City Administration can be settled jointly. I mean the problem of the supply of energy to Kaliningrad.

At present, Kaliningrad receives electricity from the Unified Energy System of Russia by transmission through Lithuania. In future, when Lithuania is disconnected from the energy network of the former Soviet Union, the situation will become more complicated. One of the strategic problems of the Kaliningrad Region will, therefore, be the need to establish our own energy system. However, this is not a realistic proposition in the near future because of the lack of finance. To create our own energy base, it would be necessary to find an appropriate international solution, suitable for all partners. This issue is complicated, and we count on the assistance of the Federal Government, the Russian electricity authorities, and, above all, on the understanding and help of the EU and our close neighbour, Lithuania.

The position of our region as an exclave creates many difficulties for the citizens of Kaliningrad in relation to border crossings. The Kaliningrad Local Authorities are seriously concerned that the residents and guests of our region have to spend several hours in a long queue of cars. The situation is especially difficult on the Lithuanian border. There are technical reasons for this. I am grateful to the leaders of the EU for financial support from the Tacis Cross Border Co-operation programme for the reconstruction of the Border Crossing Point 'Chernyshevskoy-Kibartai'. We believe that this will greatly improve the situation on the border.

But poor infrastructure is not the only obstacle in border crossings. The very complicated customs clearance procedures are also significant, although some progress has been made in simplifying them. New schemes of co-operation with border guards and railway authorities were elaborated and implemented in 1999 by the State Customs Committee. For example, in Kaliningrad permission for companies to re-export goods is now given by the local Customs authorities. Previously this was previously the task of the State Customs Committee in Moscow. But these are just the first steps in simplifying these procedures and much has still to be done in co-operation with the State Customs Committee.

We believe that this issue also has an international aspect. We are convinced that in the near future it will be vital to hold consultations on the unification of Russian and European customs procedures and also on border-crossing procedures. This will help us to make practical improvements and to achieve the final goal – being able to cross the border in less than two hours! The City Administration regards this as one of the top priorities, taking full account of the issues involved and the difficulties of implementing changes.

The list of future problems is, of course, not exhausted by the four issues mentioned above. It is much more comprehensive, and it is inevitable that other problems will arise which we cannot foresee today, simply because Kaliningrad is a unique case.

I should like to think that my comments have helped to explain the present concerns felt by Kaliningrad in connection with the forthcoming EU enlargement, and I hope that it is clear that we are considering the future seriously and are preparing for change.

In the very near future we are planning to set up a Co-ordination Group, which will include representatives of all branches and levels of the authorities in the Kaliningrad Region and of all Federal organisations, so that we can prepare comprehensive and professional proposals both for the Government of my country and for our foreign partners. We are planning to use to the full the proposal made by Lithuania that we should familiarise ourselves with what they are doing to adapt their legal and economic norms and standards to EU requirements. This will greatly help our specialists to understand the legal and economic framework of the EU.

We also hope that the Federal Government will negotiate with the EU over the possibility of a special programme for Kaliningrad. On behalf of the region, we should also like to approach the EU with a request that they should help us arrange a number of special seminars and workshops for our regional customs officials, border guards, immigration officers, transport experts, economists and lawyers.

We have a saying in Russia that if you and a friend swap apples, you still have only one apple each. But when you exchange ideas, each of you ends up with two. Once again, I would like to thank the organisers of this conference for giving Kaliningrad the chance to exchange ideas with our friends. I hope that by uniting our efforts we shall overcome the difficulties that may lie ahead.

---

[1] This is the revised transcript of a speech given by Ms Gourova at the conference in Brussels on 29 March 2000.

Chapter 6

The Regional-Centre Divide: The Compatibility Conundrum

Igor Leshukov
Centre for Integration Research
and Programmes, St Petersburg

The EU-Russia discussion on Kaliningrad has not so far produced any tangible results. Considering that the Russian side has objected to any debate for so long, the mere existence of a dialogue could be regarded as an achievement. However, results - not mere discussion - are what is needed.

Hitherto, the two sides have limited themselves to expressing their 'concerns', but have refrained from committing themselves to a joint solution. At one stage, hope for progress emerged, when a joint Russian-Lithuanian declaration on Kaliningrad was signed, but this was soon buried again. The EU Northern Dimension conference on Kaliningrad in Copenhagen on 17-18 May was prepared with high expectations, but in the event broke little new ground. Its timing was arguably wrong, shortly before the EU-Russia summit of 29 May, and there was little political commitment from Moscow.

Meanwhile, the Kaliningrad regional administration has been unwilling to take any initiatives. Some other local actors have been ready to put forward ideas, but lack the resources and authority to implement their proposals. Further progress will depend on new policies from the federal government and the regional administration. In order to understand the position, we need better insight into the domestic Russian playing-field, and in particular into the centre-regional relationship.

Federal governance

What do we know about contemporary Russian governance? Russia is a federation composed of 89 constituent entities, called 'federal subjects', and known by different names - *republics, oblasts, krays, autonomous oblasts* and *autonomous districts*. It has three layers of power - federal, regional and municipal, each with separate competences and budgets. This new Russia was born out of the dissolution of the Soviet Union, and (like the other Newly Independent States) inherited much of its polity from its predecessor. The RSFSR constitution of 1918 was the legal basis for the first years of modern Russian sovereignty. The first legal foundations of the new system were laid down in the form of a so-called Federation Treaty, signed in 1992. This provides a basic agreement between the federal centre and the regions, and regulates the division of competence and respective responsibilities.

In relation to our analysis, there are two main points that should be emphasised:

First, Russia sensibly learned the appropriate lessons from the USSR's Federation Treaty, which failed under Gorbachev. Instead of holding protracted negotiations, Russia prepared and concluded its own treaty in a strictly administrative way. Indeed, this may have been the only possible way of achieving a political settlement at a time when the risk of further disintegration was immediate. However, the shortcomings of the treaty were obvious and produced long-term effects. The treaty was not able to provide a proper legitimacy for the new relationship between the centre and the regions, and little more than a provisional consensus was reached on the balance of regional and national interests. The treaty was followed by numerous (and separate) bilateral agreements between Moscow and the regional authorities, a process which was led by such independent-minded regions as Tatarstan and Bashkiriya. The process of tough bargaining between the regional and central *nomenklatura* over property and power resulted in tailor-made arrangements which specified the division of competences (especially in the budgetary sphere), and which deviated widely from the generally agreed pattern of centre-regional relations. The outcome was that the actual relationship deviated significantly from the model in the treaty. Ad hoc arrangements (which are subject to arbitrary administrative interpretation) took the place of universal and transparent rules. This had adverse effects on the coherence of Russia as a state, and undermined the legitimacy of the existing governance. The excessive complexity of centre-regional relations has also had a negative effect on public administration and has given scope to bureaucratic arbitrariness and political intervention.

Second, it is significant that the 1992 Federation Treaty was in fact composed of three types of agreements: one – with the *republics*, another – with the *oblasts* and *krays*, and the last – with *autonomous oblasts* and *autonomous districts*. This reflects the administrative structure inherited from the Soviet Union, and the Soviet principle of making a distinction between the 'Russian' and 'national' entities and giving preferential treatment to the latter. As a result, three distinctive types of constituent parts of the state have emerged each enjoying a different set of rights vis-à-vis the federal centre.

For Kaliningrad, this means that, although it has found itself in a unique geographical and political position, this situation can not be reflected in administrative terms. Kaliningrad is simply one of many 'Russian' oblasts like Voronezh or Orel, and, constitutionally, it is very difficult to justify special treatment for it, which is normally only reserved for the 'national republics'. The latter are able to invoke the sovereignty clause and take a tough line with Moscow (as Tatarstan has done). The irony is that, at the time of the Soviet Union, Kaliningrad was deliberately left as a 'solely Russian' region. Now this absence of a 'national' status has become the main administrative obstacle to providing the region with a special status, which is well justified in objective terms.

Igor Leshukov

The 1993 Constitution established Russia as a semi-presidential republic. Under this construction - which was specifically written to satisfy Yeltsin's ambitions - the institutional balance was shifted towards the President and his administration. The approach was mirrored on the regional level - with elected Presidents in the 'national republics' and elected Governors in the 'Russian' entities (oblasts and krays). The original thinking in Moscow was that centrally nominated officials (called 'Presidential Representatives') and the federal structures in the regions should serve as a means of preventing the regional authority from acquiring too much power. However, the reality turned out otherwise, and the Governors eventually concentrated most of the power at the regional level in their own hands. The Governors also enjoyed immunity, as the Constitution gave them a seat in the Federation Council, the upper chamber of the Russian Parliament. This turned out to be another factor which strengthened the position of the regional leaders, who gained control over vast resources, substantial political autonomy and at the same time a solid insurance against prosecution. Not surprisingly, this led to an unprecedented and flourishing merger of criminality and corruption within the public service on the regional level. Empirical evidence shows that, the more remote a given region is from the centre and the greater its wealth, the more extreme and ugly will be the manifestations of abuse of power, corruption and criminality which emerge at the regional level.

The federal system in Russia has three layers: the centre, regions and municipalities. At some stage support emerged for the idea of using the third level as a means of countering the excessive power of regional bosses. The aim was to place the regional authorities between the centre on the one hand and the municipalities on the other. The sandwich effect would compel the regional authorities to react to local demands and keep them within certain limits. Although considerable efforts were put into making this system work, Moscow has not pursued this policy entirely consistently. It never managed to put enough resources and political support behind municipalities in order to help them to perform their difficult task of restraining the Governors and regional administrations. Kaliningrad is an instructive case in this regard. Typically for many regions, political opposition to the regional authorities is represented at the level of the local legislature and Mayor's Office. These bodies could be instrumental and effective, if enough federal support was provided. But, without support they have little hope of making any impact. Municipalities could become a significant political force only if parallel 'budgetary federalism' were to function properly. This is clearly not the practice at present.

Federal subsidies

Public budgets are a very broad and technically complex issue, which cannot be addressed in any detail in this paper. Nevertheless, the following comments may be helpful. The Russian Federation is asymmetric. The differences in the respective wealth of the regions (if measured by the Final Consumption Index) are enormous. For instance, Moscow is 22.3 times richer than Ingushetia. About 30 constituent parts of the federation are considered to be well off, while the situation in the rest of the regions varies from not satisfactory to very poor.[1] Insufficiency of local budgets undermines the coherence of the Federation, divides the regions into 'donors' and 'recipients' and stimulates disputes (of different sorts) between the regions and the centre, sometimes resulting in 'taxation separatism', when the regions try to keep locally collected tax for their internal use.

In contrast to other asymmetric federations, for instance Germany, no such principle as 'solidarity' has been developed that could generate the necessary public and political support for re-distributive policies. Two main instruments are applied in the pursuit of an 'equalisation' policy. The first are 'transfers', i.e. annual state subsidies allocated for given regions. The intended function of such transfers is to help non-sustainable regions to bridge the gap in their social obligations. The second instrument consists of 'budgetary loans', namely federal credits in the middle of a financial year to cover regional expenditure, if there is no money left in a local budget.

In the first years of the Russian Federal Government, subsidies were allocated on an individual basis. Eventually, a special mechanism was developed, and since 1994 financial assistance to the regions has been provided through the Financial Support Fund for the Regions (FSFR). This accounts for 16.5% of the Russian budget and is an important instrument of regional policy. However, its policy is highly politicised and badly managed, leaving considerable scope for corruption and political log-rolling. The mechanisms for allocating resources provide openings for this sort of abuse. First, the legal basis regulating the FSFR is not substantially precise and is subject to administrative 'interpretation'. Secondly, the methodology used is imperfect and highly inaccurate. The operation of the fund is even more problematic. About one third of the regions receive the transfers with a substantial delay. Some regions receive less than 25% of the transfer due to them, and others more than 120%. As a result, the main bargaining process is more to do with the level of implementation than with the level of allocating the assistance. The position over 'budgetary loans' is even worse. Although directly managed by the Ministry of Finance, these loans are not subject to any clear legal regulation, and their management provides even more scope for corruption and politically driven decisions than is the case with the federal transfers. Not surprisingly, the Government tends to use the federal financial assistance as a means not only of keeping the federation together, but also as a means of providing comfort to its political supporters and of penalising its opponents.

Kaliningrad is normally qualified as a donor region.[2] But it would be wrong to conclude that the region is less dependent on Moscow. First, it plays the game that is familiar to all donors – 'Give me my money back'. Secondly, apart from the process of equalisation, Kaliningrad (with its post-military profile) benefits considerably from federal programmes directly funded on the regional level. Thirdly, and most importantly, the structure of Kaliningrad's economy makes it extremely dependent on its relationship with the federal centre.

The present budgetary sufficiency of Kaliningrad is largely due to the continued existence of the Special Economic Zone (SEZ), which provides a favourable customs regime for the region. The SEZ is broadly criticised on the federal level on the grounds that it allegedly leads to a tax loss (estimated at 2.5 billion US Dollars for the period 1996-98) and to criminalisation. If the SEZ ended, the region would change from being a donor into a recipient. The fact that different federal bodies (the MFA, Ministry of Finance, Ministry of Economics, Customs Committee) have divergent views on the SEZ, provides the regional authorities with some space for manoeuvre. It is clear that a political understanding with Moscow is essential on this issue. The import structure (50% of the turnover is food and 15% other consumer goods) makes Kaliningrad dependent on tariff regulation which falls within the federal (not regional) competence.

This situation has a direct impact on the attitudes and decisions of the regional authority. On the one hand, as a Russian exclave, Kaliningrad has many reasons to develop its relations with its neighbours and to improve its compatibility with the surrounding political and economic environment. On the other hand, the benefits and importance of its dependent relationship with the federal centre are much more serious and immediate. The principle guiding the relations of the regional authorities with Moscow could be defined primarily as one of feudal 'loyalty', which is scarcely compatible with Russia's status as a republic.

Moscow's regional policy, as developed under Yeltsin - and as it seems likely to continue under Putin - also reflects the centrality of loyalty for the centre-periphery relations. The deal could be summarised as follows: the federal centre identifies the national priorities, especially in the field of foreign affairs, and secures the economic interests of the respective oligarchic groupings at the federal level. The regional establishment trades its loyalty in return for non-interference by the federal government in its 'domestic' affairs. Kaliningrad is a typical pattern of this logic. Since becoming Governor, Mr Gorbenko has always been quick to follow the sea-changes in the political climate in Moscow. At an early stage he was a devoted supporter of NDR (Our Home is Russia), then OVR (Fatherland - All Russia). After that he was among the first to join the Unity ('Bear') alliance.

Process of decentralisation

Until recently, the political process in Russia has been described as a process of decentralisation. It is broadly perceived as a progressive tendency, which facilitates a break with the Soviet tradition of an excessively centralised state, and which helps to make the country more open and democratic. However, the reality is less clear cut, and raises a number of controversial issues.

The Yeltsin administration managed to keep the state together, avoided a return to the scenario of the Soviet Union, and laid down the first foundations of democracy; but the cost has been high and the implications are worrying. The message to the regions of the early reforms - 'take as much sovereignty as you can' - initiated a chaotic and badly co-ordinated process of decentralisation in Russia. Instead of a clear and transparent system, the relations with the regions were regulated by *ad hoc* agreements, and there was no consistency in the implementation of the agreed arrangements: neither the regions nor the centre were prepared to comply fully with the negotiated terms. During the later Yeltsin years, the state structures became increasingly loose, the regional barons became more and more powerful and national policy remained badly co-ordinated. In practice, the decentralisation of Russia led to the emergence of many feudal-like features, and the federation in some respects came close to resembling a confederation ruled by the cynical and narrow-minded elites. Since then, the risk has (ironically) reversed itself. If, in Soviet times, the challenge originated from an excessively strong state, now the danger lies in the state becoming unacceptably weak. In the face of this, the diagnosis is simple - the state should become stronger. But how?

Administrative reform

The Putin administration is now imposing its vision as to how to make the state strong again. The suggested administrative reform that is currently under the Parliament's scrutiny provides for the following: first, there is a renewed attempt to reactivate the system of presidential representatives. Seven new 'federal districts' have been created with each presidential representative 'looking after' a number of governors. The composition of these districts coincides with the military districts, and to a certain extent resembles a scheme to govern the country under a state of emergency. Kaliningrad falls within the North-West district. What role the new structure will play in the region can be only be seen over time. Secondly, there is an attempt to review the role of the governors. There is a legal proposal to make them removable by the federal centre and to remove their immunity by withdrawing their right to sit in the Federation Council. From being elected politicians, governors will *de facto* become top regional officials whose future will be completely dependent on their loyalty to the central authority. The governors in return will have the power to remove the heads of municipalities. If this proposal is approved by legislation, the political system in Russia will in some ways revert to the Soviet pattern. The role of municipalities, although already limited, will become completely marginalised, and the notion of civil society will become obsolete.

As far as Kaliningrad is concerned, it will free the governor and regional administration from internal opposition, but will weaken their position vis-à-vis Moscow. The key to all problems will lie primarily in federal hands, but it is not clear whether they will be ready to take over the responsibility passed to them. In the most optimistic scenario, a management deficit might become even more apparent than today. It is also open to speculation whether and how the founding principles of the relationship between the federal centre and regional authorities will emerge from such a change.

Western policy dilemmas

One of the most difficult issues in western political practice towards Russia has always been how to identify and respond to the balance between the federal and regional components of policy implementation. In other words, what issues should be tackled at the centre, and what issues should be tackled on the regional level? At first glance, the theory looked very simple. There was an ongoing process of decentralisation in Russia, and the regions were gaining more weight and capacity both in the policy process and in the economy reform. So the regions should be given more attention and respect by the West in its Russia policy. The regions were also keen to exploit these new opportunities, and embarked on an easy marketing strategy of blaming Moscow and the federal government for all shortcomings in Russian politics and presenting themselves as a promising alternative, which was worth taking a gamble over. Political science also followed a well-trodden path, advocating outsiders to focus their policy on the Russian regions. Though the underlying argument behind it was sound, it soon became apparent that this issue was much more tricky than it appeared in the beginning. The problems of dealing with Moscow were well known. On closer scrutiny, however, the regions turned out to be not much better. Practice showed that regional actors were not immune from corruption and mismanagement, and abuse of laws was sometimes even more striking than at the centre. Civil society and its institutions were weaker in the regions than at the centre, and there were no effective check and balance system to constrain the regional authorities if they abused their power and began to undermine political and economic freedoms.

This also challenged a key theoretical proposition on the role of interdependence in the contemporary world. The regions of the Russian North-West are particularly exposed to western influence. Liberal expectations were based on the assumption that, through an increased interaction with their neighbours, these regions would evolve into the most advanced Russian entities, and become compatible with western norms and values. Kaliningrad is full of used foreign cars, its shops are full of imported products. Yet these features have a dubious impact on the politics and economy of the region. Further opening up to Europe, while remaining embedded in Russian practice will create a serious risk that, instead of becoming 'Europeanised', the region will provide a powerful interface channelling into Europe many unpleasant aspects of Russian life. Kaliningrad is already marked by an exceptionally high level of prostitution, drug trafficking, AIDS and organised crime. In view of this, as a pilot project for Russia-EU co-operation, Kaliningrad could display unexpected and ironic features of being a pioneer in the very spheres which the two sides least want to develop, and wish to counter by every means. Confident and long-term relations with the Russian regions cannot be envisaged without effective and trustworthy public authorities. Sadly, today's Kaliningrad clearly falls seriously short of what Europe expects on many counts.

Concluding remarks

The case of Kaliningrad is especially tricky in many respects. The dissolution of the Soviet Union made this region a desolate Russian exclave, separated by 400 km of foreign territory and two borders from the mainland Russia. As an old capital of Prussia, Kaliningrad is a conquered piece of land, received as compensation after the war, and has the fewest historic grounds among Russian provinces to remain Russian. At the same time, it is one of the most notorious regions in Russia in terms of lawlessness, corruption and criminality on the regional level. This messy basket of national pride and maladministration makes Kaliningrad a politically sensitive and technically complicated issue. The problems of delivering a solution are many times more difficult than in most other Russian regions.

There are a number of serious obstacles to progress:

First, there are problems with the profile of the political authority on the regional level. Until these issues are resolved, it is difficult to imagine that there will be significant foreign investment in the region. As discussed above, the sandwich effect on the regional authorities (converging pressure from the centre and from municipalities) will not work any more. It is not clear how the centre proposes to act. However, the situation could develop in unexpected ways.

Secondly, the Russian Mid-Term Strategy Paper on the EU presents Kaliningrad as a pilot project. For the moment, this statement looks more a declaration rather than an intention. The joint Russian-Lithuanian paper lists a number of projects ranging from AIDS programmes to cross-border check points, but it is difficult to regard these as 'pilot' issues. There are numerous examples of such activities run in other places, for instance on the Russo-Finnish border. A 'pilot' project (properly interpreted) should include activities that are new for Russia and which, for one reason or another, cannot be implemented throughout the whole country. In other words, the term 'pilot' should denote new endeavours to be tested on Kaliningrad's soil. Otherwise the term is misleading.

In any case, improved cross-border infrastructures and reduction of social problems do not provide a satisfactory answer to the enormous needs in the region. What is needed is a concept for the social and economic development of Kaliningrad. This should define what Kaliningrad should aim to become, e.g. a transport gateway to Russia, the home of hi-tech industries, services and so on. Such a concept should be based on realities and should be agreed, as the EU would say, by common accord at the regional and federal level in Russia. The region will require a structured approach. Without this, the envisaged measures could only have a palliative function, and would amount to little more than a stroll around the main issues, which would remain unapproachable. Unfortunately, this sort of clarity of thinking has not been reflected in the debate over Kaliningrad. Much of the discussion has had a distinct air of unreality.

The third point relates to the following: Russia is an increasingly asymmetric country, and the federal centre is trying, perhaps not in the most sensible way, to pursue a balancing act. The regions of North-West Russia are more exposed to western influences and closer involved with the West than many of the more remote Russian regions. Kaliningrad's case is in many ways even more complex. The question is whether Moscow will be prepared to allow Kaliningrad to go first and the others follow? Any attempt by Europe to force this issue before a clear understanding is reached internally by the Russians, would be very risky and might involve high political costs.

---

[1] The traditional figure is even less: nine or ten regions are classified as self-sufficient, i.e. are not receiving federal compensatory transfers. However, if the balance of financial flows from and to a region is taken into account, the number of sustainable regions is about thirty. See 'Federal Budget and the Regions', published in Russian by the EastWest Institute, Moscow, 1999.

[2] In the period 1996-98, Kaliningrad paid between 500-1000 Rubles (17-33 US Dollars) per capita annually to the federal budget, and received back 58-67% of the amount paid. (EastWest Institute study - op.cit.).

THE NEIGHBOURS

Chapter 7

Lithuania and Kaliningrad: Building a Partnership for the New Europe

Vygaudas Usackas
Lithuanian Deputy Minister for
Foreign Affairs[1]

Two years ago a discussion about the relationship between the Kaliningrad region and the European Union seemed impossible. Today, we are discussing this issue and asking ourselves a question - why does Kaliningrad matter? Following the re-establishment of Lithuania's independence, Kaliningrad was perceived as a potential risk and threat to the stability of the region. Over recent years, Lithuania has been deliberately working to make the Kaliningrad region be seen as an opportunity for regional and European co-operation. Our national interest is to co-operate with neighbours which share the same values. We should like the Kaliningrad region to become an attractive partner for economic and cross-border co-operation and a 'window of opportunity' for wider co-operation between Russia and the enlarging EU.

Lithuania's co-operation with the Kaliningrad region

Lithuania's co-operation with the Kaliningrad region during the last two years can be seen as a practical exercise in building a bilateral and regional partnership. Starting from humanitarian aid to the region during the 1998 Russian crisis and from the solitary links between governmental institutions, local governments and NGOs, we have succeeded in creating the institutional framework for bilateral and regional co-operation. This framework includes:

● **The Joint Lithuanian-Kaliningrad Co-operation Council** formed under the agreement on long-term co-operation between Lithuanian regions and the Kaliningrad region of the Russian Federation. This Council is composed of representatives of the central institutions as well as of the regions. The Council deals with the regular problems of our bilateral relations, supervising the implementation of joint projects and preparing plans for medium and long-term co-operative activities.

● **Euroregions 'Baltica', 'Nemunas' and 'Saule'** - multilateral cross-border co-operation structures representing the needs and priorities of co-operation on the local and regional level. The co-operation between Lithuania and Kaliningrad on a regional level is also co-ordinated by the Klaipéda Co-ordination Centre, established with the assistance of the EU's CREDO programme. Despite the short period of their existence Euroregions are already engaged in practical co-operation projects, some of which became a part of the joint Lithuanian - Russian proposals to the Northern Dimension initiative.

● **Association of Lithuanian and Kaliningrad academic institutions and non-governmental organisations** - this structure provides the possibility of engaging a wider range of political and academic elites on both sides to take an active part in shaping bilateral and regional co-operation. It also provides a framework for continuous dialogue between the politicians and intellectuals of both sides on pressing issues of our past, present and future relations. This dialogue should root out the stereotypes and prejudices still burdening our relations as well as consolidate the foundation for our future co-operative activities.

Regional frameworks: Council of Baltic Sea States (CBSS), Northern Dimension and North European Initiative

Two years ago, while preparing for the chairmanship of the CBSS, Lithuania singled out Kaliningrad and other North West regions of Russia for participation in CBSS-run activities as a top priority of our chairmanship agenda. Realisation of this programme showed that CBSS is a proper framework for identifying the priority needs of the Kaliningrad region as well as for a deeper engagement of other countries into Kaliningrad-related co-operation projects. We have also experienced the growing appreciation in Kaliningrad region itself of the possibilities and benefits of regional co-operation.

We are strongly convinced of the fact that co-operation with the Kaliningrad region should remain on the CBSS priority agenda and on the list of the forthcoming high-level CBSS meetings. The CBSS should perform a database function and accumulate institutional, technical and financial support for the regional co-operation projects, activities of the Euroregions and other initiatives. More CBSS-run activities should be organised in the Kaliningrad region in order directly to involve people on the spot.

The Lithuanian - CBSS Chairmanship priority projects, as well as the initiatives of the regional and local governments, formed the basis for joint Lithuanian - Russian proposals to the EU's Northern Dimension initiative. This document, symbolically named the 'Nida initiative', was the first ever joint Lithuanian - Russian initiative. We hope the ideas and projects of the 'Nida initiative' will be properly reflected in the Northern Dimension Action Plan. The EU conference of 17-18 May 2000 on Kaliningrad in Copenhagen should contribute to preparing a kind of 'Kaliningrad programme' within the Northern Dimension initiative. In the context of our bilateral relations the 'Nida initiative' will be translated into a joint long-term action programme supervised by the Lithuanian - Kaliningrad Co-operation Council. In this respect I would also mention the need for more synergy and interaction between Phare and Tacis programs for the effective implementation of joint projects on the Lithuanian - Kaliningrad border.

We hope that the Northern Dimension initiative will not be limited to a brainstorming exercise, but will result in a set of projects and a network of co-operative activities. The Northern Dimension should utilise CBSS expertise and mechanisms in fostering co-operation on local and regional level – and, therefore, the role and the responsibilities of the CBSS in the process of implementation of the Northern Dimension Action Plan should be clearly defined.

The United States Northern European Initiative (NEI) is yet another instrument of expanding co-operation with the Kaliningrad region. The US government and American foundations have assisted in organising training programmes for Kaliningrad local government officials and businessmen. This year, with the support of US and Swedish governments, we are planning to start training programmes for Kaliningrad Oblast officials related to the military infrastructure, focusing on management of former military bases, increasing environmental awareness, identifying environmental risks connected with military activities, pollution prevention, etc. We feel the need to design special programmes providing aid to convert Kaliningrad's military industry, minimising the social costs of this process, and to dispose of waste armaments and chemical materials. Since there remain over 30,000 military personnel in Kaliningrad, more inclusive co-operation with the Russian military is necessary. We hope that EU Northern Dimension initiative and US NEI will develop into practical co-operation programmes with a high level of co-ordination, division of labour and interaction.

Lithuania's and Poland's future membership of the European Union will open new possibilities for expanding cross-border co-operation. This has already been proved by the success stories of trans-frontier activities along the Czech - German and Polish - German borders over the last decade. Our immediate task is to increase the knowledge and professional skills of people living on both sides of the border with the aim of making the best use of those opportunities. Training programmes for Lithuanian and Kaliningrad local government officials and businessmen already serving that goal should be expanded.

EU enlargement

The process of Lithuania's and Poland's integration into the European Union and the parallel process of deepening EU - Russia relations according to the recently adopted co-operation strategies open new opportunities for expanding co-operation with the Kaliningrad region which is to become a 'pilot' region in Russia - EU co-operation. This co-operation has to minimise the risk of furthering uneven development in the region followed by negative social, economic and psychological consequences.

During my recent visit to Kaliningrad, most of the talks with our partners were in one way or another related to EU enlargement issues. We agreed to have a continuous exchange of information on Lithuania's preparation for EU membership and planned activities that could affect our relations with the Kaliningrad region. Kaliningrad officials, politicians and intellectuals showed genuine interest in EU matters and in Lithuania's preparation for the membership of the Union. Lithuanian and Kaliningrad parliamentarians had a special meeting in May 1999 devoted to European integration issues focusing on law harmonisation according to EU standards. Now we are discussing the idea of organising a special session of the Joint Lithuanian - EU Parliamentary Committee in Kaliningrad with the participation of representatives of the local Duma.

Throughout the development of co-operation with the Kaliningrad region we note increasing interest in Kaliningrad to partake and benefit rather than to ignore or be left aside from the co-operation prospects which the European integration process provides. This interest should lead to the working out of a long-term strategy on the development of the region with a practical programme of activities responding to the challenges and utilising the possibilities of EU enlargement.

Currently, EU-related matters are familiar to a relatively small group of Kaliningrad political and intellectual elites. These issues are still largely left out of public discussions. In this respect we feel the need for a continuous and comprehensive information campaign. We have already organised a couple of visits of Kaliningrad journalists to Lithuania which resulted in a series of publications in the local press giving more insight into Lithuania's integration into Western structures. We have also organised two 'round tables' with the participation of government officials, politicians, journalists and NGOs from Kaliningrad and Western countries. We are hosting a third 'round table' in June 2000, this time focusing on EU enlargement and Northern Dimension issues. We would encourage other countries of the region and EU member states actively to engage in these kinds of activities. Raising public awareness in Russia on EU issues would change the very vague understanding of what the EU represents. Those efforts would facilitate mitigation of negative stereotypes, false prejudices and unrealistic expectations about the EU enlargement process. They should also decrease the existing gap between the aspirations of political and intellectual elites of the region and the opinion of the rest of population.

Prospects for Kaliningrad region: the need for a comprehensive strategy

During my recent visit to Kaliningrad I was honoured to deliver a presentation in Kaliningrad University. This presentation included the analysis of Lithuania's experience over the last decade in transforming its state structures and introducing the principles of a free market economy. Based on this analysis and our practical experience I drew several conclusions which in my view are important for the Kaliningrad region in order to fit into the ongoing regional and European integration processes.

● A comprehensive, consensual vision of the short, medium and long term development of the Kaliningrad region should be prepared. This strategy, based on a wide political consensus and comprehensive analysis of the present situation in the region, should materialise the notion of Kaliningrad as a 'pilot' region in Russia - EU relations as it is presented in the Russia - EU co-operation strategy.

● Taking into account growing economic interdependence in the region, this strategy has to foresee the specialisation of the Kaliningrad region, not only as a part of Russia's market, but also of the regional integration processes.

● This strategy is unlikely to emerge until the overall new Russian Government's policy vis-à-vis the periphery is developed. In the case of Kaliningrad, this strategy should stimulate active participation of the Kaliningrad Oblast in regional activities as well as its co-operation with the enlarging EU. The Kaliningrad region must become open for the positive experience, knowledge and technologies of the developed countries.

● The strategy for Kaliningrad should be based on a consistent and realistic programme of reforming the economy and state structures, utilising the experience of EU member states and candidate countries.

● EU member states and the countries of the Baltic Sea region should respond with a reciprocal programme of actions vis-à-vis the Kaliningrad region. Such a programme has to emerge in the process of implementing the EU - Russia co-operation strategy and Northern Dimension initiative.

To sum up, the Kaliningrad region should be seen not as a problem but rather as an opportunity for introducing new forms of regional co-operation. In the light of the ongoing political changes in Russia, Kaliningrad presents itself as an interesting test of Russia's 'Europeanisation' vis-à-vis the processes of Euro-Atlantic integration.

---

[1] This is the transcript of a speech given by Mr Usackas at the conference in Brussels on 29 March 2000.

Chapter 8

Poland and Kaliningrad Region: The Present and Future Prospects for Co-operation

Wojciech Zajaczkowski
Department for Eastern Europe,
Polish Ministry of Foreign Affairs

The Kaliningrad Region is the only part of the Russian Federation with which Poland has a direct border. For this reason it occupies an important place - though not a privileged one - in Poland's relations with the Russian Federation. These relations are developing in three spheres:

- European dialogue, including the continent's most important international problems;
- Bilateral relations;
- Regional contacts.

The legal basis for the co-operation of Polish voivodships (provinces) with the Kaliningrad Region is formed by *The Agreement between the Government of the Republic of Poland and the Government of the Russian Federation on cross-border co-operation* and *The Agreement between the Government of the Republic of Poland and the Government of the Russian Federation on co-operation between the North-Eastern voivodships of the Republic of Poland and the Kaliningrad Region of the Russian Federation*, signed in 1992. Poland treats the Kaliningrad Region as an integral part of the Russian Federation, which means that relations are being developed on the inter-regional level and also on the cross-border level. An important element of the institutional base of the relations with the Kaliningrad Region is the Polish-Russian Commission for Co-operation between the North-Eastern voivodships of the Republic of Poland and the Kaliningrad Region of the Russian Federation, the last meeting of which took place in November 1999.

The beginnings of co-operation with the Kaliningrad Region at the start of the nineties were steeped in concern stemming from its military potential, which caused anxiety among the countries of the region. At the same time, however, the region opened itself to the outside world. That was accompanied by a rapid progress of federative trends in all of Russia and ambitious plans for the development of the region prepared by the new administration.

At that time a dilemma arose concerning the identity of the region: was it to be the most westerly Russian military base, or should it become a region enjoying prosperity by playing the role of a bridge between the European Union and the Russian Federation? Several years have passed since then, but there still is no clear answer to that question, despite significant changes in the region. Observing the transformations taking place in Kaliningrad, one gets the impression that it lacks a precise development strategy.

Perhaps that lack of clarity as to the region's identity stems from the failure of the Special Economic Zone, which - as was hoped in the early nineties - was intended to change the face of the region. But, despite its unique geographical location, Kaliningrad has not become a bridge between Russia and Europe. Moreover, the authorities have not managed to free Kaliningrad from the negative effects of the social and economic crisis afflicting the Russian Federation as a whole.

In other words, Kaliningrad, having lost its former character, has not managed to replace it with a new identity.

This situation must be considered as being totally unfavourable. The reasons for this assessment are known, and they are contained - among others - in a study on Kaliningrad financed by the EU. This refers to a broadly perceived degradation of the region and the deepening of the development gap between the region and its neighbours. Enlargement of the European Union can create an opportunity to reverse these trends. The sensitivity of EU members, and especially participants in the Northern Dimension, gives grounds for hope that an optimistic scenario will be implemented in solving the problems of the Kaliningrad enclave.

The influence of Poland and other European countries on Kaliningrad should be directed at making it more open to economic and cultural co-operation, as well as European dialogue. Much will depend here on the attitude of the central Russian authorities and the shape of the federative system of Russia. An important asset in the strivings for a new identity of the region is the growing openness of the local inhabitants to Europe.

The regional co-operation between Polish voivodships and the Kaliningrad Region dates back several years. The Warmia-Masuria voivodship - created as a result of administrative reform in Poland - appears to be a natural partner for regional co-operation with Kaliningrad. It replaced three former voivodships, and its greater economic, human and intellectual potential offers broader scope for cross-border co-operation with the northern neighbour. Such co-operation would be significantly enhanced by growing interest in Kaliningrad on the part of the European Union, with particular reference to the Northern Dimension. It is worth noting here that on 5 May 2000 Olsztyn hosted a meeting of representatives of the Government, local authorities, businessmen and scientists devoted to co-operation with Kaliningrad in the context of EU initiatives.

Poland is interested in implementation of the following undertakings – also connected with Kaliningrad – within the framework of the Northern Dimension:

- closing the energy and gas ring around the Baltic;
- development of the Via Baltica project;
- development of shipping in Vistula Bay;
- more intense efforts to protect the southern coast of the Baltic endangered by refuse and rusting poison-gas containers from World War II;
- improving methods of combating international organised crime;
- establishment of a Baltic Committee for Investment Projects;
- development of the Eurofaculty in Kaliningrad, with particular reference to academic projects in economics and law;
- creation of regional Baltica Television;
- preparation of a study on spatial development of a specific Polish-Russian cross-border area; and
- creation of wholesale markets and agricultural exchanges.

Regional co-operation with the Kaliningrad Region could benefit from certain solutions developed within the framework of Euroregions on the Polish-German border. However, making this possible would require decisions of the European Commission concerning new rules and procedures for utilisation of Phare funds on the Polish side and Tacis funds on the Russian side.

The introduction of visas for citizens of the Russian Federation coming to Poland - planned for 2001 - may have a significant impact on Polish-Russian relations directly affecting the Kaliningrad Region. These plans do not signify an intention to build new barriers in Europe. That would be incompatible with the very philosophy of transformation launched in Poland ten years ago; one of its main objectives was to remove the divisions that had existed in Europe for several decades. We do not wish to build a new iron curtain. We are motivated by an intent to put in order the mechanisms governing movement of people between the two countries, which is now conducted on the basis of a 1979 agreement with the USSR, which provides for border crossing on the basis (inter alia) of so-called tourist vouchers, records of which are not kept by any state institutions. Our actions have the goal of introducing civilised forms of registration and control of persons crossing the border of the Republic of Poland.

In addition to the introduction of visas, the following measures will also be taken:

● expansion of Polish consular missions in Russia, including Kaliningrad where a consulate-general has been operating since 1992;

● upgrading of the border infrastructure and development of existing border crossings;

● setting visa charges affordable for citizens of the Russian Federation.

In making specific decisions, we shall be mindful of the solutions adopted in this area by Finland, which have proven their effectiveness. We are convinced that the new regulations will not affect the intensity of contacts between the two nations; in the case of the Kaliningrad Region that was illustrated by some one million crossings of the border with Poland in 1999.

Firmer anchoring of the region in an expanding Europe could be served by the rearrangement of border-crossing regulations and upgrading of the border infrastructure, as well as implementation of specific Polish-Russian projects compatible with European Union initiatives addressed to the region. This could also lend an impulse to an evolution of the region which would thus turn position as an enclave into an asset and would truly become a gateway into Russia. From the Polish point of view, positive development of Kaliningrad would have an added significance, since it would create an atmosphere conducive to co-operation not only with Russia, but also with Poland's other eastern neighbours – Lithuania, Belarus and Ukraine.

Chapter 9

Kaliningrad, Borders and the Figure of Europe

Pertti Joenniemi
Copenhagen Peace Research
Institute (COPRI)

Introduction

Borders and border-related practices are central to any discussion of Kaliningrad. Wedged between Lithuania, Poland and the Baltic Sea, the Oblast stands out as an exceptional case among the eighty-nine constituent parts of Russia. It is the only part of Russia that is separated in this way from the 'mainland' of the country.

This novel feature brings forth a host of key questions. These are further compounded by the fact that Kaliningrad is (metaphorically speaking) at the crossroads of Russia and the European Union, and is influenced by both of these. The Oblast's position implies - seen from the EU's perspective - that there is not just one Russia but, in a sense, two. There is a kind of 'little' Russia increasingly inside the Union (influenced by Lithuania and Poland, which are adapting to the rules and regulations of the EU) and warranting special attention, and the 'big' mainland Russia, which remains at a distance.

The crux of the problem is that Kaliningrad can neither be completely integrated nor separated off by systemic differences. As a 'little' Russia, it calls for immediate attention in being far more exposed to the policies of the EU than any other Russian region. By contrast, the 'big' Russia forms a case that is less acute and sensitive to the Union's policies, and may therefore be tackled differently because it will not become an enclave within the European Union. And yet it is impossible to deal with the 'little' without also sorting out the 'big', as the two are intertwined. The prevailing view tends to be that Russia as such cannot be admitted to the EU, but at the same time a small part of Russia is to a considerable degree within the sphere of the Union's policies, which means that the EU and Russia will inevitably become increasingly entangled. In consequence, the distinction between a clear-cut inside and an outside will become increasingly distorted.

Russia is far more vulnerable to such a blurring of crucial lines of demarcation than the EU with its logic of governance, but Kaliningrad is a considerable challenge for both of them. Russia is called to deal with an increase in its own diversity, and on a practical level, questions arise pertaining, for example, to whether Kaliningrad can continue to serve as a credible military outpost. Is it at all feasible that such an encircled and increasingly de-bordered region can continue to function as a first line of defence? Would it not be better to treat it explicitly as an entity that mediates contacts and allows Russia to link into the rapid integration as well as regionalisation around the Baltic rim? And should not Kaliningrad's borders be understood as interfaces that mediate and facilitate contacts rather than as lines of division?

Finding proper answers is not just essential for Kaliningrad itself. There are also broader issues at stake. Russia may remain a well-bordered entity that competes for influence and fends off (perceived) efforts of intrusion, or it may embark on a kind of post-sovereign route by linking into integration and allowing its EU border to get blurred. Russia may stay with the role of an outsider, but Kaliningrad can also pave the way for a much more inclusive relationship by being turned into a backdoor for a much closer EU-Russia relationship.

The Union is equally faced with hard choices. As part of the Union's 'near abroad', Kaliningrad will gain immediate attention by virtue of being extensively exposed to the policies of the EU. The Union may in consequence be obliged to adjust its rules and regulations to a considerable degree. The EU's border practices, with Lithuania and Poland approaching membership, will to a large extent influence the future of the Oblast, and the policies pursued by the EU will also have implications for the relationship between Kaliningrad and the rest of the country. Russia will, for its part, be able to exert some influence on intra-EU relations.

With such a blurring of essential borderlines, what is the probable solution to the Kaliningrad puzzle? What are the options open for Kaliningrad, being simultaneously on the inside and the outside? What type of EU-Russia relationship is on the cards and, more generally, what kind of European configuration is on its way towards emerging as a result? Obviously, no firm answers are yet available, as the policies of the parties are still in the making, but some observations and tentative thoughts may nonetheless be aired.

Russian policies

Over recent years, Russia seems to have become increasingly sensitive to the challenges originating with European integration and region-building around the Baltic rim. In the case of Kaliningrad, relatively concrete solutions are called for. The profound nature of the challenges is evidenced for example by the new Øresund region. With such a region in place, premised on a giant bridge extending across a historical divide, both Denmark and Sweden will reach beyond their formal borders. They increasingly assume post-sovereign features. Southern Sweden will, in a way, gain two capitals. The joining of forces, with borders being turned into interfaces, means that the parties will not be pushed to the margins of Europe.

By contrast, there are only some modest 'bridges' to be discerned in the case of Kaliningrad – and yet the Oblast is exposed to challenges similar to the ones prevailing around the Baltic rim at large. Kaliningrad's borders remain, in essence, lines of division, and the Oblast tends to stay aloof from the increasing fluidity and complexity of the Baltic Sea area. They have not been moulded – at least not yet – to allow it to become an equal partner in regional co-operation. However, there are also some quite positive effects to be discerned. Adaptation of an increasingly integration-oriented agenda – evidenced for example by the treatment of Kaliningrad in the context of the EU's Northern Dimension – has caused many of the ghosts of the past to vanish into thin air. Issues of territorial belongingness and worries about excessive military development no longer stand out as crucial concerns. They have ceased to dominate the debate in the way they did even a few years ago.

The agendas have changed and one may observe, more generally, that the whole Baltic Sea region has recently become the scene for an altered type of security thinking. It has become relatively rich in innovative, low-key moves and approaches, and portrays in general what can be described as non-static images. Balances and traditional geopolitical concerns – premised on firm lines between an inside and an outside – matter less than they used to do. Such thinking has also had an (albeit slow) effect in relation to Kaliningrad. Awareness varies from actor to actor, but it can be observed that integration, region-building and trans-border co-operation are no longer comprehended as something distinct and separate from matters of security. On the contrary, for some of the key actors they form an essential part of the new, and quite broad, agenda of security.

It has to be added, however, that Russia does not rank among the actors spearheading such policies. It remains an object rather than constituting a subject in the process of turning the Baltic Sea region into an experimental area in the field of security. The Russian reading remains fairly traditional, and the political landscape in the Baltic Sea area is still largely comprehended in terms of 'them and us', with an effort to construct some neutral space in-between the (supposed) contending camps. The core entities are seen as disjointed and mutually exclusive. An ontology of fixity, stability and continuity prevails. The aim appears to be one of preserving the traditional setting that used to be there rather than actively contributing to a new and a different one.

Such a reading is quite often also applied to Kaliningrad, although it is increasingly apparent that the Oblast is misinterpreted as a result, and alternative avenues and outlooks have to be searched for. Military options have been downgraded and Kaliningrad is no longer primarily seen as a military centre. Concerns pertaining to 'hard' security have been tuned down. Instead, various hardships pertaining to 'soft' security have begun to occupy a more prominent position. The latter agenda is much more conducive to regional co-operation and a softening of borders. Preferences are increasingly those in favour of transforming Kaliningrad into an economic bridge rather than preserving it as a prominent military centre, although a duality of views prevails, thus causing a certain degree of wavering and indecisiveness in Russian policies.

The changes that have taken place are of considerable significance, although the increasing prominence of various integration-related issues also creates a major challenge. For example, should the federal centre provide the Oblast authorities with additional powers? This represents a considerable source of uncertainty. In order to be in tune with its increasingly integrated and regionalised environment, Kaliningrad should be furnished with sufficient powers and rights. This is needed for the Oblast to be able to link in with its nearby neighbours on terms that allow the evolution of a reasonably equal relationship. The Free Economic Zone (FEZ), later turned into a Special Economic Zone (SEZ), represents endeavours in that direction. However, doubts prevail as to Kaliningrad's competence and power over itself. Is it capable of choosing between the options offered? Will it be able to make proper use of the powers granted to it, and remain a loyal and constructive part of Russia? Would a transfer of authority cause further turmoil or, instead, contribute to a stable and predictable development? The dilemma is a genuine one, and no certain answers appear to be in the offing. Recent moves towards centralisation and tightening of the grip of the federal authorities over the regions seem to testify that Russia is still a long way from being able even to think of arrangements such as the Øresund region. A 'Europe of mosaics' is not what Russia is opting for.

Some of those partaking in the Russian debate have argued against any risk-taking. Better poor and an integral part of Russia than wealthy and a source of revolt and dissidence, so the argument runs. However, these critical voices have not succeeded in obstructing some cautious moves of opening up towards the nearby environment. The Oblast remains, without doubt, one of the most isolated areas around the Baltic rim as far as land and air connections are concerned. Yet small steps of progress may be discerned. Kaliningrad has, for example, been granted the right to take part in the *Baltica* and *Saule* Euroregions (although a decision is still awaited in the case of the *Nemunas* region), and it has been allowed to link in, in various ways, with the intensive network of contacts that has emerged around the Baltic rim in recent years.

But the record still remains mixed. It has been recognised, although the conviction could be deeper, that policies are needed to fend off the danger of marginalisation. The target is set as one of preserving a fairly symmetric relationship despite the fact that Russia, in terms of economic performance, is far behind the Union. Kaliningrad is, in such a perspective, emblematic of the challenges that Russia's entire position in Europe is faced with, i.e. challenges brought about by an unequal strength and the Union's eastward enlargement. Russia is not a candidate for membership, at least not in the short run. Yet policies have to be devised that allow for a close relationship with a Union that is seen as friendly but unenthusiastic.

The proposal for a 'Baltic Schengen', launched by the former Russian Prime Minister Chernomyrdin in 1998, was the first sign of new thinking. The effort was to explore whether broader arrangements, including Kaliningrad, could be set in place in order to avoid the tightening of borders and visa practices through adherence to the Schengen rules of the EU countries, especially by the Baltic States and Poland. If Norway and

Iceland as non-EU countries can be given special arrangements, why not think about the possibility of a broader arrangement around the Baltic rim as well? The proposal as aired did not yield any concrete results, but the initiative was important as such. It served as an outlet for a growing concern about increased exclusion, and signalled a will to avoid being located behind tightening borders.

Since then, the talks under the Partnership and Co-operation Agreement (PCA) and the EU's Northern Dimension have offered further opportunities to address such an issue. The Northern Dimension is particularly important in representing a horizontal and multi-pillar approach, and, due to its undefined character, the initiative offers an opportunity to think about Europe from an alternative perspective. The Russian Prime Minister entered into an agreement with his Lithuanian counterpart in June 1999 to prepare proposals on the participation of the Kaliningrad region in the activities and programmes under the EU's Northern Dimension. Russia accepted that the Union should place the Kaliningrad 'puzzle' on its agenda, and that special attention should be devoted to the Oblast. Russia's Medium Term Strategy for the development of relations between the Federation and the European Union (2000-2010) underlines the possibilities for regarding Kaliningrad as a pilot region for the EU-Russia relationship, and as a test case for this relationship in connection with EU enlargement. It mentions the option of a special arrangement for Kaliningrad in view of enlargement, and hints that, if Kaliningrad turns out to be a successful test case, co-operation could in the future cover the north-west of Russia.

Russia hence appears to be prepared to single out Kaliningrad as a special case. The previous policies, which previously amounted to a series of compromises, are no longer deemed to be sufficient. A more coherent setting is needed, and it is now the federal centre, possibly in co-operation with the EU and the neighbouring states, that endeavours to bring about a framework that really addresses the basic problems and opportunities pertaining to the Oblast, and is doing so in a symmetric and equal manner.

Requests are thus being made for policies unique to Kaliningrad. Russia is challenging the EU to restore a balance between positive cross-border co-operation and protection against risks, such as the spreading of crime, diseases and environmental problems. It has specifically asked that more favourable visa rules be considered than would normally be offered by the Schengen *acquis*. The purpose of this is to ensure that Kaliningrad residents do not to have to apply for visas in order to visit the rest of their own country. Russia seems to acknowledge, on a more general level, that borders have to be lowered and standard security thinking pushed to some extent aside, if Kaliningrad is to have a chance of coping with its problems and delivering on the potential promises that are there due to its nature as the westernmost part of Russia. The region's belongingness to Russia is taken for granted and yet it is admitted that the Oblast has turned into a joint concern between Russia and the EU.

The policies of the EU

Many of the issues pertaining to Kaliningrad are much more in line with the EU's policy of governance than any traditional statist policies. Kaliningrad may be conceived as both Russian and European, or more broadly, as a juncture in a world of networks. Yet Kaliningrad tends to present the EU with certain dilemmas as well.

The EU's relations with Russia have so far not been premised on ideas of singling out, with any clarity, a particular entity such as Kaliningrad. The PCA, which came into force in December 1997 and the Common Strategy of the EU towards Russia, adopted in June 1999, are both based on less demanding points of departure. The PCA aims to encourage political, commercial, economic and cultural co-operation. Both treat Russia as a homogeneous whole, although parts of north-west Russia have been allowed to participate in regional co-operation agreements. This is to say that they do not aim to address Russia's dual nature, i.e. with the 'big' Russia located on the outside but with the 'little' Russia increasingly on the inside of the EU. Rather to the contrary, they aim at formalising a very clear-cut point of departure by aspiring to gain the advantages of effective cross-border relations while minimising the risks. They view Russia in basically undifferentiated terms. As a corollary, these agreements have treated Kaliningrad as simply another Russian border, one that is eligible for the same programmes which apply to the rest of Russia, principally the Tacis technical assistance programme. (However, the coastal cities programme comes under INTERREG IIC.)

By contrast, the EU's Northern Dimension initiative rests on a different thinking. It constitutes the first EU move that singled out north-west Russia, including Kaliningrad, as having unique importance for cross-border relations with the EU. The initiative is premised on the idea that special EU policies are required in Northern Europe. A specific and targeted approach has been envisaged for this region, and the overall concept amounts to a proposal for a regional development policy. The move has already paved the way (although profound pessimism has in general set in as to Russia's prospects for rapid economic and social recovery) for a qualitatively new dialogue between Russia and the EU. An opening may also be traced in the Commission's document on the Northern Dimension, where both Tacis and Phare are mentioned as programmes spanning the Russia-Baltic and Russia-Poland borders. Also, there is the suggestion that 'programmes of technical assistance devoted to promoting customs co-operation, future training in administration and co-operation in the fight against organised crime should be considered through cross-border programmes for border areas, i.e. for the Kaliningrad region of the Russian Federation'.

However, there are no concrete breakthroughs, at least not yet. The border issues inherent in the EU's enlargement sets Kaliningrad apart from an otherwise quite continuous economic and social landscape. In the near future, with Lithuania and Poland having fully adopted the Schengen rules, the Union's border practices will influence not only Kaliningrad's external relations. The relationship with the rest of Russia is also at stake in the sphere of visa questions, energy problems, transit issues and the advent of a joint European currency. Or, to put it differently: due to Kaliningrad's geographic position, Lithuania's and Poland's pre-accession process unavoidably has consequences in the sphere of intra-Russian relations. This is one of the reasons why Kaliningrad does not constitute an ordinary EU-Russia border. It does not just link two neighbours, but forms a unique case that warrants special attention. The Oblast not only stands out as a transactional border, but also forms an institutional one.

As such, the Northern Dimension represents progress. It signals, in adding to the plurality of the EU, that the Union aspires to avoid the image of a closed and unattainable 'club' with fixed external borders. Instead of dividing and drawing distinct lines, the initiative aims at creating a positive interdependence between the relevant actors, although it still depends on the outcome of the Commission's Action Plan. A second ministerial meeting is scheduled to take place during Sweden's Presidency in the year 2001. Denmark organised a conference on Kaliningrad in May 2000 in Copenhagen, and recommended an ad hoc contact group to be established to study the matter further.

As observed, the EU has until recently tried to pursue two goals simultaneously. One is to attain the advantages of legitimate cross-border travel and trade with its non-EU neighbours. On the other hand, a potentially competing goal is to minimise 'soft' security risks arising from problems such as crime, illegal immigration, transmission of communicable diseases and environmental pollution. All of these are also Kaliningrad-relevant concerns.

Both efforts are understandable as such but yet there is an inherent tension between the two policies. The EU's external security concerns have caused it to encourage regional integration at all levels, but at the same time its internal security policies are having contrary effects by reinforcing barriers between itself and the outside.

The latter concern calls for an elimination of the current agreement between Lithuania and Russia, which allows

Kaliningrad residents to travel for thirty days to Lithuania without a visa, although Russians from 'big' Russia need a visa. From a Kaliningrad perspective, Schengen implies that Kaliningrad residents will need visas just to visit their own families in 'big' Russia when they travel by land. Under pressure to tighten its border, at the beginning of 1998 Poland introduced a requirement for additional documentation clearly indicating the identity of individuals crossing the border between Poland and Kaliningrad. The requirement was introduced at a holiday period and involved long delays and confusion at the border. Lack of adequate information and the expense of new documents created irritation among those crossing the border. In 1999, Poland added a requirement of a minimum amount of money which people would have to bring with them when crossing the border.

Consequently, from the perspective of local Russians, the EU is increasingly seen as an organisation that intends to make access more difficult and more expensive than the access they have enjoyed until recently. There is scarcity of accessible places where they can apply for visas (there are only two properly authorised consulates in Kaliningrad); there is insufficient sensitivity as to whether or not Kaliningrad residents can pay without difficulties; and the visa policies of the EU are not seen to be paying sufficient attention to the substantial burden these costs and difficulties impose on people involved in shuttle-trading. Simplified border crossings, important for Kaliningrad already because of its dependency on foreign trade, may soon be a thing of the past unless Kaliningrad is explicitly treated as distinct from the rest of Russia.

Kaliningrad's problems - which derive in part from its geographic location between two EU applicants - are not likely to be adequately dealt with within the current structure of the EU. There are several reasons why this seems to be the case. One of the key problems is that there still seems to be little comprehension in the EU - at least not to a sufficient degree - that Kaliningrad is as much 'in' as it is 'out'. An enlarging EU will bring with it a Russian enclave within the EU, and yet the EU still acts primarily as if Russia is something external to the EU and which the EU can either take or leave.

A second reason why the EU's current structure may find it hard to deal adequately with the problems of having a Russian enclave inside the EU is that the three pillar structure gives institutional form to the paradigm that states are either 'in' or 'out' of the EU. In the three pillars, the focus on 'community matters' and/or inter-governmental co-operation versus 'external relations' constitutes institutional reinforcement of the viewpoint that states are either 'in' or 'out' of the EU. Such arrangements create overlapping jurisdictions that are not obstacles to legitimate interaction, and offer an approach featuring more equality and parity between the 'insiders' and the 'outsiders'. This approach contrasts with a Schengen approach, which is based on a premise that the 'insiders' will create policies that the 'outsiders' will have to accept.

It might thus be argued, on a more general note, that the EU does not seem to be sufficiently aware that many of its policies contribute to an isolationist alternative, and that Kaliningrad is especially exposed to such an effect. Policy-making in the context of accession tends to have a technocratic nature, and the conditions of accession are fragmented across a range of documents and agencies. Kaliningrad is treated as an outsider, and not as an in-between case that does not fit a departure premised on the existence of a clear inside and an outside. Unconventional moves have recently been accepted both in the case of Cyprus and Gibraltar, but there are not yet signs of any breakthroughs for Kaliningrad. The idea has not sufficiently sunk in that the tension needs to be settled, and that a clear shift in the policies pursued is required. There are some signs of improvement but they do not yet manifest themselves with enough clarity.

EU, Russia and the concept of Europe: the Kaliningrad puzzle

The Kaliningrad puzzle obviously raises issues of connectivity. It offers the possibility of a very 'European' future for the Oblast.

The puzzle also contrasts views of a Schengen-Europe with strictly defined borders with an alternative concept of a Europe with a fuzzy eastern border - one that strives to open up towards the free movement of capital, services, goods and people. The border can be a sign of power to mark outer boundaries, and may confirm the ability to keep the internal and external strictly apart from each other, or it can provide space for a meeting-ground that bridges distinctions between insiders and outsiders. In any case, it appears to be one of the sites where decisions influencing the future shape of Europe are required, and where the constitutive rules of the European polity are at stake.

Kaliningrad can also be understood as being a complex case in constituting a part of the 'near abroads' of both Russia and the EU. If Russia and the Union are both depicted in terms of entities with a distinct core surrounded by concentric circles, then Kaliningrad may be seen as being located at the intersection of such circles. It would not bring about, in such an instance, any major clashes, since overlapping cases can easily be tolerated: borders at the fringes are seen as low-intensity borders with little impact on the overall configuration. They would be seen as being unavoidable within a system based on 'empires' that do not end abruptly at some specific point, but rather grow weaker in a gradual manner. Kaliningrad would thus be comprehended as a site for regulating relations where borders get blurred before fading out altogether. Whether regulated or not, the result would have marginal impact on the relations between the entities or the overall figure of Europe. It would not stand out as a kind of systemic challenge.

But the contest could also be seen as having the essence of whether there are two 'empires' facing each other, or just one imposing its will on the other (inferior) configuration. The relationship would thus be quite asymmetrical with one entity far more powerful than the other. Russia's economic weakness would speak for such an interpretation. However, there is little that supports the view that the EU would be searching for such an unequal relationship. There are certainly asymmetries present, but the Northern Dimension initiatives are there precisely to level out such differences and to introduce options for an encounter on more equal terms.

The crux of the Kaliningrad puzzle rather seems to consist of how the two entities see themselves, and the role of borders and bordering in this context. Both continue to aspire towards a relatively homogeneous quality, and Kaliningrad, in blurring essential borderlines, is seen as a nuisance. It is felt to undermine endeavours of restoring homogeneity. It thus stands out as a site that forces the EU to think more thoroughly about the tension between its internal and external security policies, and calls for systematic efforts to bring about cross-pillar coherence and to do away with an excessively fragmented approach across a range of documents and agencies. It calls for a move to transcend the established borderlines and to bend – if not break – the existing rules, thereby bringing about a more flexible Union.

This is so, since various technical remedies are hardly sufficient for settling the complex issues that arise from the fact that the neighbouring areas are provided with the prospect of EU membership, whereas Kaliningrad is not. But then, raising this question brings in its train other, more far-reaching issues. A more inclusive approach is related to Russia's position vis-à-vis European integration generally. It is neither easy to depict Russia as a future member of the EU, nor can it be excluded and treated as a total outsider. A closer relationship is called for, but within limits. One possibility would be to integrate parts of Russia.

Solutions of this sort based on differentiation already exist elsewhere in respect of the Åland Islands (part of Finland) outside the customs policies of the EU and in respect of Greenland and the Faroe Islands (part of Denmark) outside the EU. Such a diversified solution, if applied in the case of Kaliningrad, would not contradict the EU's logic of governance, although it would inject a considerable number of new elements into Russian conceptualisations of political space. Russia is, in any case, called to define itself increasingly with integration as the most essential point of departure. It is compelled to search for a differentiated essence by spurring regionalisation and linking in to the various networks that exist in the nearby environment.

To save Kaliningrad from turning into an outsider within its own region, the relevant parties have to review, it appears, their own policies and approaches. Without such a review, to be followed by clearly stated priorities and policies, the parties will tend to provide each other with the option of staying with rather modest ambitions. For example, occasional Russian worries about the Oblast's status and its belongingness allow the EU to draw the conclusion that there is only room for minimal progress. It could be taken to prove that only some limited (but joint) measures to avert negative by-products of increased cross-border interaction, such as crime and corruption, can be hoped for. Such measures are certainly needed, but they fall short of settling many of the other challenging aspects of the Kaliningrad question.

On a more profound level, the question is whether a kind of back door should be opened up for Russia, and whether Russia is interested in and prepared to accept the appearance of such a back door. Kaliningrad is bound to awaken such issues, due to its nature as a 'little' Russia. The border-breaking qualities of the Oblast places this question on the joint EU-Russia agenda. Answers are called for as to whether one part of Russia may be invited to form a somewhat different relationship with the Union from most of the other parts, and thought is required as to what kind of solution Russia, EU and Europe at large are able to produce. The challenges are obviously demanding, but that is the essence of the Kaliningrad puzzle.

PROBLEMS AND THREATS

REAL OR IMAGINARY?

Chapter 10

Myths in the Baltic

Stephen Dewar

Independent economic consultant,
Moscow

As the contributors to this book have clearly demonstrated, the issues that Kaliningrad raises are complex and challenging. It is obviously necessary in these circumstances to ensure that the basic perceptions about the situation - and the ideas for policies that these perceptions can generate - should be soundly based on facts. It is a curious feature of the 'Kaliningrad debate' that there are a significant number of what, in this author's view, are serious misconceptions about reality. Some of these erroneous ideas and beliefs are held by Kaliningrad residents, others by foreigners, and there are one or two prevailing in some Moscow circles.

The following quotation, from a respected Western newspaper, admirably manages to contain a whole string of these myths in one sentence:

> 'By any measure, Kaliningrad holds the potential to become a rich entrepot like Hong Kong on the northern rim of Europe. The region is generously endowed with a deep water harbour, a well-educated labour force, one of the world's largest deposits of natural amber, rich farmland...' [1]

This chapter tries to deal with the more common and serious of these 'myths', including the five contained in the quotation above. Inevitably, some at least of the opinions expressed in the following pages will arouse disagreement. But this is all to the good. There has been too little reassessment of some of the 'mantras' that have been unquestioningly repeated over the years. Even if some of the arguments put forward below do not convince the reader, they will, I hope, contribute to re-examining these issues and, perhaps, lead to a fuller, more realistic assessment.

No particular system has been used to determine the order in which the myths are presented, although the overall selection represents the ones that I feel are the most pernicious and widespread. In each case I follow a similar approach. Under the name of the individual myth, I discuss what it means, which main groups of actors most believe and promote it, and then what I believe the reality to be.

Myth number 1: Gateway between Russia and the West

This is a variant of the older, imagination-stretching 'Baltic Hong Kong' concept (see Myth number 2 below). The language is moderate in tone - no apparent exaggeration or hyperbole in the expression - and has a pleasing sense of common sense credibility. It is sometimes used to describe the present situation, as in 'Kaliningrad is the gateway between Russia and the West'[2] or as an aspiration for a tantalisingly close - but not quite yet achieved - state of future successful development.

The meaning of the concept is obvious: that Kaliningrad has a natural role to play, because of its geographic location, as the access channel linking trade flows between Russia and the West or, more particularly, Europe. The geographic basis of this assertion is reinforced by appeals to the excellent transport infrastructure and, in particular, the year-round ice-free port (see Myth number 3).

The main proponents of this concept are various groups in Kaliningrad, but the view has been accepted by various observers from Western countries and by some in Moscow.

However, in principle and in practice the idea is false.

A gateway is an entrance - a link between one piece of space and another. Kaliningrad is not such a link between Russia and the West, because it is cut off from Russia by a minimum of two countries. To move goods (or people) by surface transport modes to or from the Russian mainland necessitates passing through either Lithuania and Belarus, or Lithuania and Latvia, or Poland and Belarus. The difficulties, delays and costs associated with this process are sufficiently well known not to need repetition here. It is sufficient simply to note that this eliminates the possibility of Kaliningrad acting as a gateway. One might be tempted, however, to think of Kaliningrad as acting as a gateway for goods and people using air services, thereby eliminating the transit problems. But, as is discussed in Chapter 3, the services do not exist. So much for the objection in principle. It is supported by evidence regarding actual practice. Throughout the entire decade of the 1990s, Kaliningrad has failed to make any noticeable headway in winning significant shares of Russia's international trade flows in goods. Indeed, ports in Lithuania and Latvia handle significantly more Russian transit traffic than Kaliningrad (see Chart 5 in Chapter 3).

The unfortunate reality is that, far from being a gateway, Kaliningrad is, simply, an exclave - cut off from its own mainland and quite likely due to be even more isolated as its neighbours move ever closer to EU accession.

Myth number 2: The Baltic Hong Kong

This is a variant on the Gateway Myth, discussed above. Although not often heard these days, it was popular in the early 1990s with both the Kaliningrad leadership and with enthusiastic Western journalists.

The implication is that Kaliningrad would be able to turn its exclave status into some kind of golden opportunity, in an analogous manner to Hong Kong's relationship with mainland China.

I have a great deal more sympathy with the Hong Kong concept than with the gateway, because it represented the genuine, committed enthusiasm by the then Regional Administration to transform a potential economic disaster zone (arising from becoming an exclave after the dissolution of the FSU and the associated transition problems) into a shining beacon of prosperity and regional cooperation, assisted by Western expertise, especially through Tacis.

Unfortunately, the analogy was, and is, seriously flawed in a number of ways. Probably the most significant flaw is the simple fact that, while China laboured under an inefficient centrally-planned and communist system, Hong Kong was a bastion of almost totally unfettered free-market capitalism, under a very different style of extremely investor- and business-friendly government. Kaliningrad, by contrast, has continued to be saddled with the chronically business- and investor-inhospitable climate that afflicts the rest of Russia. Furthermore, despite vigorous attempts by the regional leadership in the mid-1990s to win a sufficiently large degree of economic autonomy to change this situation, Moscow thwarted these efforts continuously. For this reason alone, the Hong Kong analogy is simply invalid.

Thus, the problems were not surmounted and the vision of a thriving entrepot economy, drawing the attentive admiration of the world, have receded.

In 1998 the combined value of exports and imports were:

Kaliningrad (population 1 million): $1.6 billion[3]

Hong Kong (population 6 million): $363 billion.[4]

Myth number 3: The ice-free port

All the promotional literature produced by Kaliningrad institutions about Kaliningrad highlights the fact that Kaliningrad is 'Russia's only year-round, ice-free port on the Baltic'. As a statement of fact this is true. The implication, however, is that Kaliningrad offers the only or best access by sea to the Russian market and this, regrettably, requires something rather more substantial than an absence of ice floes.

There are four main problems with the idea that Kaliningrad is 'the' port for channelling goods in and out of the Russian mainland. First is the Gateway Myth discussed in Myth number 1 above.

Second, the competing ports along the Baltic coast are more competitive, convenient, effective and efficient. This is clearly demonstrated by their far higher volumes of cargo. (See Chapter 3, Chart 5).Third, the port of Kaliningrad is actually a number of separate ports under different ownership and management structures, without a unified port authority to develop and market them as a coherent single complex.[5]

Fourth, the main city ports are 42 kilometres upstream from the Baltic Sea, with a narrow (50 to 60 metres wide), shallow (9 to 10 metres deep) channel (dredged in the 1920s) for most of the way. This means that the traffic flow is one-way only and there is a limit on the size of vessels of not more than 15,000 dwt.[6] This poses significant size constraints on vessel-handling capacity combined with a time-consuming, and thus expensive, access bottleneck.[7]

A recent assessment of Kaliningrad Port's situation was given by the Assistant of the Director of Kaliningrad Port Administration, Vyacheslav Kukarin, in October 1999. He reported to the media that the through-put of cargo in Kaliningrad ports for the first nine months of that year had decreased by 13.7% (total amount - 2.43 million tons). According to him, this is the continuation of a trend, which has been visible since 1998. He observed that the maximum through-put of cargo in Kaliningrad ports was reached in 1997

- 6.16 million tons (i.e. three times the 1999 level). The main reasons for the fall, according to Mr Kukarin, are high railroad tariffs and difficulties with custom proceedings in Russia.[8]

A more recent assessment is gloomier:

> 'Kaliningrad ports are expected to have handled approximately 158 thousand tons of cargo by the end of February 2000. This was indicated by the director of the Kaliningrad port administration Georgy Sebev at a meeting earlier this month with the visiting Russian deputy foreign minister Ivan Ivanov. Mr Sebev also pointed out that Kaliningrad was losing to the competing ports elsewhere in the Baltic countries, handling only 4% of the overall cargo turnover in the Baltic Sea region (Estonia, Latvia and Lithuania).'[9]

In the light of these matters, it would be more constructive to dwell less on the climatic features of Kaliningrad port(s) and to look more carefully at what shippers actually require.

Myth number 4: Kaliningrad's well-educated work force

Official promotional literature produced in Kaliningrad highlights the plentiful availability of a highly skilled pool of labour just waiting to be employed by new investors. (To be fair, this is often said about the Russian labour force as a whole, not just that of Kaliningrad).

The implication is that an investor establishing a business venture in Kaliningrad will be able to hire exactly the kinds of workers required for more or less immediate productive work. In a world where high-level skills are increasingly required from all members of the work force and not just the technical 'elite', this is, indeed, something of real importance to investors. It is, for example, the reason that Ireland and Singapore, to name but two from many possible examples, invest so highly in education and training - at the State's expense.

It is true that there are tens of thousands of people in Kaliningrad who desperately want a job, especially a good job. It is also rightly recognised that the Russian labour force, as a whole, was well educated and trained for the Soviet economic system. It is true too that the intellectual standards of Russian - including Kaliningrad - educational institutions remain high. There are, for example, many young graduates in Kaliningrad who have world-class skills in IT, foreign languages, mathematics and so forth.

But, what about other disciplines? Are there in Kaliningrad the state-of-the-art-equipped laboratories where students can learn robotics, microelectronics, biotechnology, or advanced materials technologies for example, or are there educational programmes focusing on JIT, FMS, TQM,[10] and other normal aspects of contemporary manufacturing business processes? Although there are numerous scientific, engineering and technology courses available in the three principal third-level institutions in Kaliningrad, they do not have the funding resources available to keep their laboratories and equipment up to the constantly changing world standards. And despite the enthusiasm by academics and educational administrators to keep up with the changing world, not everybody necessarily supports them.

> 'Principal among the challenges facing Kaliningrad's [third-level educational] institutions are the reorientation of their course offerings to the emerging demands of the economy. The local institutions are acutely aware of this challenge and have already introduced new courses aimed at meeting the demand from students for modern management and technical education. *However, in real ways, the bureaucratic nature of the administrative system has slowed or prevented innovation in course design and introduction.*'[11] [Emphasis added].

Nor, it need hardly be said, are the financial resources available to fund brand new laboratories, pay for subscriptions to all the necessary scientific journals, finance regular attendance at international conferences, and so forth.

How well-trained, therefore, is the bulk of the Kaliningrad work force, from which new investors would recruit their skilled workers? Is there a large pool of skilled labour available to take up employment in knowledge-intensive, high-technology industries?[12]

> 'There is a very strong engineering skills base in the Region, with all the traditional primary engineering skills being available, for example, tool and die makers, paten makers, foundry men, machinists, welders, machine/electrical/ hydraulic fitters, assemblers, production and design engineers, etc. In the design offices many facilities were still using manual design methods rather than Computer Aided Design, only a few companies had made the change to CAD; and none were using CAD-CAM (computer aided design and computer aided manufacture) or CAE (computer aided engineering).
>
> It was clear that, with the structural changes taking place in the engineering industries, large numbers of well skilled workers as previously employed will not be required in the future. Re-training programmes will be needed to develop the new skills for the more advanced engineering technologies of automation, electronics, telecommunications, assembly, etc, of the future.'[13]

Much of the labour force available in large numbers for potential future investors, is drawn from collapsed or 'down-sized' traditional industries, with the skills summarised above; that is, *primary* - not *advanced* - engineering capabilities. Undoubtedly, many of these people would be well able to learn rapidly from training programmes in new technologies and processes. Equally, many would probably be able to adopt and internalise the enterprise culture that is an essential element of many successful businesses, even though this would be a totally novel concept and experience, given the previous ideology towards production. But, in the absence of State programmes, this training and retraining would have to be financed by the investors. It would also take a considerable period of time. This may not be an attractive option for the investors, especially as so many other countries really do have skilled workers readily available for instant productive employment.

Alternatively, the work force may be particularly suited to employment in old industries involving old technologies - that is, typically, low-cost, cheap labour, frequently 'dirty' and low-added-value sectors.

Myth number 5: Kaliningrad has abundant natural resources, especially amber

Locally produced promotional literature aimed at potential investors and business people invariably refer to the abundant local natural resources. The implication is that these resources are available for development and commercial exploitation.

Amber is a good example of a natural resource that has a ready market globally. Indeed, with the claim (which does not seem to be contested) that Kaliningrad is home to well over 90 percent of the world's known prime amber reserves, it is not surprising that *yantar*, the Russian word for amber, should be linked with so many aspects of Kaliningrad life - a town (where the amber is mined), a film festival, many corporate entities, NGOs, and much more. How well, therefore, is this sector being economically utilised for the benefit of the Region and its inhabitants?

Most of the amber in Kaliningrad is extracted from a large open-cast mine on the north-western seaboard of the region. In earlier times the mine, together with the monopolistic processing plant associated with it, was owned by the State. In the mid 1990s it was privatised - and then privatised again. Long-running legal disputes between the participants in the successive privatisations, about who the present legal owners are, have not been resolved, which means, among other things, that investment from external sources is impossible. The company is also, not surprisingly, technically insolvent, though it appears not to have been forced into legal bankruptcy.

In the meantime, much - if not most - of the amber is stolen by gangs of well-armed criminals and smuggled abroad. Management of the vast and antiquated processing enterprise, which is the victim of this large-scale plunder, is afraid to take appropriate counter measures because of the risk of lethal reprisals. It is certainly remarkable that neither the internal security forces (such as police) nor Customs officials and Border Guards have ever been able to apprehend the bandits running this multi-million dollar operation.

Those jewellery workshops that are able to acquire amber (by whatever supply system) are severely hampered by their effective inability to acquire the gold and silver needed for proper jewellery settings, due to what can best and most kindly be described as bureaucratic obstacles. They, therefore, largely have to rely on base-metal settings that have little appeal to customers (especially foreign ones).

Across the borders in Poland and Lithuania, it is estimated that around 20,000 jobs are supported by the availability of stolen and smuggled Kaliningrad amber.[14]

Myth number 6: ... and extensive arable land

This is another example put forward by regional authorities of the rich potential awaiting the investor. It is not quite clear why this feature of Kaliningrad is so often promulgated, as it is never accompanied by a direct invitation to acquire and develop this land. Nevertheless, something along these lines is surely implied, or there would be no point in referring to it. However, it is not possible to buy agricultural land for commercial farming purposes, thanks to legislative inadequacies, and there are insufficient mechanisms for protecting investors who would be prepared to take leases instead.

Furthermore, much of the land has been seriously degraded, partly by the gradual collapse of the old pre-War (German) pumping and drainage systems that are necessary for the large amounts of land area that are below sea level and prone to frequent flooding. Much of the rest has been degraded by pollution from landfill seepage and other contamination.

Support structures for agriculture are weak to non-existent.

For farmers producing goods for commercial distribution and sale within the region (as opposed to small-holders), there are various bandit gangs who have to be contended with, who claim monopoly rights on retail distribution and sale of such goods as tomatoes and potatoes. One commercial vegetable grower, known to me, stated that he had to equip his distributors with 'mace' and pepper sprays as forms of non-lethal protection against aggressive 'competitors'.[15]

For an overview of the situation, an appropriate example is, perhaps, the following from Kaliningrad Oblast Vice-Governor Yuri Shalimov: 'Due to the poor harvest, when only 30 thousand tons (out of 100 thousand tons required) of grain were gathered, Kaliningrad Region Administration decided to purchase the demanded gap from abroad'.[16] Thus, Kaliningrad declared it was unable to produce 70 percent of its grain needs, compared with a shortfall for Russia as a whole of 16 percent.[17] For a region which is not particularly densely populated and has such 'abundant rich farmland' - more than enough to meet its needs, if properly farmed - this failure indicates precisely how devastated the agricultural sector is. Or, to put it another way, 'there is a fall in all aspects of the agricultural sector'.[18]

In short, there is a great deal of land that is not currently being used for any kind of productive purpose, including agriculture. It is, however, extremely debatable as to whether some kind of 'green revolution' is just around the corner.

Myth number 7: The Special Economic Zone - Part 1: Stimulating investment[19]

The SEZ was intended to provide a stimulus to the Kaliningrad economy and to compensate for the economic costs of being an exclave. As with similar zones elsewhere around the world, it was hoped that the SEZ would generate significant foreign direct investment (FDI) in productive ventures, and would provide a boost to the development of international trade, especially exports. It was originally established in 1991, immediately after the region was opened up from being a closed military zone.

Its benefits to Kaliningrad are strongly propounded by all sections of the community in Kaliningrad, including groups who are normally politically strongly opposed to each other. On the other hand, the SEZ is strongly opposed by sections of the Moscow establishment and the IMF, who consider it, among other things, to be an unacceptable source of tax losses and an encouragement to large-scale smuggling. (See Myth number 9).

In this section we take a look at the investment effect. In Myth number 8 we turn our attention to international trade.

At the end of 1999 cumulative FDI in Kaliningrad during the decade had amounted to around $67 million - a fall from the previous year.[20] To put this in perspective, a look at per capita values for cumulative FDI in comparable - and competing - regions and states is informative: Kaliningrad - $70 (1999); Novgorod - $128 (1997); Russia - $63 (1998); Lithuania - $563 (1999); Poland - $260 (1998); Hungary - $1,667.[21]

There are numerous possible and probable contributing factors to the disappointing performance of the SEZ. At the overall Russian level there are the continuing deterrents to investment of macroeconomic and political instability, inadequate legal systems (including lack of investor protection legislation and the need for property rights legislation), a complex and anti-business tax environment, and the endemic problems of rampant crime and bureaucratic obstruction.

Having said that, it is important to note that tax concessions (which are all that the SEZ amounts to - and on a limited range of taxes at that) are not particularly effective in attracting investors. Indeed, an EBRD survey of FDI in Central and Eastern Europe in the mid-1990s, found that tax concessions ranked 14th in order of importance out of all the factors taken into account when choosing where, when and whether to invest.[22] Investors prefer certainty and predictability with modest taxes, rather than uncertainty and instability with low or zero taxes.

Furthermore, SEZ incentives are rarely employed as stand-alone measures. In most countries investment promotion involves a 'package' of measures, such as advance factories ready for immediate occupation, grants (for training local employees, for subsidising R&D, to cover marketing costs, etc.), access to prosperous markets, investor-friendly state institutions, investor protection legislation, concessionary corporate profits tax rates, and much more. All these are lacking in Kaliningrad.

In addition, an SEZ is normally explicitly treated as an instrument of economic policy with clearly focused goals and priorities - such as, for example, fostering high technology export-oriented industries, or promoting the development of so-called 'industry clusters' in which the host country believes it has competitive advantage that can be built upon (pharmaceuticals, microelectronics, automotive components, machine-tools, or whatever), and so forth. The Kaliningrad SEZ has never had a well-defined focus, so nobody has ever really known what it was for.

Lack of resources and expertise has also meant that the SEZ was never aggressively and effectively promoted to would-be investors, nor was there ever an appropriate institutional structure set up to do so - and which could also service investor inquiries.

But perhaps the most important reason is that the Russian Federal Government continuously and consistently threatened (and continues to threaten) to abolish the SEZ. A succession of acts and decrees have constantly changed the terms of the regime - mostly reducing or eliminating concessions, occasionally restoring them. Between June 1992 and January 1996, there were ten such interventions of significance. An attempt by the Ministry of Finance to abolish the SEZ in early 1997 was defeated by lobbying, but in July 1999 the Federal Government, in its Letter of Intent to the IMF, undertook to 'do everything within its power to ensure that a federal law eliminating excise and VAT exemptions for goods imported to Kaliningrad is adopted by end-1999.'[23]

At the beginning of the year 2000 the SEZ concessions are still in effect - but so is the Letter of Intent.

Myth number 8: The Special Economic Zone - Part 2: Boosting international trade

A major objective of the SEZ was to open up Kaliningrad to international trade, and regional authorities frequently state that this objective has been very successfully achieved.[24] In strictly literal terms, this assertion is completely true. Unfortunately, in economic terms it is a dangerously incomplete assessment.

There was a fivefold growth in exports between 1992 and 1997 (most relevant figures available - 1998 and onwards are distorted by the 1998 crisis effects) from $91.4 million to $457.7 million.[25] However, the growth in imports was of a far higher magnitude, from $54.0 million to $1,285.8 million - over twenty times greater. To put this in perspective, a *positive* trade balance of $37.4 million in 1992 was converted to a *deficit* of $828.1 million by 1997.[26]

The reason for this is not difficult to find. Kaliningrad simply did not manage to produce sufficient goods to sell competitively on foreign markets. This, in turn, is due to the failure of the SEZ successfully to attract sufficient Russian and FDI - the other key objective of the SEZ, as discussed in the preceding Myth.

But the trade figures themselves are deeply disturbing for two reasons. First, a medium-term continuation of this trend of a rapidly growing balance of payments deficit would have to be treated, at some stage, as a nationally serious problem of very considerable importance. If Kaliningrad were an independent state, it would be already in the throes of a possibly insurmountable balance of payments crisis. As it is, even if the Russian Government were happy to allow this situation to continue, the effect is that the rest of Russia is subsidising Kaliningrad's dreadful trade performance.

Second, and much more worrying, is the conclusion that these figures further illustrate the total incapacity of Kaliningrad to develop internationally competitive industries. Not only that, but there is also now a strong case to be argued that Kaliningrad has acquired a bad dose of import dependency - that is, the mindset that it is easier - and more profitable - to import rather than to produce.

The 80 percent dependence on imports to meet energy requirements is partially excusable on the grounds of the historic integration of Kaliningrad into the Soviet Union's energy systems, which are now disrupted by Lithuania's independence. (But not totally: Tacis funded a major energy study, which was completed in 1998 and which laid the foundations for getting out of this situation. Little has been achieved since then). The 80 percent dependence on imports to meet food requirements is not easily justifiable.

At any rate, the so-called booming international trade performance is, in fact, a damning indictment of regional economic failure.

Myth number 9: The Special Economic Zone - Part 3: Black hole for taxes and honeypot for smugglers

Perhaps the single biggest point of consistent disagreement between the Centre (Moscow) and Kaliningrad has been over the benefits or costs of the SEZ. We have looked above at the two biggest claims of benefits made by virtually all groups in Kaliningrad. Here we examine the other point of view, which is fiercely promulgated by much of the political and governmental establishment in Moscow, actively encouraged by the IMF.

The arguments against the SEZ take, generally, four forms as follows:[27]

1. The tax concessions allowed under the SEZ regime entail very significant exchequer losses of tax revenue;

2. The SEZ undermines local industrial producers;

3. Far more goods are imported into Kaliningrad through the SEZ regime than are consumed regionally;

4. The SEZ is a massive inducement to crime, corruption and smuggling.

As with all myths, none of these statements are totally bereft of any truth. It is what they imply that is at question. We shall look at each of them in turn.

The tax concessions allowed under the SEZ regime entail very significant exchequer losses of tax revenue

This is a tautology. By definition, tax concessions mean foregone tax revenues. It would be totally absurd to believe otherwise. The real question, of course, is whether the foregone tax revenues are *wasted*. Concessionary incentives are designed to achieve certain objectives - they may be economic (in which case there should be an acceptable rate of return on the financial investment that the concessions represent), social (in which case they should be the most cost-effective and efficient way of achieving the social goals, compared with other methods, but not necessarily required to generate a positive financial rate of return), or political (in which case totally different assessment methods may be appropriate - for instance, successfully preventing secession 'at any price').

It may be that the Centre has clearly stated somewhere its expectations from the SEZ and the criteria by which it judges whether or not these expectations have been met. If so, I have not seen them. In their absence, to the best of my knowledge, this argument is fallacious because it is unsupported by analysis. It is simply rhetoric. As such it is harmful because (a) it serves only to polarise anti-Moscow sentiment from Kaliningrad, and (b) is intellectually lazy, which is grossly irresponsible in a complex debate of this nature. Yershov[28] cites figures that the Federal Government - more precisely the Ministry of Finance - claim are the amounts of 'lost' taxes, but convincingly argues that the real value of the concessions (*not* the same as losses) are unlikely to amount to more than one-third of the claimed amounts.

The SEZ undermines local industrial producers

This is probably true, but (a) it has not been clearly proven nor (b) has the reason for this been sought. With regard to (a), the discussion of Myth number 7 demonstrates that investment has clearly not been adequately encouraged by the SEZ. But, *absence* of such investment does not necessarily mean that local producers have been *actively* harmed. Nonetheless, there are two principal arguments that could be adduced in favour of this proposition, one specific and one more general.

The specific argument is that because of an anomaly in how VAT is applied, domestic producers are disadvantaged. This occurs because, under some circumstances, importers - or producers depending on imported materials and components - are VAT-rated more advantageously than wholly domestic producers of identical goods, either paying lower or zero rates or paying at a later stage of the production chain (the latter having significant effects on cash-flow, working capital needs and, hence, profitability). If this was found to be the case it could easily be remedied by simple administrative order or decree. The fact that it has not suggests either that nobody believes that this problem exists; or, that it exists, but it does not matter; or, that nobody can be bothered to find out.

The more general argument is a version of the 'infant industries' theory. This is an argument used to justify protectionist measures for domestic producers. It runs as follows: 'Our industries X, Y, Z, etc, have the potential to become internationally competitive. Unfortunately, at the present stage of their development they are unable to compete on a level playing-field basis, because they have not yet reached their full efficiency/competitiveness/mastery-of-technology/ whatever. They need a bit more time. To give them a chance to grow up and be able to compete effectively, we [the government] are going to protect them with tariffs and/or other restrictions on foreign competitors.'

The argument is plausible and has been used by many countries to protect various industries from time to time. Needless to say, it has been used more often to protect vote-sensitive industries or to put off necessary but painful reforms, than it has been to promote genuine enterprise development and efficiency. At any rate, no analysis of infant industry needs has been carried out in Kaliningrad by either the Regional or Federal authorities. (Having said that, the Kaliningrad Regional Administration introduced a range of import quotas to protect domestic producers in September 1998. We look at this in Myth number 11).

The point here is that, although it is possible that the SEZ has damaged local producers, no effort has been made by anybody to find out. Conversely, the fact that local producers can obtain necessary imported inputs at concessionary rates, thanks to the SEZ, is an obvious *advantage*. A reliable assessment of who has benefited to what extent, and who has suffered to what extent, needs to be carried out before it is possible to say whether this argument is true or not.

Far more goods are imported into Kaliningrad through the SEZ regime than are consumed regionally

It is hard to know what to say about this one. The SEZ essentially offers three different concessionary tax regimes, depending on whether the goods involved are consumed in Kaliningrad, exported abroad, or shipped on to the Russian mainland. Given the latter two eventualities it would be extraordinary if there were not some categories of goods whose total imports exceeded local consumption.

Either this is exactly what was intended, with the associated employment and other benefits being retained within Kaliningrad, or it is not. If the latter, then it is a political matter to change the legislative basis to remove this from the benefits.

It makes no sense simply to complain.

The SEZ is a massive inducement to crime, corruption and smuggling

The first thing to be said about a statement like this is that many countries have the equivalents of SEZs and, despite the inducements to criminality which such regimes may contain, manage nonetheless to deal with the issue. To the extent that this statement is true, it is a sad reflection - though perhaps not a surprising one - that the appropriate authorities (Federal? Regional?) are implicitly assumed to be either unwilling or unable to cope with the threat.

More specifically, during the 1990s, Western observers who have attempted to chronicle serious smuggling through Kaliningrad have particularly highlighted such merchandise as drugs, weapons, prostitutes, illegal immigrants and, in one or two cases, radioactive materials such as plutonium. Also, more prosaically, this list could be extended to include amber (see Myth number 5 above). None of these 'goods' have any connection with the legitimate economy, let alone the SEZ.

The fact is that, due to its geographic location, Kaliningrad is well-positioned on the international smuggling trail, and sadly appears to be fulfilling that role more successfully than as a part of legitimate international trade routes. At any rate, it is ludicrous to blame the reportedly serious smuggling problems of Kaliningrad solely and exclusively on the SEZ.

Having said that, it is also almost certainly true that some commodities - notably alcohol, cigarettes and cars - are being smuggled on a large scale and that the gangs responsible frequently resort to violence to promote and protect their interests. Clearly, the SEZ regime has helped these criminal groups to gain access to these products, without paying excise duties, more easily than if the SEZ did not exist, but abolishing the SEZ would be unlikely to eliminate the trade, though it might diminish it. The probability is that, even if conducted on a lesser scale, such goods would simply move further into the totally black economy - along with the guns and drugs. Widespread smuggling of tobacco and alcohol products has been reported in other parts of Russia (St Petersburg and Moscow, for example).

The problem is not the SEZ, but the failures in law enforcement.

Myth number 10: The Special Economic Zone - Part 4: The wrong arguments - a synthesis

This myth shows how the three preceding myths about the SEZ have combined to create a misleading and acrimonious 'debate' between Moscow and Kaliningrad, which has unnecessarily polarised opinions and, by focusing on the wrong issues, has held back concentration on more relevant and important policy issues.

On the one hand, we have the Kaliningrad residents claiming that the SEZ is essential in order to attract investment (which has demonstrably failed - Myth number 7) and has led to a booming international trade sector (in fact a disaster - Myth number 8). On the other hand, we have the Moscow establishment, especially the Ministry of Finance, supported by the IMF, complaining that the SEZ causes massive losses of tax revenue and incites smuggling and crime (grossly overstated, over-simplified and misleading - Myth number 9).

Consequently, most of the energy and time devoted to the SEZ issue by officials in both places are devoted to bitter arguments about whether or not the SEZ should be allowed to survive, without much prospect of a satisfactory resolution, if only because facts are ignored or misused, while joint assessment of issues, that might be recognised as being of mutual concern, is not conducted.

In the meantime, any prospect of encouraging more investment, on the basis of the SEZ concessions, has little chance of success - why would any investor risk his or her money in a regime that does not know from one day to the next what it is for and, far more important, whether it will survive?

The SEZ was a good idea - the same concept has done wonders in many parts of the world - but it has been abominably mismanaged due principally to the hostility towards it from Moscow and the failure at local level to develop the other measures essential for making it a successful incentive.

Myth number 11: Import quotas protect local producers

In September 1998 - in the immediate aftermath of the August 1998 Russian rouble and financial crisis - the Kaliningrad Regional Administration introduced import quotas on 35 different categories of goods that had previously been imported free of duties and excise taxes, under the terms of the SEZ. The Administration said that it was doing this to protect local producers who had been harmed by foreign competition. The categories of goods ranged from alcohol and cigarettes through to building materials, a number of food products, industrial gases, and so forth.

This measure, as required by Russian law, was legally endorsed by the Russian Federal Government in Moscow.

The mechanism was that the Administration set quantitative limits on the amounts of each product category that could be imported free of import duties and excise taxes. Imports above these levels were permitted, but subject to normal Russian taxes and duties being payable.

These quotas were then divided into a number of lots, which were sold to the highest bidders in auctions.

On the face of it, this may not seem unreasonable and, given argument number 2 in Myth number 9 above,[29] it is perhaps not surprising that this move was supported by the Federal Government - although why anybody would think that special import controls would be necessary immediately after the 70 percent or so devaluation of the rouble, which at least trebled the price of all imports, has never been satisfactorily explained.

Import quotas, however, are not as innocuous as they look. They are one of a range of over thirty different kinds of instruments that can be used to protect local industries from foreign competition. The most common of these measures is, of course, the imposition of tariffs on imports. The other measures are collectively described as non-tariff barriers (or NTBs). NTBs can take many forms, such as outright bans on imports of the targeted goods, voluntary export restraints,[30] discriminatory procedures[31], labelling requirements,[32] medical/technological standards[33], and so forth. There is virtually no limit to the ingenuity that can be found to develop ways of restricting imports.[34]

The question is, however, *what is one trying to achieve*? This is important because different measures have different effects. If one chooses the wrong policy or the wrong measure, the consequences typically include some or all of the following:[35]

- Higher prices to consumers;
- Inferior quality and reduced choice of goods and services for consumers;
- Inefficient local producers who make no effort to improve (since they are confident they can persuade the government to retain protection from competition);
- Lack of innovation and development within the protected industries and their suppliers;

● General holding back of economic development, leading to:

   - reduced tax revenues to the government;
   - lower employment growth;
   - reduced domestic and foreign investment;
   - increased isolation from the international economy.

Protection of local producers for its own sake is meaningless and harmful

If local producers know that they can hide forever behind trade barriers - be they tariffs, quotas, or whatever - there is no incentive to become more efficient and competitive. The invariable result is more expensive and poorer quality goods for consumers. It is difficult to see how any government could justify such an objective. In the case of Kaliningrad, the only feasible justification for these quotas would be to provide an impetus to what is known as the development strategy of import-substitution industrialisation (ISI).

So, is there an ISI strategy in Kaliningrad?

ISI is a process whereby a country wishes to modernise the productive sectors of the economy, which have hitherto been dominated by imports, and enable them to develop to world standards (in terms of quality, prices and competitiveness). Normally, it concentrates on areas where the technology involved is reasonably well understood, or easily available, around the world, and where capital equipment (manufacturing equipment for example) is fairly standardised. In other words, access to appropriate technology, in terms of both knowledge and equipment, is not difficult. For this reason, initial ISI strategies tend to focus on such industries as textiles and food processing - rather than, say, pharmaceuticals or sophisticated electronics - and, for the same reason, is also known as 'initial' or 'easy' ISI. The medium-term objective is not just to substitute domestic production for imports, but to support the development of industry sectors that, having attained international competitiveness during the protectionist period, can then go on to develop thriving export markets.

Assuming, therefore, that the Administration has adopted an ISI policy with the medium-term objective of stimulating the creation of a vibrant series of exporting industries in Kaliningrad, several other questions need to be addressed. Of these, the most important are the following two.

The first question concerns timing. The infant industry argument requires acknowledgement that, in due course, the favoured industries will 'grow up' - that is, be able to compete successfully with similar industries in other countries. At this stage, of course, the protection should be removed. However, experience all over the world has shown that enterprises which enjoy protection have little incentive to modernise, innovate and become more efficient *unless* they know with *total certainty* that the protection will be removed at some future, specified date (either in one step or as a phased reduction over a particular period). The important point is that everybody - government, producers, consumers, in particular - *must* know, from the very beginning, how long the protection will exist, how and in what stages it will be removed, and that *there can be no change in the timetable except for very exceptional unforeseen reasons*, such as war or famine. Although it is impossible to be precise over how long protection should last (nobody can predict local, let alone global, economic conditions several years ahead), a rough guide is that seven to ten years tends to be a reasonable period of protection for non-durable consumer goods (longer with more complex technologies, possibly less for very technologically simple industries).

The current quota system in Kaliningrad is, on this basis, very unsatisfactory. The initial two-year period that the present regime covers is too short to enable a significant number of internationally competitive enterprises to develop. If the intention is to follow an ISI strategy, then a longer period is required - but this should have been specified at the start. Keeping the options open, in the sense of adopting an attitude of saying 'let's see how we get on over the next two years, and then we'll decide whether to extend the quotas for another two years,' etc., is a recipe for failure. This open-ended approach means that lazy producers can keep arguing for a reimposition of the quotas every couple of years, saying that they are 'not quite' ready yet.

(Of course, if the Administration is *not* following a medium-term ISI strategy, then the question arises of what the quotas are for, since there are no apparent benefits to the economy or society as a whole, only 'unearned' profit opportunities for inefficient producers at the expense of the local population - hardly a situation that any government would want deliberately to create).

The second main question refers to the other measures that are necessary to support an ISI strategy. Protectionism, on its own, is generally not sufficient to develop new, competitive industries - all it does is provide a 'breathing space' while local enterprises catch up with international standards of production.

During the protectionist period, enterprises need to gain access to appropriate technologies (both technological skills and technological equipment), and then acquire training in the new technologies. Managers (normally) require a great deal of training in management, finance and marketing, workers require training in the new skills - and plenty of 'on-the-job' learning. Possibly, third level institutions will need to introduce new educational or training courses for the new workers and managers. Enterprises will need access to capital finance (equity, and medium and long-term finance on reasonable terms) to invest in the new equipment and to fund other needs. There are many other ingredients required - several of them being specific to individual sectors. None of these other requirements are in place in Kaliningrad.

Under these circumstances the risk exists of a situation developing characterised as follows:

> 'The contact between protected industrialists and government bureaucrats ... often involves substantial degrees of corruption and bribery of officials.' [36]

There is no quantitative evidence that the quotas have done anything positive for the regional economy, nor for the people who live there. However, it is clear that a number of local businesses enjoy artificial protection from foreign competition and this, on the basis of experiences elsewhere around the world, inevitably raises the possibility of corruption.

Conclusions

My intention in this chapter has been to be somewhat argumentative and provocative in style. I have taken somewhat extreme positions with some of these myths, consciously and deliberately. I would like to be told that I am wrong - but only where such counter-claims are supported by factual evidence. For instance, at a recent seminar a senior academic from Kaliningrad challenged me over the Gateway Myth, stating that the physical gateway concept is obsolete and that the new gateway concept is about services and knowledge-based activities. Fair enough, but I do not believe that this new version is understood or accepted widely in Kaliningrad - at least, not among the present regional leadership elite. Nor do I really understand what the idea would mean in practice. But at least we are now hearing about such developments in thinking, and that is a healthy sign. Indeed, it is the essential first step towards finding real solutions to the complex problems of Kaliningrad.

Annex

Investor Motivation - Survey Results

Reproduced from FitzPatrick, Des, January 1998, Annex 6 of *'Review of Kaliningrad as a Destination for FDI'*, Tacis/IDI, Tacis Project 'Support to Kaliningrad Oblast Within the Context of the SEZ', Brussels and Kaliningrad.

Ranking	*Motivation Factor*
1	Political stability
2	Stability of macroeconomic policy
3	Regulatory environment
4	Geographical closeness
5	Skilled labour costs
6	Local market size
7	Access to other CEE/FSU markets
8	Cultural closeness
9	Unskilled labour costs
10	Opportunities from privatisation programme
11	Infrastructure - transport
12	Infrastructure - telecommunications
13	Presence of other foreign-owned or controlled firms
14	Tax/investment incentives
15	Energy costs
16	Access to EU/EFTA markets
17	Natural resources
18	Effectiveness of local financial services sector

Original source: Lankes (EBRD) and Venables (London School of Economics), 1997, *FDI in Eastern Europe and the Former Soviet Union - Results from a Survey of Investors*, EBRD, London.

---

[1] Tyler, Patrick, 5 April 2000, 'In a Russian Region Apart, Corruption Is King', *New York Times*, New York.

[2] E.g. 'The *oblast* is an economic bridge between the European countries and Russia', from the Head of the Kaliningrad Delegation, 17 May 2000, in 'Report to the Conference', *The Northern Dimension and Kaliningrad: European and Regional Integration*, Copenhagen.

[3] Kaliningrad Regional Branch of the State Committee of Statistics.

[4] World Trade Centre website.

[5] There are actually five ports, ranging from Baltiysk on the coast to three separate ports in Kaliningrad City (42 kilometres up-stream), each originally established for different purposes during Soviet times, and a further port roughly mid-way between at Svetly. Between the five of them there are separate ownership structures and responsibilities, as well as a considerable degree of competition for certain kinds of operation.

[6] Uniconsult-Kampsax International Consortium, June 1997, *Action Plan - Seaports: Appendix 1 - Multi-Modal Transport Action Plan*, Tacis Project, 'Transport Aspects of the Kaliningrad SEZ', Brussels and Kaliningrad.

[7] A short distance up the coast, the Lithuanian port of Klaipeda - which is actually on the coast - currently handles vessels up to 60,000 dwt and, when the current phase of development is completed during 2000, will be able to accommodate 100,000 dwt and more. Source: Klaipeda State Seaport, 2000, *Klaipeda State Seaport - Port Plan*, Klaipeda, and personal communication from port officials during visit to port on 3 June 2000.

[8] *Kaliningradskaya Pravda* and other local media, 6 October 1999.

[9] From *Kaskad*, No. 27 (565), 15 February 2000, quoted in Gladkov, Andrei, 14 - 20 February 2000, *Kaliningrad This Week*, Issue 7 (124), Group Transition Development, Kaliningrad.

[10] JIT stands for just-in-time manufacturing, whereby inventory stocks, and hence working capital needs, are minimised by having suppliers deliver inputs only at the times that they are actually needed. This requires, among other things, sophisticated computer-based management information systems, exceptionally good relationships with suppliers, and first-class communications and transport systems. FMS represents flexible manufacturing systems which, apart from requiring a sophisticated and highly educated work force, involves highly advanced processing technologies, with great reliance on rapid re-tooling of manufacturing lines, involving CNC equipment, robotics, and so forth. TQM stands for total quality management which, at its extreme - that is, the norm for most major and many minor enterprises - is a dedication to

zero-defect production and continuous process and product improvement. TQM depends on instilling the appropriate 'cultural' attitudes and mindsets as much as on sophisticated technologies. Achieving ISO (International Standards Organisation) certification (e.g. ISO 9000), once seen as a difficult end goal to achieve, is increasingly regarded as simply the first, necessary step on a never-ending road.

[11] O'Rourke, Bernard and Alexander Glukhov, *The Educational Infrastructure of Kaliningrad*, Tacis/IDI, Tacis Project 'Support to Kaliningrad Oblast in the Context of the SEZ', Brussels and Kaliningrad, December 1998.

[12] High-tech industries are not just the cutting-edge innovators who are creating and developing brand new industries. Many more traditional industries (oil production, textiles, food processing, etc) also are adopting and developing high-technology R & D and manufacturing processes. There are not many industries left that have not become increasingly high-tech *intensive*, even if their products and services remain 'traditional'.

[13] Widgery, Andrew and Alexander Louchinin, *Initial Review of Electronics and Engineering Industries*, Tacis/IDI, Tacis Project 'Support to Kaliningrad Oblast in the Context of the SEZ', Kaliningrad and Brussels, November 1997.

[14] This estimate was calculated by Russian and European experts who talked to the Kaliningrad amber mining enterprise, as well as well-informed sources in Poland and Lithuania. See PROMETEE II, 1998, *A Global Development Plan for Kaliningrad*, Tacis Project, PROMETEE II, Brussels and Kaliningrad.

[15] For obvious reasons I cannot divulge this person's identity, but I have no reason to doubt his veracity.

[16] *Kaliningradskaya Pravda*, 6 October 1999.

[17] Gennady Kulik, former Deputy Prime Minister responsible for agriculture, was quoted as saying that the Russian harvest for 2000 would be 10 million tons - or 16 percent - short on the total demand of 62 million tons. Reported in, *Moscow Times*, 20 June 2000.

[18] Matochkin, Yuri, Governor of Kaliningrad until 1996. Interview in *Kaskad,* 13 June 2000.

[19] This section is adapted from 'The Special Economic Zone - an ambiguous past and an uncertain future' in Joenniemi, Pertti, Fairlie, Lyndelle and Dewar, Stephen, *The Kaliningrad Puzzle*, The Baltic Institute, Karlskrona, Sweden, 2000.

[20] 'The director of the regional statistics committee Genrietta Karovaeva presented a report to the board outlining serious drawbacks in social and economic development of the oblast. In 1999 foreign investments into the regional economy, she indicated, in comparison with the previous year *had fallen by 57%* down to 68 mln USD.' (Emphasis added). From

Gladkov, Andrei, *Kaliningrad This Week*, Issue 51 (116), Group
Transition Development, Kaliningrad, 20-26 December 1999.

[21] Westin, Peter, *Foreign Direct Investment in Russia*, RECEP, Tacis/
Stockholm Institute of Transition Economics, Moscow and Brussels, 1999.

[22] The list of factors and their rankings is reproduced in the annex.

[23] 'In order to reduce losses to the federal budget, the government will,
by 10 July 1999, adopt a resolution increasing the list of commodities
whose duty-free importation into Kaliningrad is subject to quotas. The
government will do everything within its power to ensure that a federal
law eliminating excise and VAT exemptions for goods imported to
Kaliningrad is adopted by end-1999.' Paragraph 21, Letter of Intent to
the International Monetary Fund, signed by the then Prime Minister,
Sergei Stepashin, and the Governor of the Russian Central Bank, Mr.
Gerashenko, on 13 July 1999.

[24] 'The ... special economic zone ... made a good impression on the
development of the foreign trade ... foreign trade turnover has been
growing fast since 1992.' A. A. Ushakov, Deputy Governor, Kaliningrad
Regional Administration, in his address to the conference *Kaliningrad
and the Future of Russia - EU Relations*, organised by the Embassy of
Finland in the Russian Federation and the EastWest Institute Moscow
Centre, Finnish Embassy, Moscow, 7 July 1999. I am not singling out
Mr Ushakov - indeed, he deserves credit for using moderate language to
claim success in this area, compared with that adopted by more strident
exponents of this viewpoint.

[25] Preliminary figures for 1998 and part of 1999 indicate falls in both
exports and imports, largely reflecting the impact of the overall August
1998 crisis and rouble crash.

[26] All figures from Kaliningrad Regional Branch of the State Statistics
Committee. These figures must be treated with a considerable degree of
caution. Apart from some inherent methodological and measurement
problems, the sizeable black and grey economies are excluded, and it is
also difficult to distinguish between exports that truly originate from
Kaliningrad, as opposed to those in transit from elsewhere in Russia, and
vice versa for imports. Nonetheless, it is unlikely that the relative trends
are significantly misleading. Furthermore, since the regional leadership
quotes these figures as representing Kaliningrad's performance I am
treating them in the same way for the purpose of this particular Myth.

[27] The four 'arguments' and some of the analysis that follow are derived
from the excellent and only comprehensive analysis of the SEZ's tax and
other effects by Yershov, Alexander, 'The SEZ in Kaliningrad: Pros and
Cons', in *Kaliningrad and the Future of Russia - EU Relations*,
conference materials, EastWest Institute Moscow Centre and Embassy
of Finland in the Russian Federation, Moscow, September 1999.

[28] *Ibid*, page 9.

[29] i.e. 'The SEZ undermines local industrial producers'.

[30] This is where the exporting country 'voluntarily' agrees not to export above a certain quantitative level to the affected country - the classic examples being Japanese export restraints to America, first with cars, later with semi-conductors.

[31] France at one time required all Japanese VCRs to be imported through a single, small, under-staffed customs post. The delays, costs and frustration this caused greatly reduced Japanese exports of VCRs to France.

[32] Ireland once ordered that chinaware products made in Japan should be clearly labelled as being made in Japan - but written in Irish, which caused delays in production runs as manufacturing lines were reset to accommodate this particular need.

[33] The EU ban on US beef treated with growth hormones, the French ban on British 'mad cow' beef, various bans on genetically modified food products, etc.

[34] The European Commission categorises NTBs as physical, technical or fiscal - see Commission of the European Communities, *Completing the Internal Market*, COM (85) 310, Brussels, 1985.

[35] The reader may like to consider whether any of these consequences are observable in Kaliningrad and, if so, to contemplate whether import quotas may have contributed to such a state of affairs - especially the first two consequences listed.

[36] Cypher, James M. and James L. Dietz, *The Process of Economic Development*, Routledge, London, 1997, p 287.

Chapter 11

Kaliningrad and the European Union: The Clash of Expectations

Andrew Dolan
International Institute for Policy
Development, Edinburgh

Judging by the number of symposia and conferences and the quantity of research devoted to the issue of Kaliningrad and its relationship with the European Union (EU), one could be forgiven for thinking that Kaliningrad matters. Certainly, this is an impression fostered by the Oblast Administration and the local business community and frequently reinforced by analysts inside and outside the Baltic region. The unique geographical position of Kaliningrad in relation to the future enlargement of the EU, so the argument goes, demands an imaginative solution for the future of Russia's enclave within the European Union's space.

Yet, when compared to the EU's limited response, there is an unmistakable impression that this claim to uniqueness has failed to generate a commensurate view from Brussels. Indeed, in relation to the many other thorny issues associated with the EU's future enlargement, the Kaliningrad problem has yet to feature on the 'most pressing list'. By inference, Kaliningrad does not matter.

The truth of the matter probably lies somewhere in the middle of these two extremes. Certainly for the people of Kaliningrad, one would hope that proximity to an economic superpower would bring its own benefits. Yet, why is it that, after so many years of dialogue and discussion on the question of Kaliningrad, we are no closer to a modus vivendi? Is the problem insurmountable, or are we merely prisoners to a clash of expectations?

A major stumbling block facing both parties in this issue is the asymmetrical fault lines which are always present, but which dare not be spoken of in any transparent way. In this context, I refer to the lack of understanding and appreciation of the cultures, practices and policies which drive both the EU and the Russian Federation.

Despite many years of exposure to EU policies and practices, the administration in Kaliningrad still cannot accept the fact that a special relationship based upon derogation of the *acquis communautaire* is out of the question. For example, the EU will not permit any concessions over visas. Similarly, those well-intended economic development studies undertaken on behalf of the Commission and which offer a future of Kaliningrad as the service industry hub of the Baltic, based upon Singapore-type offshore tax and investment regimes, fail to take account of the delicate relationship between Moscow and the regions. In reality, independence in the fields of economic and legal action will not be countenanced by the Russian Federal Government, if only because of the potential precedent that this would set in relation to other Russian regions.

If this level of asymmetrical appreciation is an obstacle to realistic progress, then what can and should be done to encourage mutual appreciation of the other's position and aspirations?

As far as the EU is concerned, there should be a clear recognition that part of the solution to Kaliningrad's future lies in Moscow. For the foreseeable future, the Region will remain part of Russia and indeed, if the early actions of President Putin are any indicator, the room for independent action by Kaliningrad in relation to the EU will be severely curtailed. Any imaginative solution to the future of a Kaliningrad surrounded by EU Member States must, therefore, start at the centre.

Yet there is no certainty of finding Moscow in a receptive mood. Slowly but surely, Russia is beginning to realise that the European Union is more than an economic experiment in single markets. The introduction of the euro and the beginnings of a nascent defence and security identity have already overturned the accepted Russian view of Brussels. Therefore, as enlargement proceeds, Kaliningrad may once again become a geo-strategic pawn in Russian security policy.

With regard to the substance of any EU-Russian discussions on Kaliningrad, the emphasis from Brussels must be on the integrity of the Union's regulations concerning relationships with non-Union states. The provisions of the Single Market, and for that matter Schengen border control, cannot and should not be compromised. However, to characterise the EU's position as a new fortress Europe would be to neglect the very positive efforts being made by Brussels, through its Partnership and Co-operation Agreement (PCA) and Common Strategy with Russia, to regulate the relationships between both parties in a positive manner. A thorough examination of both documents should reassure the Russians that having a single market and a tightly-controlled border management policy does not stymie developments in the economic, social and political spheres. Keeping the bad out does not prohibit letting the good in. However, the very fact that the PCA exists between the Union and Russia would suggest that any separate PCA or 'Europe Agreement' solely for Kaliningrad is most unlikely.

Of course, one could argue that, despite the PCA and the Common Strategy, there is still a requirement for more imagination when it comes to Kaliningrad and that Brussels could offer greater assistance. Indeed, the pressure for greater responsiveness from the EU is inherent in the comments and local initiatives of the Lithuanians and Poles, and is to some extent reflected in the Northern Dimension initiative. More needs to be done. However, for the Union to even begin contemplating new initiatives would require a degree of consensus on behalf of the Member States which to date is simply not present. Ask any Italian or Portuguese what Kaliningrad means to them, and the starkness of the answer belies the impression that somehow Kaliningrad matters. Therefore, if the EU were to set about developing a Kaliningrad strategy, it is essential that this should be based on a unanimity of purpose by the member states, a clear recognition that there will be no dilution of the *acquis* and finally an acknowledgement that this issue is as much related to the internal politics of Russia and its geo-strategic view of the region as it is to any economic context.

So much for the Union's position, but what of Kaliningrad and its responsibility as an active partner to this process? Three main considerations immediately come to mind and focus on questions of transparency, a willingness to face harsh reality and finally an acceptance that doing existing things better may in the long term prove more beneficial than promoting unrealistic initiatives which are inevitably doomed to failure.

Whilst it is understandable for government officials and business elites to seek to 'sell' Kaliningrad, to present it to the outside world at its most attractive, it is equally wrong to present a false image. The fact is that Kaliningrad is not, at least for the moment, an attractive business magnet either for trading or investment. This is understandable to those who know the region. However, if Kaliningrad is ever to become a viable economic region, then it must open up more to outside inspection and influence. Investors and traders need to know what they are getting into before committing themselves to commercial intervention and this picture must be accurate. Perhaps it is simply asking too much for Kaliningrad to offer greater transparency, but I fear that, without it, most commercial risk takers, faced with an incomplete economic route map, will simply turn away. No amount of artificial stimulation through grants or tax breaks will reverse this.

Allied to this question of transparency is the preparedness of the Kaliningrad Administration to accept some hard and uncomfortable truths. The region is economically unattractive. There is little possibility that Moscow will allow it the freedom to introduce more trading-friendly legislation, including a trade stimulating tax regime. Soviet-style bureaucracy is not up to the task of generating internal economic reform. Corruption levels are unacceptably high. Sadly, this is by no means an exhaustive list but it does amply demonstrate that Kaliningrad, in its present condition, holds no allure for those who may have an eye for investment or trade. No one likes to hear such negative views, and the people of Kaliningrad will be no exception, even if privately many of them are prepared to acknowledge the unfortunate circumstances in which they find themselves. However, a failure to acknowledge this set of debilitating circumstances can only lead to false expectations and frustrations when improvements fail to materialise.

A less-than-transparent Kaliningrad, with a reluctance to accept the reality of the situation, is unlikely to initiate the reforms needed to transform social and economic conditions to the extent that the region becomes attractive to both internal and external inward investment. Yet reform is badly needed, if only to the degree that will make Kaliningrad administratively capable of partnering the EU in significant technical assistance programmes. Much criticism has been laid at the door of the European Commission for its lack of deep and sustained efforts in Kaliningrad, particularly in relation to the Tacis Programme. Whilst some of this criticism may be justified, it usually fails to appreciate the difficulties Commission officials have in managing technical assistance projects in areas where public administration is weak or underdeveloped. Kaliningrad cannot afford to look at the positive social and economic developments taking place in neighbouring countries such as Lithuania and Poland and assume that this is merely a reflection of subsidy from Brussels. On the contrary, this transformation required and still requires considerable internal reform for progress to take off and be sustained. This provides an example for Kaliningrad to follow.

Admittedly, such a transformation of thinking and policy in Kaliningrad will not come easily. For many, there will be little or no incentive to change; old ways die hard. For others, change can seem inherently dangerous and destabilising, and furthermore will not guarantee a positive outcome. Where are the obvious incentives? It is the answers to these questions that will, I believe, largely determine whether or not Kaliningrad can become a viable region in the Baltic and provide sufficient reason for the EU to offer an imaginative partnership.

If anything positive is to come out of this rather depressing assessment, it is the fact that goodwill exists on both sides to do something. Despite facing its own hardships, Lithuania is continuing to support Kaliningrad as far as circumstances will allow. This support has been notably holistic, and ranges from humanitarian assistance to facilitating small trading ventures. Finland too has been keen to champion the cause of Kaliningrad inside and outside the Northern Dimension.

For its part, the Kaliningrad Administration has tried to stimulate internal SME development and offer limited concessions to inward investors. It acknowledges problems in economic and business legislation but rightly points out that such matters are controlled by Moscow and not the Region. Setting up a Representative Office in Brussels was also a bold initiative, even if the results to date have been limited.

To return to the question posed at the beginning of this chapter, is there a solution to Kaliningrad's problems, or is the clash of expectations too great an obstacle to progress? On reflection, there is probably no clash of expectations between Kaliningrad and the EU. The expectation, if any exists, probably only remains in the minds of a few Kaliningrad players and even then reflects a faint hope rather than positive expectation. What can the EU reasonably expect from Kaliningrad? That it should not challenge the single market or breach the EU's future external borders may be sufficient.

Is there any scope for an imaginative partnership between the enclave and a future enlarged EU? Such a scenario cannot be discounted, although at present it is rather difficult to gauge what form any relationship would take. Certainly significant levels of investment could stimulate limited economic growth, and possibly create artificial markets. Investment in structural reform and public administration could also make a difference. This is hardly imaginative.

If I were to speculate on this matter, then I would suggest that this is not the time for an imaginative solution. Developments in Moscow and Russia will determine a possible timetable for discussion on Kaliningrad's future, and not any enlargement timetable determined by Brussels. If Russia moves towards greater integration with Europe and develops her democratic institutions and market economy accordingly, then the conditions for imaginative solutions will improve. However, a Russia ill at ease with herself, insecure and under a dictatorship of harsh laws, a Russia more suspicious of the enlarged EU, may not be so willing to be imaginative - irrespective of Kaliningrad's wishes.

Chapter 12

Kaliningrad from a Security Perspective

Chris Donnelly[1]

Special Adviser for Central and
Eastern European Affairs, NATO

Perhaps the most striking thing about Kaliningrad these days is that the region no longer features as a classic security concern.

From being an area of great strategic interest to military specialists during the Cold War, by virtue of its geographic position and its role as a forward garrison for the Soviet Armed Forces, Kaliningrad today is no longer an issue on this count. The fundamental change in East-West relations may not have resulted in perfectly harmonious relations between the West and Russia, but it has completely removed any fear in the West of military confrontation with Russia. Russia is no longer seen as a threat, and this has changed the perception of Kaliningrad. It has now in very large measure lost its military significance.

The second thing to note is that, in the West, there is absolutely no questioning of Kaliningrad's status as a subject of the Russian Federation. This is not an issue of debate.

But for those who study Russia and the Baltic region, some security concerns do arise over developments in the region, and there is a strong interest in seeing that the region does not become a political or an economic problem area - in other words a hindrance to the improvement of Russia's relations with the West.

Kaliningrad's geographical situation is both a challenge and an opportunity. It is a challenge in that it is a region of Russia beset by many problems, which borders on a NATO member [Poland] and on Lithuania, an aspiring member, while both these countries are also applicants for the EU. It is an opportunity in that, as a region of Russia, it offers the chance for East and West to collaborate on the solution of Kaliningrad's problems and thereby to develop a good relationship between Russia and the West, addressing the new security issues which face us all at the beginning of the new millennium.

The first element of these concerns is the nature of the relationship between Moscow and Kaliningrad. Western specialists are very interested in seeing Russia establish an effective and stable relationship between the Centre and the regions. This is essential if the Russian Federation as a whole is to flourish and prosper, and to develop along democratic lines as a country which sees fruitful and co-operative partnership with the West as a sensible option. For this to happen, Moscow's relationship with the regions needs to evolve in a way that satisfies both parties. There is always tension between the regions and the centre in any federation. The US and Switzerland provide very good, if very different, examples of this. But developments in Russia over the past few years have demonstrated that the Federation has a long way to go to reach an equilibrium in its sharing of power between central and regional authorities, and this can certainly be seen in the example of Kaliningrad.

The Kaliningrad regional Duma is in favour of Baltic integration, envisaging a future as an autonomous 'Baltic region within the Russian Federation'. Kaliningrad has an observer's seat on the Baltic Assembly. The Chechen war, however, has recently created concern that Russia may not allow such local autonomy. But Moscow has yet to produce a solution to Kaliningrad's economic problems.

As a result, there is today a question mark hanging over the region. Many Western specialists have expressed great concern that organised crime and corruption within the region have reached such a level as to threaten its economic viability. Neighbouring nations fear not only the spread of criminal activity, linked especially with drugs, prostitution and smuggling, but the potential for economic migration should the region suffer a sharp economic decline – a serious possibility in the opinion of many regional experts.

There are now some 18,000 active military in Kaliningrad. The previous chaotic state of the armed forces has been brought under control as numbers of serving officers have been drastically reduced. The great number of retired officers gives an impressive capacity for mobilisation. However, there is no sense at all of the military establishment now being a threat, either to neighbouring states or to the existing social order in Kaliningrad. The military does not have a 'Soviet' attitude, but on the contrary shares the attitudes of the population in general.

Poor economic performance coupled with the growth of criminalisation could present a problem vis-à-vis the armed forces in the region. There have already been examples of weapons proliferation from this (as from many other regions of the Russian Federation) as the armed forces sell off their equipment. The international community is now alert to the dangers of conventional weapons proliferation, but it is not yet fully geared up to combat this trade, and Kaliningrad's maritime location makes it an ideal location for export if the central and regional military authorities cannot or will not enforce control.

There has been a great deal of discussion about the location of Kaliningrad and its importance for NATO enlargement. In fact, given the nature of NATO and the lack of any real military tension in today's Europe, this need not be a substantive problem. But it is very easy to see how it could be made into a problem, if certain political forces in Russia had an interest in creating tension and hindering the development of better East-West relations. It is also easy to see how, even without any such serious intent, there could be a misperception of the situation in Russia which would lead Russians to believe that the region was being surrounded and therefore threatened. The most serious security issue is that neglect or ill-will could create an artificial tension between Kaliningrad and her neighbours which made the region an obstacle to East-West partnership.

If political or economic problems encourage migration, even on a modest scale, this would be of greatest concern to Lithuania. This is ironic since relations with Lithuania are very good and continue to improve all the time. The Kaliningrad football team has applied to join the Lithuanian league, tourism is increasing and Lithuanian farmers are applying to farm uncultivated land in the Kaliningrad Region. Lithuania is now the second largest investor in the region after Germany, having recently pushed Poland into third place. Residents of Kaliningrad feel comfortable with Lithuania, and Lithuania could become the goal of many economic migrants precisely because, just north of the Lithuania-Kaliningrad border, Lithuania has a sizeable Russian-speaking population that is both economically prosperous and socially contented. But a sudden influx of economic refugees might upset this delicate economic and political balance, especially if it occurred at a difficult time of year or during a difficult political situation.

The dilemma of Kaliningrad is that both geographic and economic logic plus the inclination of the local population are pushing the region into the West, whilst in Moscow there are growing fears that Kaliningrad will be 'encircled and cut off' as NATO and the EU expand. This situation requires our attention. We need to find a way to reconcile these different attitudes. At the moment the main target of Russian suspicions is NATO enlargement. But EU enlargement (with its attendant threat to control borders more effectively hence curtailing the current relatively free movement of population and goods between Kaliningrad and Lithuania) is really more problematical.

In terms of the real security concerns of the region in the immediate future, it may also be the EU that will be most closely involved. It is the EU, not NATO, which addresses the crucial aspect of economic development and political evolution. Organised crime and governmental corruption, smuggling, immigration and the problem of insecure borders are all issues which are most appropriately dealt with under the EU Justice and Home Affairs umbrella. As the EU further develops its CFSP with its attendant crisis management capability and its capacity to deal with specific security issues, it will be more and more the EU which looms large in the consciousness of both Moscow and Kaliningrad region.

As far as security is concerned, what should our interest in the region be? First, that the area should become an example of co-operation, a stepping stone between East and West. Secondly, that the Kaliningrad region should itself become more capable of resolving its own problems and that it should establish a more efficient political and economic system which promotes regional recovery. Thirdly, that Moscow should improve its relationship with the region, establishing a judicious balance between regional autonomy (that is in its positive aspects - not one occasioned by Moscow's lack of interest or neglect) and effective enforcement of law and order in a manner which is both satisfactory to the locals and acceptable to the international community.

---

[1] Disclaimer: The following views are purely personal and do not in any way represent an official view either of NATO or of any of its member nations.

THE WAY FORWARD

Chapter 13

Kaliningrad: A European Challenge

Dag Hartelius[1]
Department for Central and
Eastern Europe,
Swedish Ministry of Foreign Affairs

When most European Cold War truths were radically
overturned a decade ago, there was one area that seemed to be
changing at a very slow pace. The Kaliningrad region, the
Soviet Union's and later Russia's far West, had played a role
as a military fortress - sealed-off to foreigners - for a long
time. With the withdrawal of the Russian troops from the
independent Baltic countries, the region's military - in
particular naval - importance to Moscow appeared to grow in
relative terms. Initial Russian reactions, in particular from
military quarters, seemed to confirm a feeling of increasing
sensitivity and uneasiness with the new geostrategic situation.
Fears were expressed about a deliberate Western encirclement
aiming at the eventual secession of Kaliningrad from Russia.

Western countries could see a problem emerging on the horizon
but were generally discouraged to act for two main reasons -
they were absorbed in other more burning issues and were
unwilling to add to Moscow's concerns at a time when more
important issues regarding Russian-Western co-operation were
at stake. Engagement was limited to a handful of senior-level
visits with a fairly general agenda. Although no-one in the
West could find any credibility in the irredentist statements on

the status of Kaliningrad made by some individual German and Lithuanian groups or individual politicians, almost all Western declarations on Kaliningrad in the early to mid 1990s included a mantra stating that Kaliningrad was and would remain an integral part of the Russian Federation. Statements of reassurance to, and of encouragement for, intensified direct co-operation between Kaliningrad and her Baltic Sea neighbours was as far as anyone would go.

Being economically more or less left to their own resources by Moscow and realising the need to attract foreign direct investments, local political leaders in Kaliningrad tried to obtain special tax and customs exemptions. The results were bleak, however, reflecting Moscow's old fears of losing control over Kaliningrad in particular, but also of encouraging other Russian regions to follow suit with similar requests for special arrangements, thereby stimulating a disintegration of the federation. The latter was a worst-case scenario to many political leaders in Moscow, and also one that was perceived by many at the time to be quite real.

With only little development that encouraged foreign direct investment (FDI), Kaliningrad's relative competitiveness was shrinking from low to zero. The brave statements of the early 1990s about creating a Baltic Sea Hong Kong and a Euro-Asian transportation hub in Kaliningrad sounded more hollow than ever in the mid to late 1990s. Why would anyone invest in Kaliningrad with its uncertain legal and economic environment when the situation was much more promising just a few miles away, in the booming economies of neighbouring Lithuania and Poland?

It was not until 1998-1999 that one could witness a turning-point. The Russian financial crisis in the autumn of 1998 exposed Kaliningrad's vulnerable situation. Although it felt psychologically awkward to many Russians (in particular to those in Moscow), Kaliningrad (including its garrison of military forces) was largely left to rely on assistance from Lithuania and other neighbours. Even though concerns about centrifugal trends were looming large in Moscow at the time, it was not until the autumn of 1999 that the wind changed.

This was mainly due to two developments - one specific and the other more general.

The first, and important, trigger for change regarding Kaliningrad was the EU's work on defining guidelines for its new Northern Dimension, with its stated geographic focus on co-operation with the countries bordering the Baltic Sea and on North Western Russia including Kaliningrad. The second was a clear breakthrough in Russian understanding of the EU, which was reflected in much new thinking and later culminated in the Russian EU Strategy that was presented to the EU troika at the EU-Russia Summit on 22 October 1999. For the first time, Moscow was not only encouraging direct co-operation between the EU and Russia's regions but was also proposing to make Kaliningrad a pilot project in EU-Russian relations. It is not hard to guess that EU policy development in Moscow was also partly triggered by increasing awareness of the ongoing EU enlargement process.

For the EU, this was a welcome development, not least with regard to Lithuania's and Poland's steady accession process, which were bringing to the fore a number of issues relating to Kaliningrad.

In this context we also need to reflect on Russia's views on the enlargement process. The initial Russian reactions to EU enlargement were highly political and in stark contrast to its reactions to the opening of NATO of which Moscow took, and still takes, a negative view. EU enlargement was almost by definition seen as something positive or at least harmless. It was not until later, when Russia started to look into the potential economic effects of EU enlargement, that her comments became more cautious or nuanced in certain respects. This applies, for example, to different aspects of EU-Russian trade where the EU share of Russia's foreign trade is expected to grow from just under 40% to between 45-50% after enlargement. Although it is beyond doubt that the positive effects of enlargement on Russia will far outweigh the negative ones, Moscow still needs to be convinced about a number of aspects and the EU will have to address the whole complex of issues in a more detailed way with Moscow – not in the form of negotiations but in an open, attentive and informative dialogue.

Against this background, the case of Kaliningrad is special. Nowhere else will the consequences of EU enlargement for Russia be as deep and direct as here. But this conclusion applies both ways: nowhere else will relations with a third country have a more concrete impact on enlargement and on new member states. This makes Kaliningrad a particular challenge. At the same time, it presents an obvious opportunity to the EU to demonstrate the positive effects of enlargement to the Russians. For the moment, the ball is very much in the EU's court.

Indeed, it takes two to tango. To leave Kaliningrad as a 'wallflower' (even if this were a self-inflicted condition) would hardly be helpful either to the EU enlargement process or to EU-Russian relations. This is where we stand today. Moscow has eventually begun to push Kaliningrad onto the dance floor. The EU has welcomed this and has realised the importance of taking a few turns, but is at the same time somewhat reluctant to make a pass at her because she could turn out to be a tricky and possibly expensive partner.

Yet neither Brussels nor Moscow has any real choice. An isolated and underdeveloped Kaliningrad region would be harmful to the interests of both. Kaliningrad is indeed a challenge to us, but to leave her on her own would become politically, economically and socially much more expensive.

What needs to be done and who should do what? First of all, we need to set our priorities. Kaliningrad's special situation consists in being a Russian enclave surrounded by what will soon be EU members with an internal market and no internal frontiers. Finding practical solutions in order to make cross-border travel, trade and co-operation, if not free, at least simple and easy should be at the top of the agenda. Managing the consequences of Polish and Lithuanian implementation of the Schengen Agreement and internal market *acquis* does not necessarily mean breaking or even bending the rules. Visas will be needed but practical access to Schengen visas can be improved for Kaliningrad residents. As a means of stimulating contacts and co-operation, Russia should be expected and asked to reciprocate on a unilateral basis, by providing ready access to visas to Kaliningrad for EU citizens. Further, efficient border crossings applying modern procedures need to be organised. The Polish and Lithuanian transit agreements with Russia concerning Kaliningrad should be re-examined in the context of the Partnership and Co-operation Agreement (PCA) between the EU and Russia.

The internal market regulations and the possibility of extending some of them to Kaliningrad will probably be a more difficult issue to handle. Some kind of solution is urgently needed, however. If we want Kaliningrad to prosper and participate in regional and EU co-operation, we need to find some practical solutions concerning imports and exports of goods and services. However, the potential solution at hand is not an obvious one. It is easy to identify the principal and practical obstacles. Could and should the EU in any way accept derogations from some of its core rules? What effect would this have on the Union's relations with other partners? Would we risk undermining basic EU policies? And, in practical terms, how could we avoid any special internal market solution for little Kaliningrad being tacitly extended to its huge parent country, Russia proper? Maybe part of the answer lies in regarding Kaliningrad as a testing ground for longer term solutions for extending some new openings to the EU internal market to Russia as a whole.

These issues deserve to be analysed in depth. However awkward we – the EU – find this, we need to tackle them with an open mind but also paying full attention to possible negative consequences. At the same time, Russia will have to consider what she can do unilaterally – because, as in the matter of the consequences of EU enlargement for Russia, this can hardly become a subject for formal negotiation between the EU and Russia, but should be a parallel process of (unilateral) step-by-step actions.

Having proposed that Kaliningrad become a pilot project for EU-Russian relations, Moscow will need to put legal and economic reform as well as an advanced anti-corruption programme for Kaliningrad on a fast track. The EU could and should provide substantial technical assistance for such efforts but only when a decisive and credible Russian initiative is on track.

The Northern Dimension for the policies of the European Union is a horizontal, multi-pillar concept and uniquely well suited to providing a framework for the many concrete problems of a specific region such as Kaliningrad. If Kaliningrad is to become a pilot project for a new era of EU-Russian relations, the region would at the same time become a fully-fledged pilot project for the Northern Dimension. This seems to be the ideal platform for developing and managing concrete projects. As the Northern Dimension is also very much a political, visionary concept, it can be used to give the EU's Kaliningrad policy a central role in its Russia policy. It is very much aimed at finding new models for managing and developing the Union's external relations with its northern European partners at both national and sub-national level. Kaliningrad (with its limited population, economy and territory) could become something of a laboratory for new forms of co-operation between the EU and Russia as a whole.

However, the EU is not the only important external player with regard to Kaliningrad. Sub-regional organisations such as the Council of Baltic Sea States (CBSS) and the Task Force on Organised Crime in the Baltic Sea Region are already involved in practical co-operation projects with Kaliningrad and have the potential to do more in promoting Kaliningrad's regional integration. Both the CBSS and the Task Force have been given prominent operational roles in implementing the Northern Dimension. The CBSS includes the same seven partner countries – Estonia, Latvia, Lithuania, Poland, Russia, Norway and Iceland – as the Northern Dimension. In addition, four member states – Finland, Sweden, Denmark and Germany – and the Commission are CBSS members. Having developed practical co-operation in several fields on the Northern Dimension's priority list over almost a decade, the CBSS is well experienced and flexible enough to make substantial contributions to the process ahead. In this context, it might perhaps be worth considering the creation of a CBSS working group on Kaliningrad that could discuss new ideas and project proposals.

The key stakeholders in this process are, of course, the neighbouring EU candidate countries, Lithuania and Poland. Vilnius has been increasingly active in developing concrete and imaginative initiatives together with Moscow. Such initiatives need to be supported by the EU, and the initiators – for instance Lithuania – should be given a lead role and responsibility in specific fields. This would enable them in their capacity as candidates to contribute to the EU's Northern Dimension and to the Union's stability and external relations.

Other important facilitators will be NGOs that provide a platform for informal creative thinking on trans-frontier co-operation between Kaliningrad and her neighbours. Especially in a complex case such as EU-Kaliningrad relations, NGOs with an ability to think out of the box and to bring policy-makers and experts together, such as the EastWest Institute (which has plans to open a new Centre for Transfrontier Co-operation in Kaliningrad), could really prove their usefulness to the EU and to the governments concerned. Also, NGOs specialising in key problem areas such as Transparency International (which focuses on anti-corruption measures), could be extremely useful working with both local administration and local NGOs.

* * * * *

Kaliningrad is a challenge to the EU, to neighbouring countries – and to Russia. To leave the region to its own devices would be detrimental in the long term. To present Kaliningrad as an opportunity could be seen as a rather far-fetched statement at first glance. In many ways the region is in an almost frightening economic and social condition. Still, one could argue that few other functional or geographic areas present such a multi-faceted interface between the EU and Russia as does Kaliningrad. If we – the EU and Russia – succeed in managing EU-Kaliningrad relations in a visionary, but also very practical and constructive way, this could develop into a best practice model for long-term EU-Russia relations. Despite all the difficulties, Kaliningrad is of limited size, has a small population and economy and this should make a joint effort manageable and easy to monitor for all concerned. Co-operation projects would be controllable and relatively easy to monitor and adjust.

Kaliningrad is not a military fortress any more and is not likely to become one again in the foreseeable future. It is not, and is scarcely likely to become, a Baltic Hong Kong. But it is, and will remain, a piece of Russia at the heart of Europe. What we do, or do not do, with this Russian region is likely to have strategic consequences for northern Europe and for the whole range of EU-Russian relations.

---

[1] The author has earlier served at Swedish Missions in St Petersburg, Moscow, Berlin and London and as Vice President for European security at the EastWest Institute in New York. The views in this chapter are his own, and do not necessarily reflect those of the Swedish Government.

Chapter 14

'What is to be Done?'

Stephen Dewar
Independent economic consultant,
Moscow

1. Introduction

a. A Russian question

In 1864, while imprisoned in the Peter and Paul Fortress in St Petersburg, the Russian revolutionary, Nikolai Chernyshevsky, completed and smuggled out of prison his novel, 'What is to be Done?' Chernyshevsky's grim, revolutionary prescription inspired Lenin's intellectual development to such an extent that he, in turn, later wrote his own revolutionary tract and honoured his inspirational debt to Chernyshevsky by using the same title.

The question, consciously echoing these forebears, is frequently asked today, as Russians contemplate the seemingly insoluble problems they face. Kaliningrad seems ideally suited to have this question addressed to it. The best answer to date is probably given in the words of Viktor Chernomyrdin who, during his tenure as Prime Minister, once famously remarked when asked why something had gone terribly wrong, 'We wanted the best, but it turned out the same as usual [disastrously]'.

Over the last ten years nobody has really known what should be done. What was actually tried - most importantly, the SEZ - has failed.

In this chapter I try to answer the question. I make recommendations for policy developments and changes in Kaliningrad, Moscow and Brussels. I suggest institutional changes and initiatives. And, to support these measures, I propose the establishment of a development fund – the Kaliningrad Equalisation and Development Fund – to be set up, funded and managed by concerned countries, initially and most probably, the richer states in the Northern Dimension territory.

I should make two points before presenting my case. First, I recognise that opinions are divided over the nature and degree of importance of the Kaliningrad issue. I think that this is reflected in the diversity of views offered by the contributors to this volume. I myself am firmly on the side of those who feel that there is a serious problem, that it is going to get worse, and that there are powerful arguments – based on moral and humanitarian concerns, as much as on self-interest and pragmatism – for all the actors concerned to start addressing the issue with firm commitment right now.

The second point is that there is no simple recipe of ingredients that can be simply added together, stirred and baked, in order to produce a guaranteed solution. This is a novel situation and so we have no precedents for how to handle it. Consequently, I can only offer my own views on what I consider to be essential conditions that must be fulfilled, together with some suggested steps forward. Others can undoubtedly improve on and add to these proposals. The important thing is to agree on the goal - successful transformation of Kaliningrad into a prosperous and stable region, enjoying mutually beneficial relations with its EU neighbours, thereby eliminating the risks of cross-border destabilisation, while assuring continued and unquestioned Russian sovereignty and, at the same time, developing new modes of thinking and models of behaviour that could act as templates for other areas of developing EU-Russian relations. We also need to recognise that this can only be achieved by the committed involvement of all the relevant actors – and that, not on the basis of grudging concessions to be traded and bargained over, but in a spirit of constructive and innovative generosity – in the same spirit, that is, that has underlain all that is great and worthy in the European heritage, and not that spirit that made the last century the bloodiest in all of Europe's turbulent history.

b. Key considerations

The starting point is to set out the principal assumptions and foundations of my arguments; they are as follows.

- Kaliningrad is a legitimate issue of real concern for both Russia and the other states in the overall region.
- This has been recognised and accepted by all main parties.
- A solution cannot be found without the co-operation of all the major (and the more important minor) players.
- *Nothing at all can be achieved without the active and constructive engagement of the Kaliningrad Regional Administration* (and, to a lesser extent, the Regional Duma).
- The EU has a specially important role to play – but this role needs to be defined in a new way, not by relying solely on existing and historical rule-bound approaches.
- Where the EU is unable to act, other states and/or multilateral groupings need to fill the gap.
- The only economic solution that, in my view, is viable (and without which, there can be no solution to social, cultural, security and environmental problems) lies in harmonising Kaliningrad with the expanding EU economic space.[1]

This much is simple. The sticking points come in two areas: one, turning these generalisations into policies, strategies and operational programmes and, two, obtaining the political will and means to overcome bureaucratic inertia and other obstacles to their implementation.

Later on in this chapter I will address these two issues, but before doing so there are some other matters to be dealt with first. These deal with the economic context and with what it means to be (or not to be) a candidate state for EU membership.

c. A brief reminder

In Chapter 3 I have argued that Kaliningrad's transport infrastructure is not competitive with that available in the neighbouring states and in one important respect (aviation) is virtually non-existent. I have suggested that there are signs that, rather than being on an important trade cross-roads, Kaliningrad is actually located on an economic 'fault-line' – with Polish trade flowing strongly to the west, and Lithuanian and other Baltic State trade flowing primarily to the north-west; in other words, the trade flows are moving *away* from Kaliningrad, rather than past or through it, which would have offered some opportunities for enterprise development.

In Chapter 10 I have argued that most of the supposed competitive advantages that Kaliningrad possesses – being a natural gateway between Russia and Europe, having an ice-free port, offering an investment-friendly and trade-supportive SEZ regime, and so forth – are, in fact, simply a set of 'myths' that are effectively false and misleading.

In brief, Kaliningrad lacks the infrastructure, opportunity and advantages to stimulate sustainable economic development.

Assuming, as I am suggesting, that Kaliningrad's successful future is inextricably tied up with the encroaching EU economic space, there is a fundamental defining question that will decide Kaliningrad's freedom of choice. This is whether or not Kaliningrad is treated (*de jure* or *de facto*) as a candidate member of the EU – in the same practical ways as the other states in the region.

Of course, there are numerous other possible half-way houses between these, but focusing on the extremes helps in identifying the most important issues and variables. Thus, I will now suggest what it would mean for Kaliningrad, in terms of assistance, if it were a candidate territory for EU membership, and compare it with the current situation.

2. (E)U or non-(E)U

The aristocratic English writer, Nancy Mitford, popularised the use of the terms 'U' and 'non-U', depicting the vast and essentially unbridgeable gulf between those lucky people who, by accident of birth, are 'one of us' (i.e. the upper classes) and the rest (everybody else). By simple accident of geographical location, we can divide the territories around the eastern Baltic into EU and non-EU. As with Nancy Mitford's distinctions, there are profound differences between the two groups.

The simplest way of imagining what candidate status would entail is to look at what the immediate neighbours, Lithuania and Poland, are getting to assist their applications, and adjust this appropriately to Kaliningrad's situation.[2] While looking at what Kaliningrad would be eligible for, I also show the actual situation.

a. Strategic issues

During the current EU planning period of 2000 to 2006, the strategy towards candidate states comprises three elements:

> 'Establishing a comprehensive pre-accession strategy with a view to preparing the countries for accession to the European Union;
> bringing the various forms of EU aid together within a single framework (the Accession Partnerships);
> familiarising the applicant countries with EU procedures and policies in order to enable them to take part in Community programmes and to help them to comply with existing Community legislation.'[3]

The first element covers an enormously wide range of issues, including establishing an economic development/transition programme, supported by legal, institutional and other changes. It involves assisting these states in complying with the requirements set out in the 80,000 pages that constitute the *acquis communautaire*. Included in this work is, for example, the adoption of the more than 300 directives that have established the tens of thousands of standards, procedures, regulations, and so forth, that make up the Single Market.

There is no 'comprehensive strategy' to show Kaliningrad how to prepare for being surrounded by the EU – let alone for joining.

The second element leads to the development of the Association Agreements, which tie all the different aspects of EU involvement into a coherent, integrated programme. The equivalent mechanism for Kaliningrad is the EU-Russia Partnership and Co-operation Agreement (PCA), which focuses mainly on EU relations with Russia as a whole, and not on the specific characteristics of the extremely diverse 89 Federal Subjects that make up the Russian Federation, including Kaliningrad. On the other hand, the EU's Northern Dimension (ND) policy calls for increased 'co-ordination' and 'synergy' of existing EU programmes within the ND states and territories, but does not suggest how this will be achieved – that is, there is no (if greatly more modest) equivalent of an Accession Agreement.

The third element highlights the vital importance of continuous institutional strengthening, familiarisation, training, and so forth, that is necessary for enabling the candidate countries' administrations, and societies as a whole, to understand the complexities of EU 'life' and play an appropriate role. There is no equivalent programme for Kaliningrad to learn what will happen to it when it becomes an enclave within the EU. There is an EU Information Office in Kaliningrad (located in Kaliningrad State University), which is being supported with one-off grants of 10,000 euro for equipment and 5,000 euro to purchase publications. It is also intended to establish a Tacis Technical Office at a later date, which will help to promote awareness of Tacis and how it works, and will provide a greater degree of co-ordination of Tacis activities in the region. It is not, however, likely to have the additional role of preparing Kaliningrad for the implications of EU accession by the neighbouring states.

It is difficult to overestimate the degree of support being offered to the candidate countries – indeed, 'imposed' would be a better term, given the need for the new members to be able to participate effectively in the workings of the EU. There simply is no equivalent support for Kaliningrad to deal with the implications of enlargement for its own situation.

b. Resources

In terms of resources, the EU has committed 21.8 billion euro over the period 2000 to 2006 to support the pre-accession strategies of the candidate countries. Shortly, we will look at how this money will be distributed and estimate the kind of support Kaliningrad could reasonably expect if it was also a candidate country. But, before looking at the amount of assistance Kaliningrad might have been entitled to, it is useful to look at what it is currently receiving.

According to figures compiled by the Danish Foreign Ministry, as a contribution to the conference it sponsored on Kaliningrad (Copenhagen, 17 – 19 May 2000), for the period 1998 to 2000 a total commitment of 25.24 meuro[4] has been entered into by various donors for projects in Kaliningrad. Denmark and Sweden, followed by Germany, are the most active bilateral donors. EU support is recorded as follows:

Tacis: Study of Kaliningrad Port	1 meuro
Tacis: Support to Kaliningrad Regional Development Agency	1 meuro
Tacis: Health system reform	2 meuro
Tacis: Border crossing programme	6 meuro
Tacis/CBC[5] : Water quality management	2.4 meuro
Tacis/CBC: Development of Kaliningrad Zoo	0.2 meuro
Interreg II C[6] : SEABIRD – Baltic air transport project	0.65 meuro
Interreg II C: Waterfront urban development in eastern Baltic	1.35 meuro

This amounts to 14.6 meuro from the EU over a three-year period (approximately 60 percent of the total) or around 5 meuro a year. But this is a bit misleading – erring somewhat on the high side. For instance, project number 3 – health system reform – involves three Russian regions (Murmansk, Archangelsk and Kaliningrad) with a central project office in Moscow. Thus, the allocation to Kaliningrad (assuming equal sharing of resources) will be around 0.7 meuro.

Project number 4 – border crossings – by definition involves foreign partners (in this case Poland and Lithuania). Kaliningrad's 'share', therefore, will be somewhat less than the figure given. Even if the expenditure takes place entirely on the Russian sides of these borders, the benefits will be shared between the three countries. On this basis, the net benefit to Kaliningrad could be, let us say somewhat arbitrarily, 4 meuro – around two-thirds of the total.

Project number 5 – water quality – involves Kaunas and Klaipeda in Lithuania as well as Kaliningrad. Assuming a fifty-fifty allocation, the benefit to Kaliningrad would be 1.2 meuro.

Projects 7 and 8 – from Interreg – are spread over a wide number of locations around the Baltic. SEABIRD, for instance, involves 25 airports and numerous airlines in all the countries around the Baltic Sea. It would be generous to assume that, out of the 2 meuro total, Kaliningrad's 'share' would amount to even 0.2 meuro.

Projects 1, 2 and 6 are exclusively within Kaliningrad.

These considerations lead me to suggest that the actual level of EU support for Kaliningrad over the designated period, amounts to 8.3 meuro. Because of the somewhat arbitrary way in which I have 'reallocated' resources, it is probably prudent to increase this figure to, say, 10 meuro, or 3-3.5 meuro a year.

We can now look at what Kaliningrad might expect to obtain if it was a candidate territory for EU membership.

Table 1 below is, I hope, self-explanatory. On the basis of the assumptions used, Kaliningrad could reasonably expect to benefit by something in the (admittedly very wide) range of

23 to 53 meuro a year. This is seven to 16 times higher than the current allocations. Even if one adds in all the bilateral assistance that Kaliningrad receives, the total would still be only between one-fifth and one-eleventh of the candidate state allocation from the EU.

Table 1: Proposed financial assistance from EU to candidate states, 2000 to 2006, with estimated allocations to Poland and Lithuania, and hypothetical allocations to Kaliningrad.

	2000	2001	2002	2003	2004	2005	2006
1. PHARE[7]	1560	1560	1560	1560	1560	1560	1560
2. SAPARD[8]	520	520	520	520	520	520	520
3. ISPA[9]	1040	1040	1040	1040	1040	1040	1040
4. TOTAL	*3120*	*3120*	*3120*	*3120*	*3120*	*3120*	*3120*
5. Poland's proposed share	936 to 1154	936 to 1154	936 to 1154	936 to 1154	936 to 1154	936 to 1154	936 to 1154
6. Lithuania - proposed share	125 to 187	125 to 187	125 to 187	125 to 187	125 to 187	125 to 187	125 to 187
7. Poland – euro per person	23.4 to 28.85	23.4 to 28.85	23.4 to 28.85	23.4 to 28.85	23.4 to 28.85	23.4 to 28.85	23.4 to 28.85
8. Lithuania – euro per person	35.7 to 53.4	35.7 to 53.4	35.7 to 53.4	35.7 to 53.4	35.7 to 53.4	35.7 to 53.4	35.7 to 53.4
9. Kaliningrad[10]	23 to 53	23 to 53	23 to 53	23 to 53	23 to 53	23 to 53	23 to 53

Source: derived from European Commission, 2000, op. cit., page 126. See footnote 3.

Notes: (a) Rows 1 – 6 and 9 in meuro. Rows 7 and 8 in euro. (b) The ranges of figures in rows 5 and 6 (and hence 7 and 8) are from the Commission's proposed distribution, whereby Poland will be allocated between 30 and 37 percent of the total, and Lithuania will get between 4 and 6 percent. (c) The hypothetical range for Kaliningrad in row 9 is obtained by taking the lowest of the four per capita figures in rows 7 and 8 and the highest, and then multiplying these by the size of Kaliningrad's population. (d) The Commission has simply divided the total proposed financial assistance into equal amounts for each year of the programme.

c. Assessment

I think that it is very important to stress that this analysis does not in any way purport to be critical of the level of EU assistance to Kaliningrad. In fact, Kaliningrad has done well from the Tacis Programme in Russia, since it commenced in 1991, and the continuing levels of support clearly show that the *oblast* has by no means been abandoned. And, to keep things in perspective, if Russia as a whole were to obtain comparable levels of funding as the accession states, the amounts involved (using the per capita figures applied to Kaliningrad) would be in the range of 3.4 billion to 7.7 billion euro a year – up to two-and-a-half times the total available!

What these figures indicate, however, is that there is an enormous difference between what candidate states receive as opposed to non-candidate states. The significance of the analysis is solely concerned with making the point that Kaliningrad's neighbours, who are competitors for much the same trade and investment opportunities, (a) are receiving greatly more resources to assist their economies and societies develop in such a way as to make them even more competitive than Kaliningrad than they are already[11], and (b) are becoming more and more integrated with the EU (in terms of, for example, the Four Freedoms) and, concurrently, isolating Kaliningrad.

In practical terms, the accession states are getting major support in 'learning' how to manage their economies in such a way as to be able to participate and compete effectively within the EU. They are also getting major capital funding to invest in essential infrastructure development. In due course, they will participate in the Schengen *acquis*.[12] Kaliningrad, although getting the assistance described in the list earlier, is not getting any of these kinds of fundamental, structural assistance. This can only lead to Kaliningrad falling further and further behind its neighbours – unless remedial actions are taken.

The issue, therefore, is to decide whether the special circumstances affecting Kaliningrad, as it becomes increasingly surrounded by the EU,[13] merit some kind of additional or compensatory support from Brussels. On this matter, opinions are divided. My view is that such support is merited, on pragmatic as well as moral grounds.

3. Possible strategies and programmes

a. Designing and developing strategies

Kaliningrad needs a strategic development plan and programme – and it needs technical assistance (TA) in the form of expertise, advice and, perhaps, training to help both design and implement such a plan. The first step should be to carry out an up-to-date assessment of the economic situation, so that the right information is available to guide the planning process. Such a step is envisaged in the Northern Dimension Action Plan[14]. The next step along this way is planned with the forthcoming 1 meuro Tacis project to support the newly-established Kaliningrad Regional Development Agency (KRDA).[15] A useful further move would be to provide substantial additional assistance to the KRDA. This could be conditional on satisfactory progress in the initial KRDA project and, not only would be meeting the conditionality criterion increasingly stressed in the Tacis programme, but would also be reflecting another current requirement– the focus on larger, more strategic, but phased or staged projects.

Quite clearly, a significant element of the KRDA's work must be to monitor the implications of EU accession by Poland and Lithuania for Kaliningrad and formulate policy responses. But, the most important challenge to be addressed by the KRDA is to determine the fundamental policy orientations for Kaliningrad. In economic terms, the most effective approach will be to forge closer economic links with the neighbouring states of the enlarging EU. This, however, poses serious difficulties. For one thing, as already suggested, there are no obviously burgeoning regional economic activities to 'tap into' – the economic fault-line I have referred to earlier. Nonetheless, all neighbouring states around the world find areas where the international trade principle of comparative advantage comes into effect and there is no reason, *a priori*, why Kaliningrad should necessarily fail here – subject to the conditions for trade and investment being improved. Indeed, as wage rates increase in Poland and Lithuania, reflecting progression towards EU accession, the principle of absolute advantage should also become increasingly important – notably in the area of labour-intensive industries (though not necessarily high added value or knowledge-intensive industries).[16]

Two major options exist, in terms of developing economic relations with the neighbouring states. One is to become, *de facto* if not *de jure*, a part of the EU economic space. This would imply, for example, adopting EU standards in manufacturing processes, labelling, packaging, and so forth, in conformity with Single Market directives covering these issues. It would not necessarily, however, imply adoption of, say, EU public procurement policies – although a unilateral move in this direction would be an interesting and remarkable initiative.[17] In other words, Kaliningrad could move closer towards harmonisation with EU standards of as much of its economic processes as possible.

This does not preclude regional legislative reforms. The more successful Russian regions (Moscow City, Novgorod, Samara, for example) have demonstrated that a great deal can be done at regional level in key areas such as land reform and investor support. Indeed, if Kaliningrad is to attract investment, be it Russian or foreign, it is essential to introduce legislative and regulatory changes to develop a more welcoming business environment. The KRDA should study 'best practice' in these areas in other parts of Russia and propose appropriate measures for Kaliningrad.

The other option would be deliberately to exploit areas where the new member states would be barred from certain kinds of activities or from offering certain kinds of incentives. For instance, the EU is increasingly hostile towards export processing zones, preferential corporate taxation incentives, and so forth, as tools for attracting FDI. As such incentives are eliminated, Kaliningrad could introduce them.[18]

These two options – harmonising with the EU in some areas and going in the opposite direction in others - are by no means mutually exclusive. Indeed, for the second approach to be truly effective, the first approach is necessary as well.

Policy initiatives along the above lines are an essential first step towards economic restructuring and eventual growth. It needs to be stressed that much else also needs to be done. Critically, urgent attention must be given to dealing with the poor state of Kaliningrad's infrastructure.

b. Infrastructure

Some of the fundamental issues that must be addressed include the following:

i. Energy

Kaliningrad imports around 80 percent of its energy needs from Russia via Lithuania. This imposes very significant hard currency costs and, anyway, Lithuania will become disconnected from the Russian electricity grid in the short to medium-term future. Within the context of their Association Partnerships, it is intended that the accession states of Estonia, Latvia, Lithuania and Poland should 'integrate their energy markets and networks and ... connect them with those of the enlarging EU.'[19] For example, it is planned that these countries should participate in the Baltic Ring for electricity. This means that Kaliningrad will be an imported energy-dependent 'enclave' within an integrated EU energy network. Despite moves towards increasing natural gas supplies from Russia to Kaliningrad, by laying a new pipeline through Lithuania, dependence on imported energy will remain a feature for the foreseeable future, and these Baltic/EU developments will pose significant technical, legal and financial problems, not least acquiring the substantial amounts of hard currency to pay for supplies.

ii. Transport

Transport is important, not so much for its own sake, but because it is a vital component of economic activity. Furthermore, not only does it merely have to exist and function, it needs increasingly to become faster, smoother, more efficient, more flexible, provide greater value for money and the like. This is an imperative of international and domestic business needs.

I have already commented on transport in Chapters 3 and 10: Kaliningrad's transport infrastructure and services are inferior to those in neighbouring states, and are likely to continue to fall further behind. Tacis is funding a study to recommend how best to modernise the port complex. The other key needs are to establish how to develop aviation services (a project to deal with this is currently being prepared for submission to Tacis) and how to ensure that the development of the accession states' TEN road and rail networks do not simply by-pass Kaliningrad and cut her off. For example, Tacis is funding a large number of projects in Russia, Belarus, Moldova and Ukraine, concerned with the development of Corridor IX, which links Helsinki with Moscow, via alternate routes through St Petersburg and Pskov, before going on down through Kiev and south to the Black Sea. At Kiev Corridor IX joins with Corridors III and V, which provide the links into the whole of eastern, central and western Europe. From Kiev there is also a 'backward' spur running through Minsk and into Lithuania and Kaliningrad. No projects are currently being funded for the Kaliningrad stretch of Corridor IX, nor indeed for the Kaliningrad spur of Corridor II, which runs down through the three Baltic States and directly into Poland.

In the past, Tacis funded a major project to develop a multi-modal transport strategy for Kaliningrad, so much of the analysis has been done, although significant updating is now required, since this project took place before the 1998 crisis, which has affected transport usage and volumes, and there have been developments in the neighbouring countries which need to be assessed. Nevertheless, a large body of information and, more importantly, well-researched development proposals have already been formulated. A key requirement here is to ensure that the appropriate Russian transport authorities (road and rail for the Corridors) are actively working on this issue. Modest Tacis support would be sufficient to update project proposals for investment.

Other issues relating to transport include modernisation and harmonisation of customs regulations and procedures. It would be wrong to regard this issue as being solely about Kaliningrad – it cannot be dealt with solely at local level. Customs issues must be determined between the EU and the federal authorities in Moscow, since this is primarily a legislative and regulatory matter. However, insofar as follow-up support of training of Customs officials, installation of computerised systems, improved border facilities and so forth, might be available, Kaliningrad should be involved as a 'pilot region'.

The fundamental need is to ensure that Kaliningrad can offer a multi-modal transport system and services that are compatible and competitive with those offered elsewhere. Without this, trade, and hence investment, will wither away. Technical assistance (planning, design, etc.) and investment are needed.

iii. Telecommunications

The region's telecommunications system must be modernised, including ensuring adequate bandwidth to support new generation services (Internet, video, etc.). This is an essential requirement for ensuring that economic (and social) development, incorporating the 'new' high-technology industries, can take place at all. Fortunately, there is already a detailed plan for telecommunications, drawn up in an earlier Tacis project.[20] Some updating will be necessary, but much of the preparatory work has already been done.

This needs to be set within a broader context at Russia-EU level. Thus, the planned integration of the Baltic regional national telecoms networks with each other and with those of the EU, 'requires inter alia the adoption of common international standards as agreed in the ITU and implemented through the European standardisation process and its institutions… This is a requirement for accession for the candidate countries. *The acceptance of these standards by Russia would facilitate closer business and social ties.'* (Emphasis added).[21] This latter issue can, obviously, only be dealt with at federal level in Moscow.

iv. Comment

Most of the rest of Kaliningrad's infrastructure – water, waste disposal, and so forth – is in serious need of repair and improvement, and deficiencies in some areas (e.g. reliable sources of good quality water) are serious impediments to certain kinds of industrial activity. On the positive side, a 55 million dollar loan agreement, co-financed by the EBRD, the Federal Government and the Nordic Investment Bank, will finance the construction of a new water plant, while Tacis is funding a waste water monitoring management project. Nonetheless, the three areas above – energy, transport and telecommunications – are vital to all kinds of economic activity, so should be given the highest priority.

It is also the case that in each of these three areas, there are sub-committees of the PCA (i.e. groups of senior EU and Russian officials), who have responsibility for dealing with these issues – on an overall Russia-EU basis. It is valuable that there exists an institutional framework already within which these matters of vital importance for Kaliningrad can be discussed. However, even if formal requirements are placed on members of these sub-committees to give particular attention to Kaliningrad, these sub-committees only meet twice a year and have extremely large agendas. Furthermore, if responsibility for Kaliningrad is divided between nine sub-committees (the total number), nobody has real responsibility at all – let alone for ensuring that there is a coherent overall approach, consistent with Kaliningrad's development policies and strategies. I return to this matter later.

c. Attracting and stimulating investment

The fundamental requirement is to attract investment. This is the most central issue. Without investment, nothing else will have any value whatsoever.

i. How can Kaliningrad attract domestic and foreign investment?

There are several approaches to this. They start with resolving the status of the SEZ once and for all. Either the Federal Government gives an unequivocal commitment to ensuring the SEZ survives (whether or not in a modified form) for a period of at least twenty-five years, or it agrees to provide a less generous concessionary regime, or it decides to abolish it altogether. But, whatever the decision, the time is long past that the uncertainty that has plagued the regime can be allowed to continue. In the meantime, the Regional Administration should propose legislation to the Regional Duma, similar to that already enacted in Novgorod, which provides a more investor-friendly legislative and regulatory environment. Even if it takes a long time to obtain satisfactory reforms at Federal level, the experience in more successful regions shows that progress can be made at regional level.

ii. Other investment-promotion initiatives

Bonded warehouses, industrial estates, and other superstructure are of significant value in attracting investment. Furthermore, if the EU would support the establishment of a centre that can train local business people in what is required to meet EU (e.g. Single Market) product standards *and* provide company and product certification to those enterprises that meet EU standards – this, in itself, would be of value in attracting (a) Russian exporters from elsewhere (since they would have the advantage of on-the-spot certification and proximity to EU markets – a 'reverse gateway', so to speak, compared with the 'traditional' one) and (b) international manufacturers who are looking for low-cost locations for supplying the EU. Naturally, customs procedures would also need to be significantly improved.

iii. Which sectors should be targeted?

There are obvious possibilities for import substitution in a range of sectors, most notably food processing. In turn, this requires a task-force approach to redeveloping the agriculture sector. But there are other opportunities in other sectors, such as building materials. Software development has excellent potential to grow as a significant export industry and as an attractive alternative location from Moscow for foreign software companies interested in operating within Russia. More added-value, high-tech sectors, such as pharmaceuticals, are unlikely to be serious prospects until the infrastructural problems, among others, are sorted out. Besides, as argued in Chapter 10, the workforce, though plentiful, does not have the appropriate skills. In turn, this requires looking at the need for developing new higher education courses, relevant to contemporary business needs.

iv. Restructuring existing large enterprises

Considerable assistance has been provided by Tacis to help large enterprises that were privatised during the 1990s to adapt to market conditions, notably through a Post-Privatisation Centre (a free consultancy service to selected firms, funded by Tacis). Even though considerable achievements were accomplished, a number of profound problems were – as elsewhere in Russia – impossible to surmount. Companies that make products that nobody wants to buy cannot be made profitable simply by improving management skills. Those that see opportunities for developing new product lines are frequently thwarted by lack of access to adequate finance. Nor has the general investment climate provided encouragement to foreign investors to buy stakes in such enterprises and finance the conversions to new technologies. Furthermore, even when enterprises have managed to manufacture products that could be marketed successfully, lack of knowledge of how to penetrate foreign markets - indeed, which ones to go after – is often lacking. Not least of the problems is the inability of many managers, educated and trained in the Soviet era, and with most of their professional lives spent in the command economy system, to develop the necessary attributes of initiative and risk-taking – even decision-making. Nonetheless, possibilities do exist, as the experience of Baltkran demonstrates. This is a company that makes cranes and, thanks to German investment and technology, now successfully manufactures high quality products, most of which are sold in EU markets. Less potential exists for the paper and pulp factories that use obsolete, energy-intensive and polluting technologies and which rely on raw materials (wood) brought in from thousands of kilometres away at increasingly great expense.

v. Small and medium-sized enterprises (SMEs)

This is a priority area for support, partly because around the world SMEs have rightly gained the reputation of being 'engines of growth' and partly because there are virtually no large enterprises already in existence, or likely to start up, that could lead the overall transformation process (see subsection above). The biggest problem here is the hostile business climate. This needs to be drastically reformed and support could then be provided through well-known instruments such as business centres, incubators and the like. Furthermore, such supporting instruments can be partly or fully funded with private investment, thereby reducing or eliminating the need for public funding – but this can only occur if investors have adequate protection and are confident that their SME clients will operate in a favourable business environment.

vi. Comment

There is a great deal more to the question of investment than the matters touched briefly on above. However, this gives a feel for the range of issues involved. They are many, complex and expensive to solve.

4. Making it work

In this section, I make my proposals for answering the core question which this chapter tries to address. I do this under three headings – policies, institutions and resources. This is because, although economic development is an extremely complex and far from fully understood process, getting these three issues 'right' is an essential starting point.

a. Policies

New policies are required from all parties. Kaliningrad needs investment in productive enterprises and the ability to export its goods abroad, primarily to the enlarging EU. Some people in Kaliningrad have called for a free trade agreement between Kaliningrad and the EU.[22] I think there are two problems with this proposal. First, European Commission officials and other experts have repeatedly stated that this idea is a non-starter on the grounds that agreements of this nature can only be entered into with sovereign states – in this case, with Russia. There is a formal aspiration set out in the Partnership and Co-operation Agreement to establish a free trade agreement between Russia and the EU, but this currently appears to be something of a long-term prospect. The second problem is that Kaliningrad makes very little in the way of exportable goods that would benefit from such an agreement, many of its exports being either commodities such as oil that are sold on world markets, independent of EU tariffs and other trade barriers, or which are goods that are subject to bilateral trade deals in sensitive sectors like textiles and steel. Furthermore, successive rounds of GATT/WTO negotiations have enormously lowered average tariffs over the last few decades such that the EU estimates the average tariff on Russian exports to the EU to be 0.3 percent.

On the other hand, Single Market directives have created enormous numbers of non-tariff barriers to exporters from outside the EU.[23] Thus, while welcoming any concession from the EU in terms of preferential trade access for goods manufactured in Kaliningrad, I think that there would be a more immediate benefit if the EU would support appropriate measures for enabling Kaliningrad enterprises to be aware of what standards apply to their particular businesses (there are tens of thousands of such standards), providing the know-how and training (where appropriate) for these enterprises to be able to adapt to these standards, and certifying the products as acceptable in EU markets when these standards are achieved. If all this could be done in Kaliningrad it would not only greatly reduce trade barriers for existing local enterprises, it would also act as a powerful incentive for Russian manufacturers elsewhere to locate their ventures in Kaliningrad.

It is also important to try to reverse the trade flow fault-line I have referred to in Chapter 3, wherein Lithuanian and Polish trade is primarily flowing away from Kaliningrad, rather than through or past it. The measure proposed in the paragraph above could well help to attract Baltic regional investors, seeking low-cost manufacturing locations with close proximity to the EU. But in addition, further measures for developing joint Kaliningrad-Polish and Kaliningrad-Lithuanian links should be explored. One idea that might merit investigation is the development of cross-border export processing zones – industrial estates spanning the border areas and enjoying a range of incentive measures relating to tariffs, taxes and the like. I will not offer detailed prescriptions here, but the idea might be attractive particularly to Poland if, as I have suggested in Chapter 3, there is a migratory shift of the Polish population to the west, reflecting the burgeoning growth of EU trade relations and, thereby, depopulating the areas furthest from the heart of the EU.

Furthermore, even though western companies are extremely cautious about investing in Kaliningrad – indeed, in Russia as a whole – there are numerous enterprises in CEE countries which are more inclined to consider this option seriously. These firms should be targeted for marketing by the KRDA.[24]

All these measures would, of course, put great pressure on the transport system. It is therefore essential that the TENs are developed. In addition, it should be investigated whether it would be feasible to develop a port network, linking Gdansk (Poland) with Kaliningrad and Klaipeda (Lithuania), with each port specialising in pre-agreed and complementary port-related activities. This would, if successful, not only provide powerful competition from these south-eastern ports against their northern neighbours in Latvia, Estonia, St. Petersburg and, perhaps, in Finland; it would also help to maintain the through-traffic after Poland and Lithuania join the EU, which will introduce the customs-free internal border that could isolate Kaliningrad. Informal discussions in 1998 and 1999 with Lithuanian officials suggest that the idea would be examined seriously if the Kaliningrad side were to promote it.

As well as land and sea transport developments, successful investment and trade promotion would also provide the demand to make feasible the development of better international air passenger services and this, in turn, could help to stimulate demand for air cargo services. I have argued in Chapter 3 and Chapter 10 that this is not commercially feasible at present, but an upsurge of international investment and trade activities could change this. Kaliningrad could, in principle, become a useful staging post for air cargo in and out of mainland Russia. This would require major infrastructural investment as well as significant private sector investment in carrier and freight services.

Within the region, phased development of fully serviced, international standard, industrial estates with attractive incentives would act as useful magnets for the kinds of investment to be sought. I explored this idea with the Kaliningrad City authorities in 1999 and found it was enthusiastically received.

In short, despite the enormous difficulties that exist there are numerous possibilities for trying to integrate Kaliningrad into the international economy. I have no doubt that there are many more – and better – ideas that could be developed if enough attention and expertise were focused on this matter.

There are, finally, major policy issues concerning Schengen and Third Pillar – JHA – matters. All the economic development initiatives will be seriously thwarted if Schengen leads to prohibitively expensive and difficult regimes for enabling Kaliningrad residents to cross borders easily for economic purposes, let alone for humanitarian purposes, such as visiting friends and relatives in the rest of Russia. This is a very complex area. However, it must be addressed in parallel with the other policy initiatives suggested here. Finland, as the only Member State so far to have a common border with Russia, has shown that a practical approach can be devised that works. However, some doubts must remain as to whether the Finnish model can be applied without adaptation to Kaliningrad once it becomes an EU enclave – the question of intra-Russian travel must be solved. But, on the other hand, the Finnish experience clearly shows that where there is the political will, solutions can be found to complex problems such as this.

b. Institutions

The key leadership role should be played by the Kaliningrad Regional Administration. Since 1996, however, when the gubernatorial elections led to a change in Governor, there has been no obviously coherent development strategy and, even more apparent, none towards developing trade and investment relations with neighbouring states at the level required. Rather, there seems to be an approach towards attempting to achieve self-sufficiency through, for example, the introduction of import quotas (see Chapter 10).

However, even if the current preference for a predominantly isolationist approach continues, the KRDA, jointly established by the Federal Ministry of Economy (now Ministry of Economic Development and Trade) and the Regional Administration in late 1999, is decidedly oriented towards developing international economic links. Unfortunately, it is very small at present and is significantly short of funding. Nonetheless, it has support from numerous researchers, analysts, economists, business leaders, and so forth, which augurs well for its potential to develop good policies. Whether it can obtain the funds to turn these ideas into operational programmes remains to be seen.

A further concern relates to the need to introduce new economic legislation in the Regional Duma, as several other Russian regions have successfully done. The relationship between the Regional Duma and the Regional Administration since 1996 has generally been bad with, for example, the Chairman of the Duma, Valeri Ustyugov, reportedly asserting that the administration is closely linked to organised crime, and the Governor threatening to sue Mr Ustyugov for libel, among many other such incidents.[25] Such activities have understandably distracted both parties from agreeing on a legislative programme that would benefit the region. The KRDA is completely outside these matters, as such agencies should be (i.e. apolitical and non-partisan), but it is not clear that it would be in a position to push through its own legislative ideas. Nonetheless, the KRDA is undoubtedly the most promising institutional development to have taken place in years and deserves international support.[26]

A matter of concern is that the regional 'ministries', which deal with matters such as transport and utilities[27], are directly under the authority of the Regional Administration and may, therefore, be unwilling to play their necessary role in the development process.

Turning now to Moscow, there are several institutions that have roles to play. First is the Ministry of Economic Development and Trade which, as mentioned above, is a co-founder of the KRDA and takes considerable interest in the region's development. Second is the Ministry of Foreign Affairs that is the ministry primarily responsible for Russian-EU relations and, therefore, would have a key role to play in negotiating any changes in the status of Kaliningrad's economic relations with the EU. Third, there is the transport complex of ministries and state bodies, all of whom have important developmental and funding roles to play in the region's transport system. Then there is the Ministry of Finance which, apart from being the source and recipient of fund transfers between Moscow and the regions, is the main negotiating body with the IMF and, thus, has a crucial role to play over the future of the SEZ. There are, of course, many other ministries which have roles to play.

As elsewhere in Russia, Kaliningrad's future is strongly influenced - in some areas, controlled - by numerous federal ministries, committees, agencies and so forth. What is clearly lacking is any one body that represents and co-ordinates an overall federal policy towards Kaliningrad.

But for Kaliningrad there really does need to be some kind of authoritative central structure to pull together all the different threads. This is not only in order to enhance and co-ordinate Moscow's policies and actions towards Kaliningrad – since the same argument applies for all the regions – but to ensure that initiatives involving, among other things, new economic relations with neighbouring states and the EU in general, are not thwarted or dissipated in Moscow. There are good reasons for fearing that there are some elements in the Moscow power structures that are opposed to any special treatment for Kaliningrad. These reasons vary from fear of losing tight control and hence allowing secessionist tendencies to develop unchecked, to the belief that Kaliningrad already benefits unduly from its SEZ status, to the more general view that it is wrong to single out one region for preferential treatment. For instance, as I have shown in Chapter 10, the Ministry of Finance wants to eliminate the SEZ. It is also widely believed in Kaliningrad (rightly or wrongly) that the authorities in St Petersburg are opposed to any special privileges for Kaliningrad in order to promote the interests of their port against their southern neighbour. For this reason, there is concern in Kaliningrad that, in the new 'super-regional' structure established by President Putin in mid-2000 (i.e. grouping the 89 Federal Subjects into seven administrative regional blocs), the power centre for the North-West region, in which Kaliningrad is located, is St Petersburg.

What matters in this situation is not who is opposed to what measure and why – there will always be such circumstances, that is human and political nature – but the fact that to get any significant new measures approved by the Federal Government requires assent from numerous structures, virtually any one of which can veto, block or delay such measures. It is one of the paralysing features of centre-region relations.

In my view, therefore, there is a strong case for the Government or the Presidential Administration to establish some kind of unit, secretariat or whatever, with the responsibility and the authority to 'look after' Kaliningrad issues. What and where this unit should be located is an internal matter for the Russian authorities. Given the wide-ranging changes in power structures currently being introduced by President Putin, it is impossible for an outside observer to pinpoint exactly the right solution. Having said that, there are good arguments for suggesting that the Presidential Administration would probably be the most appropriate part of the system in which to locate this structure. This is partly because it would be possible to give it more power and strength against factional lobbying and partly because, by attaching it to the President's office, it would show Mr Putin's personal endorsement of, and commitment to, the policy of treating Kaliningrad as a 'pilot region' in Russia-EU relations, as called for in the Russian Medium-Term Strategy to the EU.

The other aspect of the institutional arrangements in Moscow concerns the role of the PCA. There are nine sub-committees responsible for dealing with the issues covered by the PCA, including transport, energy and telecommunications, as mentioned earlier, but also trade and investment relations. These sub-committees are made up of senior officials from the Russian Government and counterpart European Commission officials. Within the Russian Government, a 'PCA secretariat' handles co-ordination and implementation of policies. This is currently answerable to Deputy Prime Minister Khristenko who, among other responsibilities, oversees Russian relations with the EU.[28] This secretariat could also have specific responsibilities assigned to it to ensure that there is a coherent – and high priority – consideration of Kaliningrad issues in all sub-committee affairs.

Because of the complex, changing and somewhat confused nature of Russian governmental structures and responsibilities, both at federal level and between the federal level and the regions, it is immensely difficult to be confident about recommending a particular arrangement for meeting the needs of Kaliningrad. At any rate, it is an internal Russian matter.

The most important point is that Moscow needs to do something effective in this area. There are no adequate existing structures to handle the issue satisfactorily.

Moving now to Brussels, the situation is not that much clearer. At least three major elements of the Commission and European Council need to be involved – External Relations, Enlargement and the High Representative, Mr Solana's Office for the CFSP. But many other parts of the Commission also have a role to play – in telecommunications, transport, energy, environment and so on. Arguably, there are two existing institutional structures that could take on the responsibility of dealing with Kaliningrad – the Commission's side of the PCA structures and the unit that is responsible for Northern Dimension matters.

I see this as *primarily* an external relations issue so, for me, this is the logical place to assign overall responsibility. But there are no especially overwhelming arguments to suggest that this is necessarily the only option. The key issue is for the EU Member States and the Commission itself to accept the concept that Kaliningrad is sufficiently important to merit separate treatment and establish the appropriate mechanism for dealing with it. That is the most important aspect of the EU's involvement in the matter – political acceptance of the idea and commitment to action.

In summary, therefore, I am arguing that all three major actors – Kaliningrad, Moscow and Brussels – must introduce institutional arrangements for dealing with the Kaliningrad problem. The details are less important than the principle and, it need hardly be said, failure by any one of these actors to take such steps will neutralise the effects of positive steps taken by the others – it is a case of 'all for one, and one for all'.

c. Resources

Assuming that the policies are established and agreed, and that appropriate institutional structures are established: what next? The critical issue is money. Kaliningrad needs funding to improve and modernise its infrastructure and to support the activities of the KRDA, to suggest just two of many requirements – although the former will need vastly more funding than the latter. But where will this money come from?

Much can be obtained from private sector sources – given the right investment environment. Toll roads, air cargo services, port developments, industrial estates and the like, can all, in principle, be financed by risk capital – if the risk can be made acceptable. (And, it is worth noting here, even though much investor apprehension stems from problems at federal level, if Kaliningrad can make itself more attractive – less risky – than most of the rest of Russia, this in itself will be a powerful incentive).

But there will still remain a need for capital from non-private sources. Clearly, the Federal budget has a major responsibility here, but it is well known that the Russian exchequer has inadequate resources to meet all the demands placed upon it and, further, it would be politically extremely difficult to justify significantly more generous treatment for Kaliningrad than elsewhere, when so many other parts of Russia are almost literally falling apart – with major power and heating 'outages' and much more. And this quite apart from the 'pork barrel' trade-offs that are a common feature of federal political systems.

Inescapably, it is apparent that major funding must be sought from abroad. While it must be hoped that improvements in the region will persuade the major international financing institutions (IFIs), such as the World Bank and the EBRD, to upgrade their assessment of Kaliningrad for loan agreements,[29] this on its own will be not enough to secure the level of funding necessary in the rapid time-scale that is also called for.

How much money is required? Frankly, I do not know, although it is easy to prepare a 'shopping list' just from past Tacis projects that have identified important investment projects totalling many hundreds of millions of dollars. For guidance, therefore, I return to an earlier part of this chapter in which I reviewed the assistance being offered to Poland and Lithuania as part of their pre-accession support programmes. I suggested that if Kaliningrad were in the same situation, it could look forward to 23 to 53 million euro a year for the next six years. Let us be arbitrary and take a figure roughly in the middle – 40 million euro.

The absorptive capacity of Kaliningrad is fairly weak at present.[30] But, with the policy and institutional reforms I have suggested above, this should improve. So where can Kaliningrad get 40 million euro a year from for six years – some 240 million euro in total?

The ideal solution is for this money to come from the same source as the other countries get it – the EU. The mechanism would be simply to extend the same procedures to Kaliningrad as to Poland, Lithuania and the other candidate states.

Of course, this is a – probably – hopeless aspiration. The list of powerful objections and incontrovertible arguments why this could not possibly be done would probably be enormous – on political, economic, legal, and other grounds. It will be 'impossible'.

I suggest, therefore, that a fund should be established that would aim to match the EU programme for the other states and which would be applied solely to Kaliningrad. The fund would obtain its financial resources from those states which, on a voluntary basis, believe that Kaliningrad merits such support. These countries need not be limited to EU Member States or candidate countries – if the United States, in support of its North European Initiative wanted to contribute, then why not? Nonetheless, the obvious supporters would initially be most likely to be found from those countries that are most closely interested in Kaliningrad – the Northern Dimension countries.

The richest of these – Germany and the Nordic states – might take the lead, but there is no reason why Lithuania and Poland, for example, should not also contribute within their means. In order not to create the impression that this would be some kind of unlimited source of money, and to ensure that it is not treated as a precedent for funding requirements in the other Russian regions which, though not exclaves, will also in due course have a common border with the EU, I would propose that this be called the 'Kaliningrad Equalisation and Development Fund'. This would give the clear message that the fund exists solely for developments in Kaliningrad, nowhere else, and that the *maximum* sums available would not exceed those available to the candidate states, calculated on the same basis as is applied to them (see footnote 2).

I am asking a lot from these countries, but they do already provide significant amounts of bilateral support – some 10 million euro over the period 1998 to 2000, according to the Copenhagen conference (see section 2(b) above). Thus the precedent exists, albeit on a far smaller scale than now proposed. If these countries were prepared to adopt this recommendation it would also have the benefit, through pooling resources, of improving the optimal co-ordination and hence use of the available funds. Furthermore, by operating with the sole objective of developing Kaliningrad and lessening or eliminating the 'development deficit', this fund could design its own rules for eligible projects without being bound by existing procedures for EU funding activities.

I believe such an approach is the only feasible one in the present circumstances.

5. Conclusions

I lived and worked in Kaliningrad from January 1996 to November 1999 – nearly four years. During that period I came to identify more and more closely with the issues that I encountered there. I often discussed what could be done to improve the future of the region with Russian friends there – business people, academics, politicians, journalists, public servants, NGO workers, bankers, students and many more.

I do not think that I have expressed any opinions in this book which are not shared by at least some of these people, although I cannot claim that any of them would necessarily agree with everything I have said. What I do know for certain is that there is a large body of thoughtful opinion in Kaliningrad which believes fervently that to make progress must involve deepening the links with Europe. Ultimately, the future of their home is in their hands. But they will not be able to realise their aspirations without our help.

This must take more substantial form than the expression of concern. Kaliningrad and the other actors involved need to agree on what should be done and then find the will, the means and the resources for implementation. Where the EU cannot act, for whatever reason, other states should try to play the appropriate role. Russia, too, must be fully involved, not only because Kaliningrad is an integral part of her sovereign territory, but because there cannot and must not be an over-reliance on foreign assistance to solve this problem. We all have a responsibility in this matter and we must now, all of us, accept that responsibility.

---

[1] The alternatives are (a) that Kaliningrad could become economically self-sufficient, with little or no interaction with anywhere else or (b) that a prosperous future could be achieved by re-establishing close economic links with the Russian mainland and CIS economies. The former option – barring a Botswana-style 'miracle' discovery of diamonds or something similar on a vast scale (but look what has happened to amber) – is inconceivable. The latter is not an optimistic scenario. These economies are having a bad enough time themselves. Kaliningrad's exclave situation would merely continue to be exacerbated by the already serious structural problems they suffer from, as performance to date amply demonstrates.

[2] Actual allocations of EU assistance to each country depend on a combination of population size, GDP per head (adjusted for purchasing power parity) and land area. However, for the purpose of this exercise population size will be a sufficient indicator. I am using 'rounded' totals of Poland – 40 million people; Lithuania – 3.5 million; Kaliningrad - 1 million.

[3] European Commission, 2000, *Structural Actions 2000-2006, Commentary and Regulations*, Office for Official Publications of the European Communities, Luxembourg, p. 126.

[4] Meuro stands for million euro.

[5] CBC is the Tacis Cross-Border Co-operation programme, which

supports projects involving any of Russia, Ukraine, Moldova and Belarus and a neighbouring state or states.

[6] Interreg II was one of the EU Community Initiative programmes from 1994 to 1999, focusing on cross-border co-operation between Member States, accession/candidate states and some others. It had three strands: A – cross-border co-operation; B – energy networks; C – co-operation on regional planning. Interreg III, with similar objectives, applies from 2000 to 2006.

[7] PHARE is the EU technical assistance programme for EU candidate states. It is analogous, but not identical, to Tacis – the EU technical assistance programme for the NIS and Mongolia.

[8] SAPARD is the EU programme to support the modernisation of agriculture and the promotion of rural development.

[9] ISPA is the EU programme to support development of transport and environmental protection measures.

[10] Based on the lowest per capita figure (Poland) and the highest (Lithuania).

[11] Widening the 'development deficit', a term coined by Professor Ivan Samson, Project Director of a Tacis project 'Developing a Global Economic Development Plan' in Kaliningrad, 1997-1999.

[12] Membership of Schengen is non-negotiable for the accession states – they *must* join – unlike existing Member States, the UK and Ireland, which have successfully derogated from this requirement for now. However, the date of joining Schengen may be later than the date of formal accession to the EU itself.

[13] Some observers, both Russian and EU, think that such problems as these may arise will start on the day(s) that Lithuania and Poland actually accede to the EU. This is incorrect. Both these countries are steadily adapting their economies, administrations, legal bases, and so forth, so that when they are admitted they will *already* have instituted most of the changes that will affect Kaliningrad. The tightening up of border procedures by Poland in January 1998 is an obvious example. Thus, at some as yet unknown date in the future Kaliningrad residents will wake up to find themselves legally surrounded by the EU. In practice, however, they are already being increasingly encircled.

[14] 'An EU study on the prospects of the Kaliningrad oblast, the support already provided to the region and the possible steps to further promote co-operation between Russia and the enlarging EU could be considered', Council of the European Union, 30 May 2000, *Draft Action Plan for the Northern Dimension with external and cross-border policies of the European Union 2000-2003*, European Commission, Brussels, page 47. While this does not explicitly call for a study leading to a policy and strategy programme, it seems to me that such an interpretation could be accommodated within this recommendation.

[15] The KRDA was set up in November 1999 by the then Federal Ministry of Economy (subsequently restructured) and the Kaliningrad Regional Administration, with the dual mandate of (a) monitoring and supporting the implementation of the Federal Programme for the Implementation of the SEZ (primarily a capital works programme, suffering from post-1998 crisis funding shortages) and (b) supporting the regional economic development process. The KRDA, however, has only a very small staff (less than ten people) and limited funding. The Tacis project will give valuable assistance, but probably not enough to help launch a sustainable development process.

[16] The principle of absolute advantage proposes that when two or more countries have different input-utilisation structures (e.g. different amounts and ratios of labour and capital to produce a given quantity of identical products) in the production of goods, each country should specialise in those products in which it is more efficient than the other(s). This leads to an increase in the total output and, through trade, each country ends up with more goods than if each were to try to make everything it needed on its own. The principle of comparative advantage takes this argument a step further. It proposes that even when one country can make all goods more efficiently than another, it still leads to an increase in total output if each country specialises in the production of goods at which it is *relatively* more efficient. The mathematical proof of these propositions is simple and can be found in any introductory textbook dealing with international trade theory.

[17] The Single Market rules require Member States to open up tenders for publicly-financed works (building schools, supplying telecommunications equipment, supplying army boots, and so forth) to bidders from other Member States – not just bidders in the offering state.

[18] This does not mean that Kaliningrad should encourage industrial activity that is banned on certain other kinds of grounds, such as being environmentally hazardous or in other ways posing threats to public safety and health. Further, Russia's planned accession to the World Trade Organisation (WTO) will lead to restrictions in the kinds of incentives that can be offered to investors. The WTO is also moving towards trying to establish 'level playing fields' for internationally mobile FDI. Nonetheless, it seems very probable that there will be 'arbitrage' opportunities in this policy area.

[19] Council of the European Union, 30 May 2000, *Draft Action Plan for the Northern Dimension with external and cross-border policies of the European Union 2000-2003*, European Commission, Brussels, page 14.

[20] O'Reilly, Brian, 1998, *Review of Kaliningrad's Telecommunications Needs*, Tacis/IDI, 'Support to Kaliningrad Region in the Context of the SEZ', Kaliningrad and Brussels.

[21] European Council, May 2000, *op. cit.*, page 17.

[22] This idea was developed in the late 1990s by Alexei Ignatiev, Chief Executive of the Yantar Regional Development Foundation.

[23] In fact, they have caused considerable problems and costs for enterprises inside the EU as well, but at least there have been institutions to assist them to overcome the difficulties and to comply with the regulations.

[24] This assertion is based on field trips carried out in Lithuania, Poland, Hungary and the Czech Republic during 1998 by consultants working for the Tacis project 'Support to Kaliningrad Region in the Context of the SEZ'. I was the Team Leader for this project.

[25] See, for example, Gary Peach, 'Letter from the Enclave', *The Moscow Times*, 30 September 2000, which summarises the more notable libel cases that the Governor has initiated, but generally withdrawn.

[26] Tacis will be the first source of such international support, with a new project, valued at 1 meuro, expected to commence in early 2001. It will provide technical assistance (primarily consultancy expertise and training) to the agency.

[27] Such matters are divided between federal, regional and, in some cases, municipal authorities.

[28] However, international relations issues between the two are handled by the Foreign Ministry under the Foreign Minister, Mr Igor Ivanov.

[29] At present, the EBRD has committed itself to a co-financing deal for construction of a water treatment plant. As far as I know, the World Bank is not currently financing or committed to any projects in Kaliningrad.

[30] Absorptive capacity refers to the ability of the local authorities to identify and manage good projects that could usefully utilise or 'absorb' the funds available. Excessive funding can be as harmful in its own way (white elephants) as inadequate funding.

APPENDICES

Appendix 1

Brief History of Kaliningrad

1255: Teutonic Knights build a castle in Königsberg (now Kaliningrad City) around which the town grows.[1]

1333: Building begins on the cathedral.[2]

1340: Königsberg becomes a member of the Hanseatic League.[3]

1457: Castle becomes the residence of the Grand Master of the Teutonic Knights.[4]

1525: Castle in turn becomes the residence of the Dukes of Prussia.[5]

1544: Founding of the university (Collegium Albertinium, later the University of Königsberg).[6]

1701: Elector Frederick III of Brandenburg is crowned in the chapel of the castle as the first King of Prussia – Frederick I.

1724: Immanuel Kant, the city's most famous son, is born. He spends his entire life in the city, teaching at the university.[7]

Early 19th century: Königsberg suffers severely during the Napoleonic Wars.

Mid 19th century: The opening of a railway system in East Prussia and Russia gives renewed life to the city, making it the principal outlet for many Russian staple products and Prussia's (and later Germany's) main naval base on the Baltic Sea.

1871: East Prussia (with Königsberg as its capital) becomes part of the German Reich.

1919: Treaty of Versailles turns East Prussia into an enclave, separated from the rest of Germany by the 'Polish corridor'.

1944-45: German forces in the city are attacked by the Royal Air Force and then by the Soviet Army. The bombing and fighting caused extensive damage.

April 1945: The city eventually falls to the Soviet Army.

July 1945: The northern third of East Prussia - now Kaliningrad Oblast - is ceded to the Soviet Union under the terms of the Potsdam agreement. Most of the remaining German population is deported, being replaced by Soviet settlers.

July 1946: The city and Oblast are renamed after the recently deceased Mikhail Ivanovich Kalinin (Chairman of the Government of the Soviet Union, 1919-1946).

1945-1991: Kaliningrad is closed off to foreigners. It becomes home to the Soviet Baltic fleet (at Baltiysk, 32 km from Kaliningrad City) with up to 200,000 soldiers based in the region.

Jan 1991: The region is reopened. The first direct train since 1945 runs from Kaliningrad to Berlin.

1991: Most of the Oblast is declared a Free Economic Zone (FEZ).

Jan 1996: The Oblast subsequently becomes a Special Economic Zone (SEZ).

Oct 1996: In elections, Leonid Gorbenko becomes Governor, replacing Yuri Matochkin.

Nov 2000: Date for new elections for Governor.

---

[1] The fortress, badly damaged in the Second World War, was finally razed to the ground in 1967-69 to make way for the House of Soviets, never occupied due to structural problems.

[2] The cathedral is currently being restored.

[3] A mercantile league of medieval northern European towns which in the 14th century dominated Baltic and North Sea commerce. The Hanseatic League fell into decline in the 17th century.

[4] When the Order loses its capital at Marienburg. The Order is finally dissolved in 1618.

[5] Until 1618, when the Prussian Duchy is united by marriage to the German State of Brandenburg.

[6] The State University of Kaliningrad is its successor, founded in 1967.

[7] His grave lies next to the cathedral.

Appendix 2

Facts and Figures

Geography and Population[1]

Size: 15,100 km^2

Kaliningrad Oblast (pop.): 1,000,000

Kaliningrad City (pop.): 419,000

Ethnic Composition: 78% Russian, 10% Belarussian, 6% Ukrainian, 4% Lithuanian, 0.8% of German origin[2]

Life expectancy (1996):[3] Male: 59 years Female: 71 years

Principal natural resources[4]

Amber: Over 90% of the world's amber deposits are found within the oblast (reserves estimated to be 275 million tons).

Fish: major stocks in the large inland lagoons (Kurskiy and Vistular Lagoons) and in the Baltic Sea.

Arable land: 314,000 ha under cultivation (1997), well under half the potential total.

Timber: covers 18% of the oblast, although little is cut down for commercial use.

Oil: 650,000 tons per annum (1999) – down by over half since the previous decade.

Brown coal: reserves estimated at 50 million tons.

Rock salt: there are around 10,000 km^2 of salt containing areas.

Peat: estimated at over 3.0 billion cubic metres.

Other natural resources include sand, clay and gravel.

Major industries

Engineering, machine tools, ship-building and repairs, pulp and paper manufacturing, fishing and agriculture.

Structure of regional economy (1997)[5]

	% contribution to Gross Regional Product
Manufacturing	19.4
Agriculture	9.3
Building and construction	5.7
Other industry	1.8
Services	59.8

Structure of employment[6]

Sector	1990 (%)	1999 (%)
Industry	30.4	19.1
Agriculture (incl. forestry)	12.0	10.5
Construction	9.7	6.9
Transport/communications	8.7	7.8
Commerce, public catering	9.0	19.8
Utilities, certain services	4.4	6.6
Public health, social security	6.7	7.4
Education, science, culture, arts	13.6	11.4
Banking, finance, insurance	0.7	1.3
Government, administration	1.8	7.4
Other	3.0	1.8

Unemployment[7]

1993	1994	1995	1996	1997[8]	Dec 1998[9]
			(%)		
1.8	4.5	5.8	5.2	3.2	3.5

Percentage change in industrial output (1990-1998)[10]

-61%

Trade figures (1995-1998)[11]

	1995	1996	1997	1998
		Million US dollars		
Exports	459.4	480.8	452.0	429.3
Imports	585.1	1030.0	1285.6	1187.9
Total foreign trade	1044.5	510.8	1737.6	1617.2
Balance of merchandise trade +/(-)	(15.7)	(380.8)	(833.6)	(758.6)
Cargo handled by Kaliningrad port (ml. tonnes)	3.5	4.4	4.0	3.4

Principal import and export markets (1997)[12]

Exports		Imports	
Poland	26.1%	Germany	24.2%
Germany	9.4%	Poland	17.0%
Lithuania	7.9%	Lithuania	16.0%
Nordics	2.9%	Nordics	6.0%
Latvia	1.5%	Latvia	1.8%
Lithuania	0.7%	Estonia	0.6%

Principal exports (1997)[13]

Oil	22%
Ships/boats	10%
Fertilisers	6%
Fish/crustaceans	6%
Cellulose	5%

Cumulative Foreign Direct Investment (FDI) over past decade – comparison with neighbouring countries[14]

	Per capita, US dollars
Kaliningrad	70 (1999)
Russia	63 (1998)
Lithuania	563 (1999)
Poland	260 (1998)

EU Tacis support towards Kaliningrad

	Million Euro
1995-1998	13.3[15]
1998-2000	12.6[16]

---

[1] *Kaliningrad In Your Pocket* travel guide, 2000.

[2] Mostly Volga Germans – originally encouraged to settle in Russia by Catherine the Great.

[3] Tacis/IDI, *Kaliningrad Region: Proposed Strategic Development Framework* (December 1998).

[4] Figures taken from *Kaliningrad – your Gateway to Russia* at www.klgd.ru and Matochkin, *Kaliningrad Today – the report on Forum Kaliningrad-96*.

[5] Kaliningrad Region State Committee on Statistics, *Social and Economic Situation in Kaliningrad Region, 1997*, Kaliningrad, 1998

[6] *Op cit*, note 5.

[7] Official unemployment figures.

[8] Methodology for calculating unemployment was changed in 1997, which largely explains the apparent improvement over 1996.

[9] Hanson, Kirkow, Sutherland and Troyakova, *Kaliningrad and Primorskii Krai*, May 1999. Figures taken from *Goskomstat SEPR99 II*. Calculations using International Labour Organisation (ILO) methodology give a significantly higher figures, e.g., 10.5% for 1996. Other estimates suggest that real unemployment may be as high as 25%.

[10] Hanson, etc., *op cit*, note 9.

[11] *Op cit*, note 5 and Hidrosfera-Klaipeda Port Services. See Chapter 3.

[12] *Op cit*, note 5.

[13] *Op cit*, note 5.

[14] Westin, *Foreign Direct Investment in Russia,* RECEP, Tacis/ Stockholm Institute of Transition Economics, Moscow and Brussels (1999).

[15] Tacis, *op cit*, note 3.

[16] Before 1 January 1999, the basket of currencies was known as the ECU. The figures are provided by the Danish Foreign Ministry to the conference on Kaliningrad, Copenhagen, May 2000. These figures include projects involving other states and Russian regions and are, as such, slightly inflated. See Chapter 14.

Abbreviations

CBSS	Council of Baltic Sea States
CEE	Central and Eastern Europe
CFSP	Common Foreign and Security Policy
CIS	Commonwealth of Independent States
CMEA	Council for Mutual Economic Assistance
COPRI	Copenhagen Peace Research Institute
CREDO	Cross-border co-operation between CEE countries and NIS
EBRD	European Bank for Reconstruction and Development
ECU	European Currency Unit
EES	See *UES* below
EIB	European Investment Bank
EMU	Economic and Monetary Union
ESDP	European Security and Defence Policy
EU	European Union
FDI	Foreign Direct Investment
FEZ	Free Economic Zone
FSFR	Financial Support Fund for the Regions
FSU	Former Soviet Union
GATT	General Agreement on Tariffs and Trade
GDP	Gross Domestic Product
GRP	Gross Regional Product
IFI	International Financial Institution

IMF	International Monetary Fund
INTERREG II	Inter-Regional Assistance (EC initiative concerning border development, cross-border co-operation and selected energy networks)
ISI	Import Substitution Industrialisation
ISPA	Instrument for Structural Policies for Pre-Accession
ITU	International Telecommunications Union
JHA	Justice and Home Affairs
KRDA	Kaliningrad Regional Development Agency
KLN	Kaliningrad Air Enterprises
LDC	Less developed country
MECU	Million ECU
MFA	Ministry for Foreign Affairs
NAFTA	North Atlantic Free Trade Association
NATO	North Atlantic Treaty Organisation
ND	Northern Dimension
NDR[1]	Our Home is Russia (Russian political party)
NEI	Northern European Initiative
NGO	Non-governmental Organisation
NIS	Newly Independent States
NTB	Non-tariff barrier
OECD	Organisation for Economic Co-operation and Development
OSCE	Organisation for Security and Co-operation in Europe
OVR[2]	Fatherland – All Russia (Russian political party)

PCA	Partnership and Co-operation Agreement
Phare[3]	Poland and Hungary: Action for the Restructuring of the Economy
RSFSR	Russian Soviet Federal Socialist Republic
SAPARD	Structural Adjustment Programme for Agriculture and Rural Development
SEZ	Special Economic Zone
SME	Small and Medium-sized Enterprise
SVOP[4]	Russian Council for Foreign and Defence Policy
TA	Technical assistance
Tacis[5]	Technical Assistance for the Commonwealth of Independent States
TEN	Trans European Network
TEPSA	Trans European Policy Studies Association
UES	Unified Energy System (the electricity monopoly in Russia)
UN	United Nations
USSR	Union of Soviet Socialist Republics
WEU	Western European Union
WTO	World Trade Organisation

---

[1] *Nash Dom Rossiya.*
[2] *Otechestvo – Vsya Rossiya.*
[3] Phare now means the EC programme of aid to all CEE candidate countries applying for EU membership.
[4] *Sovet Vneshnyei i Oboronitelnoi Politiki.*
[5] TACIS was originally Technical Assistance to the Commonwealth of Independent States, but is now written as Tacis and means technical assistance to the NIS and Mongolia.

Background to Contributors

James Baxendale   First Secretary, British Embassy, Brussels

Yuri Borko   President of the Association of European Studies, Moscow

Stephen Dewar   Independent economic consultant, currently working in Moscow

Andrew Dolan   International Institute for Policy Development, Edinburgh

Christopher Donnelly   Special Adviser for Central and Eastern European Affairs, NATO

Sylvia Gourova   Deputy Mayor, Kaliningrad

David Gowan   Senior Associate Member at St Antony's College, Oxford during the 1999-2000 academic year

Dag Hartelius   Director, Department for Central and Eastern Europe, Swedish Ministry of Foreign Affairs

Pertti Joenniemi   Senior Research Fellow and
Programme Director for Baltic-
Nordic Studies, Copenhagen Peace
Research Institute (COPRI)

Igor Leshukov   Research Director, Centre for
Integration Research and Programmes
(CIRP), St. Petersburg

René Nyberg   Ambassador, Head of Division for
Eastern Affairs, Finnish Ministry of
Foreign Affairs

Alexander Songal   Deputy Head of Analytical
Department, Kaliningrad Regional
Duma

Vygaudas Usackas   Deputy Minister for Foreign Affairs
of Lithuania

Wojciech Zajaczkowski Department for Eastern Europe,
Polish Ministry of Foreign Affairs

Notes on TEPSA and the British Embassy Seminar Series

TEPSA

TEPSA (Trans European Policy Studies Association) was established in 1974. It is an independent, non-profit making research and academic network aiming at the promotion of international research on European integration in order to stimulate discussion on policies and political options for Europe. TEPSA links affiliated national research institutes from all European Union Member States and from the candidate countries. TEPSA projects include research, studies and conference series commissioned by the European institutions, foundations and national public and private authorities.

British Embassy Seminar Series

The British Embassy Seminar Series is organised by the British Embassy, Brussels. It aims to address a wide range of contemporary European policy themes. Previous events have included seminars, round table discussions, debates and talks. In the near future, it also hopes to host a series of internet debates on Europe.